Return to God

CHARLES MICHAEL

GIFTED BOOKS AND MEDIA

Copyright

Printed in the United States of America

E-book ISBN: 978-1-947343-02-3
Paperback ISBN: 978-1-947343-03-0

Published by Jayclad Publishing LLC
www.giftedbookstore.com

Table of Contents

Introduction

Have you ever wondered why God wants his children to confess their sins to a Catholic priest? Practicing Catholics around the world, during Advent and Lent, make it a point to confess their sins to a priest. Many wouldn't receive communion on Sundays without making their weekly confession. Non-Catholics see this practice as unbiblical, manmade, and unnecessary. The Jews, who saw Jesus forgive the sins of people, couldn't believe what they were witnessing and spoke out by saying, "Who can forgive sins but God alone?" Jesus replied to them that he indeed had the authority to forgive sins and reconcile the sinner with God. Jesus passed on this authority to the Church, giving them the ministry of Reconciliation. The words of absolution, "Go your sins are forgiven," spoken by Jesus to many, continue to be spoken in a confessional with the same authority. A priest receives this authority directly from Jesus.

Since then, this practice has been around and has evolved into one of the seven sacraments of the Church. What is so remarkable about this sacrament? Why does the Church give such an important place for this sacrament in a person's life? People who have experienced this sacrament and those who go to confession regularly know how it changes their lives each time they visit the confessional. At the same time, the present younger generation finds it challenging to balance the demands of the real world and faith. Godly values and spiritual activities have taken a backseat. Churches in most developed countries struggle to stay open. Church attendance is at an all-time low. In recent years, a lack of teaching, a shortage of vocations, scandals in the Church, and other issues have discouraged many young Catholics from being involved. That being said, we have the promise of Jesus that the gates of hell will not prevail against it (the Church).

Jesus who is alive and active, works in us through the sacraments. Confession is one of them. The blessings and the benefits of the Sacrament of Reconciliation are manifold. Confession is not merely the saying of one's sins to a priest. It is an act of conversion. The main reason why people have stopped confessing their sins is that they did not do it correctly and hence did not reap the full benefits of it. Without the results or the fruits of the activity, it is quite natural for us to quit any habit. I can identify with such people because I too was a victim of "Being Catholic without the Sacraments." Our Catholic call cannot be fulfilled without a life of Sacraments. Obedience to Sacraments is obedience to Jesus.

Born in a Catholic family, I was not regular to Church from the time I learned to say no to my parents. I would find the lamest excuse to stay away from Church and Holy Mass. At the age of 22, I had a divine encounter with Jesus when I attended a retreat. It was a homecoming experience. It drew me closer to God and the sacraments. I became more regular to church, especially the Holy Mass, Eucharistic Adoration, and confession. A deep longing for the Eucharist made me visit the confessional more often. Slowly, I began to see God for who he is. His love and mercy became visible to me in the confessional. God's forgiving love became evident to me each time I failed and ran to him for pardon.

For years, I too found it hard to gain victory over many sins. Sin always got the best of me for a very long time. My visits to the confessional were always marked with guilt and fear. Although I was regular to confession, for the most part, I was not walking in freedom. I read many books, attended many seminars, but to no avail. It made me wonder if I was missing something. Does God only forgive sin, or can he also free us from sin? One day, I decided to search for answers. I immersed myself in studying the word of God. Soon I realized that hidden in Scriptures, is the answers to all our life's problems. Life comes with many challenges, and sin is one of them. The secret to living a God-centered life lies in total dependence on God and relying on him for the smallest need in life. Enlightenment in the areas of sin and salvation led me to become a teacher of the Word of God wherein I can help others identify their Christian call.

Guided by the Holy Spirit, I was able to put together this book, which in most parts is my own experiences about sin, repentance, and confession. I sincerely thank God Almighty for inspiring me to write and publish this book. I also thank God for all my well-wishers, spiritual directors, and family members without whose support this book would not have materialized.

It is my sincere desire that as you read this book, you too will experience the ocean of God's love that flows into us through his mercy in the confessional. His love for us is the force by which we can escape the evil and corruption of this world.

Amen

God Bless You

Charles Michael

Let the words of my mouth will be so as to please, along with the meditation of my heart, in your sight, forever, O Lord, my helper and my redeemer. (Ps 19:14)

Pre-Confession

Let us imagine that Jesus had appeared in your dream last night. He showed you his palms and his feet and told you that it was your sins that caused those wounds, and Jesus wanted you to go for a confession at the earliest. The dream ended there, and you woke up troubled. You are Catholic, and you are convinced that it was Jesus who appeared to you. You decide to go for confession, but it is still three days away. You are not regular to confession and also not familiar with the format. You don't exactly remember when you confessed last; months, maybe years ago. But this time, since you are convinced, it was Jesus, you are inspired to make a sincere confession. As you pondered over it, some legitimate questions came to your mind.

Question 1: Why should I confess my sins to a priest?

Question 2: Why can I not just say sorry to Jesus directly?

Question 3: How do I confess?

Question 4: How do I make a "sincere" confession?

Question 5: What do I confess and what sin is Jesus talking about?

Question 6: How do I know if I have sinned or not?

Question 7: How do I prepare myself for a sincere confession?

Question 9: Will I receive God's forgiveness at confession?

Question 11: Do priests have the authority to forgive sins?

Question 12: Can confession free me from sin?

Question 13: How frequently must I go for confession?

These are some valid questions about confession that we may have had from time to time, and without an answer to these questions, we may have stopped going to confession, or we may be making an insincere and heartless confession. This book is an honest effort to give the reader an in-depth knowledge of the Catholic Sacrament of Reconciliation in an easy-to-understand language suitable for people of all nations. Each of the above questions is answered in this book with the help of the Holy Bible and other available resources.

How Do I Know if I Have Sinned or Not?

This is a valid question to which many of us can relate to. When I was a kid, my mother used to force me to go for a weekly confession. At times, I would argue with her and tell her that I had not sinned since my last confession. My mother would not listen to me and still insisted on me going. I would go only to make her happy or to get what I wanted. Many of us have had a similar experience. We find it hard to see our sins most of the time. In the first section of this book, we will focus on sin and how and where to look for it.

Before we make a trip to the Church and confess our sins, we must make a list of them. Take the example of a household. The person who cleans the house collects the garbage from all the rooms, bundles it, and then takes it to the dumpster. The person does this regularly to keep the house clean and tidy. The house is thoroughly checked and cleaned, including every nook and corner before the garbage is removed. Similarly, every area of life must be carefully examined before we head to the church; our thoughts, speech, actions, relationships, etc. Now, sin may not be readily discernible or detectable. Thus, to detect and identify its seriousness is the first step.

Knowledge of Sin

Common sense tells me that when I am driving on the highway, I must be familiar with the traffic rules and know at what speed I should be traveling. Similarly, in our faith journey, we as Christians should know the laws and regulations set forth by God to attain eternal life; what God likes and does not like, and what he has allowed and rejected. Many of us have a poor understanding of sin. Our definition of sin and evil comes from the society and culture around us. We think of sin as something that is prohibited by the law of the land. Sin is often confused with what is legal and illegal in a country. For example, Marijuana was illegal to consume in many countries; therefore, people saw it as something wrong and sinful. Recently, it has been made legal in some developed countries, making it acceptable to society, and people have started to perceive it as good. People live with a wrong idea of sin and evil. Even if a practice is legal in a country, it does not mean God has allowed us to take part in it. God's law is above every other manmade law. The writer of the book of Hosea, speaking for God, writes that we destroy ourselves because we lack knowledge. To begin with, we have to unlearn certain beliefs and teachings that is close to our heart. Of the many titles of Jesus we see in the Bible, teacher is one of them. Jesus taught many things to his disciples. God continues to teach us through his word and the Church. We will look at some misconceptions and wrong teachings about sin and evil that we have adopted from the world around us.

The hawk in the heavens has known her time. The turtledove, and the swallow, and the stork have kept the time of their arrival. But my people have not known the ordinances of the Lord. (Jer 8:7)

My Thoughts are Harmless

Although our mind and thoughts are our personal space, we are still accountable for every single thought that we have entertained. No thought or idea of ours escapes God's attention. The psalmist rightly puts it this way,

You have discerned my thoughts from afar. (Ps 139:2)

99% of our sins are committed in our thoughts. Jesus says that even if we look at a woman with lust, it is equivalent to adultery.

Similarly, our sinful thoughts are real sins. Our words and actions will see a change only if our thought life is purified. St. Paul, in his letter to the Philippians, speaks about how one's thoughts ought to be.

Whatever is true, whatever is chaste, whatever is just, whatever is holy, whatever is worthy to be loved, whatever is of good repute, if there is any virtue, if there is any praiseworthy discipline: meditate on these. (Phil 4:8)

Our sinful thoughts may not affect others, but certainly harms us and hurts God. A good Christian strives to attain purity and holiness in his mind and thoughts.

It is Legal

We look for what is legal in the place where we live. It is the most popular standard by which people live. In countries where fornication and consensual sex is permissible, people do not look at it as sinful and evil. There is a widespread endorsement to the same. Sexuality existed long before any of the modern nations came to existence, and the one who created it has given specific laws concerning it. Sin can blind us if we do not look at God's law and go by what the law of the land dictates about morality and values.

The Professionals Have Approved it

There are some practices either supported or proven harmless and even beneficial by certain medical professionals, giving people the right to indulge in it. Masturbation is a good example. People see it as a simple and safest method of having sex. But the Word of God warns against and forbids any sexual practice outside of marriage. St. Paul, speaking about sexual sins, adds that, although it may be lawful or legal, it is not beneficial or useful for the person.

All things are lawful for me, but not all things are beneficial. (1 Cor 6:12)

My Spouse is OK With it

There are families where the husband and wife both indulge in the practice of watching pornography. Approval from spouse or family members does not mean approval from God. Some wives are OK with their husbands' habits of smoking or drinking, and men take this as a green signal to sin. The world and the people around should not decide what is right and wrong for a person, but God's word should be the standard.

Where Does it Say That it is a Sin?

People always look for a clause or provision to legalize their sin. The alcoholics have their verses to defend their habit. A person addicted to tobacco/ smoking will say that no verse in the Bible condemns their habit. People always look for ways to justify their actions, beliefs, and habits.

It is "My Life."

These are the "I know what is good for me" people. They live by their rules and decide what is right for them. They let nobody rule over or give directions to them. They are spiritually blind. These are people who do not repent or go to confession as they cannot see their sin. Jesus used the phrase, "blind guides leading the blind" when he referred to such people.

It Helps me or Makes Me Feel Better

People sin because it offers them temporary relief or comfort. The consolation and pleasure trick them into believing that it is good. They fail to see the long-term harm and damage it can cause. All sin is temporarily good. Eve saw that the fruit was good, but this fruit stole the whole garden from them. Some of us are introduced to sin by others just as Adam was offered the fruit by Eve.

Sin is Camouflaged

The main reason why people get deceived and cannot see sin as sin is because it is sugar-coated and appears entirely different and appealing to them. As a result, people have accepted it as a way of life. The fruit that Adam and Eve ate was very eye appealing, tasty, and desirous. But it stole their God-given blessing. They were deceived by the external appearance. So is it with every sin we commit. Although sin may appear to be satisfying, it robs everything from us. Due to ignorance and lack of knowledge, sin has become acceptable to many. There is a sin culture around us. Life is even considered boring and mundane without sin.

I am Not Addicted to it

Another excuse people give is; I will not get addicted to this habit. I only do it as a social commitment. I do drugs only at parties or get drunk with alcohol on occasions. A person need not be bitten every day by a snake to die. One bite is enough. Sin operates in the same way. Each sin we commit takes us closer to our death. We who belong to the light cannot afford to have any fellowship with sin even if it is a venial sin.

Abstain from every kind of evil. (1 Thes 5:22)

It is a Small or Minor Sin

The seriousness and gravity of any sin are decided by God alone. Every sin breaks fellowship with God to some degree. No evil can be taken lightly. Every sin puts us on the path of bondage, slavery, sickness, and death. Every sin robs our God-given blessings. The smallest sin we commit has the power to separate us from God. It takes only one cancer cell to spread and kill a person. Often, it is the little sins that go undetected and unchecked. Every venial sin we commit can grow to become a mortal sin one day.

The Whole World Does it

Just because something is acceptable and practiced by the world around us does not mean God approves it. The world and the things are passing away, and those who follow this world cannot follow Jesus. We, Christians live in the world but cannot belong to it. We bear the image of God and belong to him alone, and we are the property of God.

Do not choose to love the world nor the things that are in the world. If anyone loves the world, the love of the Father is not in him. (1 Jn 2:15)

Conclusion

We have studied some misconceptions and wrong ideas about sin, which prevent us from seeing them as they are. In the next chapter, we will move on to identifying, detecting, and discerning the sin in us. It introduces us to the examination of conscience, which is a scan of our whole being. A thorough and in-depth examination is a must for an effective and fruitful confession.

Examination of Conscience

Let us test and examine our ways and return to the Lord.
(Lam 3:40)

Basics of Examination of Conscience

Examination of conscience is a vital step in preparing for confession. The word examination means a detailed inspection or investigation. One should not merely visit the confessional to confess the occasional major mortal sin one has committed that is preventing one from receiving the Eucharist. Each time we go to confession, we must examine ourselves thoroughly and write down all the areas where we have fallen from grace. Every minor sin counts. Just as every cancer cell is harmful to the body, every evil is detrimental to us.

Examine yourselves to see whether you are living in the faith. Test yourselves. Do you not realize that Jesus Christ is in you? (2 Cor 13:5)

Examination of conscience is

- The practice of analyzing one's thoughts, words, and actions in the light of God's word
- A prayerful reflection into one's life and identifying any sin
- Allowing the Holy Spirit to reveal to us all hidden sins
- Going over the Ten Commandments to see if any sin is committed against them
- Analyzing one's life in the light of the great commandment; love of God and love of neighbor
- Examining one's life by reflecting on the teachings/ precepts of the Church

Additional Reading: Sir 18:20

Tools for Examination

This section lists some basic methods by which one can examine one's conscience. Each of these tools helps us in identifying our sins and evil tendencies within us. Each of these tools is inspired by the Word of God, which makes God's word the source of all truth and enlightenment.

Word of God

God's word is also God's law, and it is like a mirror which enables us to see our sins and weaknesses. The book of James uses the example of a mirror when referring to the Word of God.

Those who look into the perfect law, the law of liberty, and persevere, being not hearers who forget but doers who act – they will be blessed in their doing. (Jas 1:25)

Reading scriptures every day and meditating on them will help us see and repent for our sins. A Christian must spend time at least twenty minutes every day reading the Word of God. A Christian who doesn't read the Bible regularly exposes himself to the lies and corruption of this world. The book of Proverbs and Sirach are very good resources that cover many important areas where we tend to fall into sin.

Additional Reading: CCC 1454

The Ten Commandments

The Ten Commandments are laws given by God to the Israelites through Moses on Mt. Sinai. It is an excellent tool to examine ourselves before a confession. It is by far the most popular tool used by Christians to prepare for confession. The ten commandments deal with laws concerning the love of God and love of neighbor. The first three commandments focus on our relationship with God, and the rest focuses on the love of neighbor. The ten commandments are obligatory for all Christians. A detailed explanation of the commandments and its relevance and blessings are covered in the next chapter.

The Ten Commandments state what is required in the love of God and love of neighbor. The first three concern love of God, and the other seven love of neighbor. (CCC 2067)

Capital Sins

Capital sins are also known as cardinal sins or the seven deadly sins. They are hidden in nature and hence can be detected only by their manifestations, which can either be in the thought or speech or action. A list of the capital sins is covered in a separate chapter in the book.

Precepts of the Church

The precepts of the Church are laws which are binding on all Catholics with regards to worship. There are five precepts of the Church listed in the Catechism.

The precepts of the Church are set in the context of a moral life bound to and nourished by liturgical life. the obligatory character of these positive laws decreed by the pastoral authorities is meant to guarantee to the faithful the indispensable minimum in the spirit of prayer and moral effort, in the growth in love of God and neighbor (CCC 2041)

It speaks about the minimum effort a Catholic should take to grow in love of God and neighbor.

Sermon on the Mount

The Beatitudes and the sermon on the mount are a series of teachings given by Jesus in the Gospel of Matthew, chapters 5 to 7. St. Augustine calls them *"a perfect standard of the Christian life*[1]*."* They cover a variety of topics and serve as a useful tool to examine our conscience.

Conclusion

The above-listed tools are the best ways to examine one's conscience. Our knowledge of sin comes from God's word and sacred tradition. We will proceed to the next section, which is a detailed study of the commandments. As mentioned earlier, this book is not a novel, but a study guide or a manual of reference. We read a novel only for the plot. To study means to take some knowledge out of it, which requires revisiting the material, highlighting key texts, taking notes, and even memorizing.

The Ten Commandments

Introduction to The Ten Commandments

What are the Ten Commandments?

The Greek word for Ten Commandments is *decalogue.* The Ten Commandments, as it is known, were laws or instructions given by God to Moses on Mount Sinai, by which, the people of Israel must live. The law of God holds an essential place in the Jewish faith and most Christian denominations. The law was intended to be written not on stone alone but every human heart. All the spiritual laws and sins are contained within the Ten Commandments. Every kind of sin that humankind has ever committed or will commit is stated within one of these commandments. The Ten Commandments is the best tool to examine our conscience, and it is the widely used tool in the Church to prepare for confession.

There are rules everywhere we go. Every institution has its rules. Every country, state, county, and town has its own set of rules and regulations for the good of its citizens. There are rules in each home. We tell our children what to do and what not to do. As a parent, I see that these rules are in the best interest of my children, although they may not understand or grasp them – the same works with God. Our heavenly Father has given us rules and regulations for our good while we are here in this life.

Where in the Bible, Do We Find the Commandments?

The Ten Commandments are listed in two places in the Old Testament and multiple places in the New Testament in parts. It is listed in Exodus, chapter 20 and Deuteronomy, chapter 5.

List of Ten Commandments

1. I am the Lord your God, who brought you out of the land of Egypt, out of the house of slavery. You shall have no other gods before me
2. You shall not make wrongful use of the name of the Lord your God

3. Observe the sabbath day and keep it holy, as the Lord your God commanded you
4. Honor your father and your mother
5. You shall not kill
6. You shall not commit adultery
7. You shall not steal
8. You shall not bear false witness against your neighbor
9. You shall not covet your neighbor's wife
10. You shall not covet your neighbor's goods

Obedience and Blessings

God has hidden blessings in each of the commandments that he has given us. We tap into these blessings when we obey God. The secret of financial success lies not in toiling or running after money but being obedient to God and doing his will. Many people question the relevance of the Biblical laws and do not see a point or purpose in today's world. God's law is relevant and rewarding even today as it was during biblical times. With the help of Bible verses, we will look at some of the advantages and benefits of obeying God's law.

Long Life and Wellness

Adam and Eve's disobedience and sin cost them everything and also brought sickness and death into this world. Deceived by Satan, they chose death over life. Sin leads to death, whereas obedience to God's law leads to long life and abundant welfare. There is much toil these days to be healthy and fit. The whole world is health conscious. People are running in various directions to find a cure for many sicknesses. God gives an easy way to be healthy and complete our lifetime in this world.

My child do not forget my teaching, but let your heart keep my commandments; for the length of days and years of life and abundant welfare, they will give you. (Pro 3:1-2)

The writer of the book of Proverbs also echoes the same thought.

The commandment is a lamp, and the law is a light, and the reproofs of discipline are the way of life. (Pro 6:23)

Long life and good health are not acquired by beauty products or cosmetic surgery or age-defying products as some suggest, but by obedience to God and doing his will in all things.

Our Prayers Will be Answered

Sin is an obstacle to prayer. Our pleadings go unanswered because of unconfessed sin in us. Each time we approach God in prayer, it is important that we repent and forsake our sinful ways and be obedient to his commandments. We read in the first letter of John that if we are diligent in obeying his commandments, whatever we ask in prayer will be done for us.

Whatever we shall ask of him, we shall receive from him. For we keep his commandments, and we do the things that are pleasing in his sight. (1 Jn 3:22)

Blessings Upon our Descendants

One who fears the Lord and obeys his commandments will see his children and grandchildren being blessed. Below are some verses that validate this claim. Fear of God and obedience bring blessings to the whole family.

If only they had such a mind as this, to fear me and to keep all my commandments always, so that it might go well with them and with their children forever! (Deut 5:29)

Additional Reading: Ps 128, 2 Kgs 10:30, Deut 5:10

Eternal Life

Jesus promises eternal life to those who keep the commandments. God gave us the law for our good, and those who obey the law find life. Attaining eternal and everlasting life is the ultimate goal and purpose of this life. We may have gained the whole world, but without eternal life, all our accomplishments and achievements will amount to nothing. The reward of obedience is eternal life.

If you wish to enter into life, observe the commandments. (Matt 19:17)

Additional Reading: Deut 4:1, Lev 26:3-13, Luk 10:25-28

Commandments and Financial Blessings

The book of Deuteronomy, chapter 28 (verses 1 to 14) speaks about the blessings and reward associated with obedience to God's law and commandments. Prophet Isaiah writes that prosperity and financial blessings will flow into a person's life when he heeds to God's law.

O that you had paid attention to my commandments! Then your prosperity would have been like a river, and your success like the waves of the sea. (Is 48:18)

Additional Reading: Jer 11:3-5, Deut 5:32

The Commandments Tell Us What is Right and Wrong

Our whole life is a journey with many twists and turns. Imagine that we are on a highway, and there are many exits with no signs or indicators. We do not have a GPS with us and do not know which exit to take and how far to go. That is scary. Thanks to technology and the signs that are out there that make our journey reachable. Similarly, we are on the journey of life, and many wrong turns and exits can take us away from our destination. God's commandments act as a signpost to tell us which way to go and warns us of the things we should avoid. There is an excellent reward in keeping the law. The reward is eternal life.

The law of the Lord is perfect, reviving souls. The testimony of the Lord is faithful, providing wisdom to little ones; the justice of the Lord are right, rejoicing hearts; the precepts of the Lord is clear, enlightening the eyes. (Ps 19:7-8)

Blessings Within Each Commandment

When we study the commandments in the next chapter, you will notice that there are blessings built within each commandment. Every commandment has blessings and reward attached to it. We unleash these blessings by obedience to God's law. For example, when we honor and respect our parents, the Bible promises wellbeing and long life. Tithing promises financial blessings, and keeping the Sabbath law comes with its blessing. The opposite is also true; every sin and disobedience come with its consequence.

Healing

Obedience to God's law also brings healing to our mind, body, and soul. Repentance and confession heal marriages and relationships. Families that keep God's law are blessed in every way.

Blessed shall you be among all peoples. No one will be barren among you of either gender, as much among men as among your herds. The Lord will take all sickness away from you. And the very grievous infirmities of Egypt, which you have known, he will not bring upon you. (Deut 7:14-15)

Obedience brings Wisdom and Knowledge in us

Obedience to God is the source of all spiritual gifts. One who is rebellious and living in sin is left to his own wisdom. God pours his gifts of wisdom and understanding on all those who seek to live a holy and blameless life. Wisdom cannot dwell in a sinner's soul.

My child, if you would accept my words, and conceal my commandments within you, so that your ears may listen to wisdom, then bend your heart to understanding. For if you would cry out for wisdom and raise your voice for understanding, if you will seek her like silver, and dig for her as if for treasure, then you will understand the fear of the Lord, and you will discover the knowledge of God. For the Lord bestows wisdom, and out of his mouth, prudence and knowledge. He will preserve the salvation of the righteous, and he will protect those who walk blamelessly. (Pro 2:1-7)

Additional Reading: Wis 1:5

Obedience Brings Protection

Obedience to God fills us with the presence of God and the presence of God keeps us safe from evil. He who walks according to the will of God will also have the protection and safety of God.

Additional Reading: Ps 19:11

Obedience and Holiness

Holiness is not about how many prayers I say each day or how many meals I skip each week. It also has nothing to with how many crucifixes I wear around my neck or how often I go for pilgrimages. To be holy is to be Christ like. Christ was without sin and we who desire to become like him must also strive to keep the commandments and stay away from sin.

The law itself is indeed holy, and the commandment is holy and just and good. (Rom 7:12)

Obedience and Family Blessings

A man who fears and obeys the lord will have his whole family blessed by God. God will shower his graces and blessings on the family line of one who is obedient and strives to live a holy life. His wife will be a blessing and his children and grandchildren will bring immense joy and gladness.

Happy is the man that fears the Lord: who delights greatly in his commandments. His descendants shall be mighty upon the Earth: the generation of the righteous shall be blessed. Riches and wealth shall be in his house: and his righteousness endures forever and ever. (Ps 112:1-3)

Obedience to God Expels and Drives out Evil

Satan cannot dwell where God's presence and anointing dwells. When we obey God and follow his commands, we automatically cover ourselves with the presence and protection of our God. No evil presence can overcome us when we are under the care of our God. Evil and darkness will flee from us when we are obedient to God.

If you keep the commandments which I command you, and do them, to love the Lord your God, and walk in all his ways, cleaving unto him, The Lord will drive out all these nations before your face, and you shall possess them, which are greater and stronger than you. (Deut 11:22-23)

Additional Reading: Deut 6:18-19

Obedience brings the presence of God

God cannot stand evil and therefore he separates himself from one who lives a sinful life. He waits for him to give up his sin and return to him. At the same time, God fills his presence on the one who lives a holy and blameless life. God has no sin and he does not tolerate sin of any kind.

Those who keep his commandments abide in him, and he in them. And we know that he abides in us by this: by the Spirit, whom he has given to us. (1 Jn 3:24)

Are the Commandments Relevant for Our Times?

Commandments are Valid till the End of Time

Many people put forward this theory that the biblical laws are outdated and irrelevant to our times, but this is not what the Bible teaches. The Church, from the time of its conception, has taught and practiced the commandments and laws of God. The law was given not just for the Jews, but for all humanity and all ages. Times have changed, but God and his law never change. Jesus reiterates this in the Gospel of Mathew.

Until heaven and earth pass away, not one letter, not one stroke of a letter, will pass from the law until all is accomplished. (Matt 5:18)

God's Law Does Not Change

Human laws change according to the convenience of the people and the lawmakers, but God, the divine lawmaker, does not change with time. The reason why we find it hard to follow God's law is because of our evil desires and selfish motives within us. We have become lovers of ourselves. To love God is not a priority for us anymore. The first letter of John informs us that when we love God, his commandments will not be difficult to follow.

The love of God is this, that we obey his commandments. And his commandments are not burdensome. (1 Jn 5:3)

Jesus Did not Abolish the Law

Today's Christians are of the understanding that being a Christian or having a parish membership is enough to get them to heaven. They go to church every Sunday and do whatever they want with their personal life. According to them, the commandments were abolished by Jesus, and faith in Christ alone is enough for salvation. It is another lie that has spread over Christianity. If Baptism alone is enough, why did Jesus institute the Sacrament of Reconciliation?

Do not think that I am come to abolish the law, or the prophets. I am not come to abolish, but to fulfill. (Matt 5:17, DRA)

Know the Commandments

Jesus, preaching the sermon on the mount, stresses the importance of the least of the commandments. The commandments of God were not abolished in the new covenant as many claim.

Whoever breaks one of the least of these commandments, and teaches others to do the same, will be called least in the kingdom of heaven; but whoever does them and teaches them will be called great in the kingdom of heaven. (Matt 5:19)

Do not Tweak the Commandments

The term "Cafeteria Catholic" refers to a person who picks and chooses what he or she wants to believe and follow. Unfortunately there are many such people in the Church today.

You shall not add to the word which I speak to you, neither shall you take away from it. Keep the commandments of the Lord your God which I am teaching to you. (Deut 4:2)

Additional Reading: Deut 12:32

Love and Commandments

To obey the commandments is not difficult for the one who loves God with all his heart. In fact, God himself will make us his dwelling place and give us the grace and strength to do his will. Through the Eucharist, we invite Jesus into our hearts, and he will set our hearts on fire for God. We will no longer be hungry for sin, but righteousness. God's law will be deeply engraved in our hearts and minds.

This is the commandment which I will make with them after those days, says the Lord. I will instill my laws in their hearts, and I will inscribe my laws on their minds. (Heb 10:16)

Jesus goes on to say that, we prove our love for God by keeping and obeying his commandments.

Those who accept my commandments and obey them are the ones who love me. My Father will love those who love me; I too will love them and reveal myself to them. (Jn 14:21, GNT)

Obey all the Commandments

We live in a day and age where each one is his own boss and each one dictates what is good and bad for himself. Everything is relative these days. People are unwilling to submit to any kind of authority even it is for their own good. God's Word is clear that the laws given to us are relevant for all ages and must be followed in its entirety.

Today the Lord your God commands you to obey all his laws; so obey them faithfully with all your heart. Today you have acknowledged the Lord as your God; you have promised to obey him, to keep all his laws, and to do all that he commands. (Deut 26:16-17, GNT)

Additional Reading: Deut 27:11-26, Matt 28:20

Teach the Commandments

We, as Christians have the responsibility to not only obey the commandments but also to teach the law of God to others.

Assemble the people. I want them to hear what I have to say, so that they will learn to obey me as long as they live and so that they will teach their children to do the same. (Deut 4:10, GNT)

God's Spirit Enables us to Obey the Commandments

The Holy Spirit is our helper given to us by God to do his will, which includes strengthening and enabling us to follow the commandments. Therefore, we must pray and seek the help of the Holy Spirit actively to grow in holiness. Jesus knew very well that it is impossible for us to become righteous and attain sainthood without the Holy Spirit.

I will place my spirit within you, and make you walk in my precepts and be careful to observe my ordinances. (Eze 36:27)

Conclusion

God's law is not burdensome or difficult to those who love him. His blessings will flow in and through us if we are obedient to him. The next chapter is the beginning of the study on each of the commandments. Each section or subsection has a Bible verse or other references to validate a claim or statement. There are also additional references given for further reading. Each section also comes with an examination of conscience to help prepare for confession.

The First Commandment

I am the LORD your God, who brought you out of the land of Egypt, out of the house of bondage. You shall have no other gods before me

---

The first three commandments deal with our relationship with God. Every commandment is rooted and built on the first commandment, making it the most important of all. It speaks about the oneness and supremacy of our God. There are many religions in the world, but only one God who is the creator of heaven and earth (universe). He is almighty, omnipresent, omniscient, and omnibenevolent. This commandment also deals with how one must approach God.

Knowledge of God

God desires every human being to foremost spend time knowing him. Throughout time, God has revealed himself to man in various ways and continues to show his presence, love, and power in and through his works in our lives. He tirelessly and lovingly invites everyone to know, seek, and love him.

He calls man to seek him, to know him, to love him with all his strength. (CCC 1)

Knowledge of God is the gateway to eternal life. Knowledge of God is knowledge of the truth because God is the truth. One who seeks God will receive insight and truth about the origin, purpose, and destination of life.

This is eternal life, that they may know you, the only true God, and Jesus Christ whom you have sent. (Jn 17:3)

Most of us have limited our faith life to information and facts. We know when Christmas is and how to celebrate it. We know when to sit, stand, and kneel in Church. We know who the pope is, where our Church is, and when to go to church. We have memorized all the prayers and many of the basics of our Catholic faith, but our knowledge of God is weak and shallow. St. Paul in his letter to Timothy says,

Having the appearance of piety while rejecting its power. (2 Tim 3:5)

God equates the destruction of man to lack of knowledge and warns us through the prophet Hosea,

My people are destroyed because of lack of knowledge. (Hos 4:6)

All the doctrines, dogmas, our mother Church, tradition, worship, liturgy, saints, Blessed Mother, angels, feasts, Scripture, sacraments, relics, sacramentals, novenas, prayers, and ministries, all point to our creator and our God. However, we fail to see God's hand behind all this. God shares his grief and pain through the prophet Isaiah,

The ox knows its owner, and the donkey its master's crib; but Israel does not know, my people do not understand. (Is 1:3)

How Does One Know God?

Creation is the foremost witness to the awesomeness and power of God. By carefully looking at the world around us, we can come to a basic understanding of God. Creation itself is a sign that there is a creator behind it, yet we fail to comprehend and deny the existence of the Almighty.

All people who were ignorant of God were foolish by nature; and they were unable from the good things that are seen to know the one who exists, nor did they recognize the artisan while paying heed to his works. (Wis 13:1)

We are ignorant if we fail to see the nature and person of God around us. God has put his character and personality in the created world. The sun shines every day without charging a penny for its light. The earth is abundantly giving us minerals, medicines, and many other products. The trees give us fruits, vegetables, medicine, chemicals, wood for our furniture and homes. Nature is ever giving itself selflessly. The ocean supplies us with seafood. The clouds provide us with rain. And if we were to look closely at our human nature, we as parents provide everything for our children for free; food, clothing, shelter, books, toys, etc. We receive this nature from God. His likeness is in all created things.

From the greatness and beauty of created things comes a corresponding perception of their Creator. (Wis 13:5)

God's power and his divine nature, though invisible he is, can be understood just by looking at the world around us.

Ever since the creation of the world his eternal power and divine nature, invisible though they are, have been understood and seen through the things he has made. (Rom 1:20)

God, in his conversation with Job, reveals this truth for our understanding. There is order and discipline in nature. The spinning of the earth and the movement of the planetary bodies bear witness to it. If we look closely into the smallest of particles within an atom, there is beauty and order.

Even birds and animals have much they could teach you; ask the creatures of earth and sea for their wisdom. All of them know that the Lord's hand made them. (Job 12:7-9, GNT)

Creation speaks volumes about the wisdom of its creator. The world around us could not have come to exist by itself. There is wisdom in creation, which shows to prove that somebody wise created it.

He poured her (Wisdom) out upon all his works (Sir 1:9)

Prayer and Revelation

Prayer is powerful. It lifts us to God and into his spiritual realm. Prayer helps us see and understand the truths that we cannot grasp with our senses. It also gives us access to divine knowledge. We will appreciate the depths of God only when we spend time with him. The psalmist says,

When I thought how to understand this, it seemed to me a wearisome task, until I went into the sanctuary of God; then I perceived their end. (Ps 73:16-17)

and again, we read in the book of Jeremiah,

Call out to me and I will answer you, and will tell you great and hidden things that you have not known. (Jer 33:3)

Prayer opens us to the mysteries of God. It helps us understand our human nature. Prayer gives us wisdom, knowledge, and understanding to see beyond what the eye can see. John the Apostle, while he was on the island of Patmos, spent his time in meditation. It is during this time of prayer that God reveals to him the course of events that will happen at the end of time.

I was in the spirit on the Lord's day, and I heard behind me a loud voice like a trumpet saying, "Write in a book what you see and send it to the seven churches. (Rev 1:10)

Apostle John, while he was in prayer, received the command to author the book of revelation, which shows that it is through prayer, we gain insight and knowledge of God and life.

Word of God and Knowledge

Light, as we all know, makes it easy for us to see. Without light, this world would be chaotic. The psalmist compares the Word of God to light. God's Word reveals to us more about his nature, our human nature, the present life, and the life to come. Somebody beautifully said that the word BIBLE stands for "Basic Instruction Before Leaving Earth." Scripture gives us insight into divine matters which cannot be known otherwise.

Your word is a lamp to my feet and a light to my path. (Ps 119:105)

Sacramental Life

Every sacrament takes us closer to Jesus and reveals his love for us. Frequent confession helps us to understand the mercy and forgiving love of God. Through the Sacraments, God reveals himself to us. Frequent communion helps us understand the self-sacrificing, unconditional love of Jesus.

He sat down to eat with them, took the bread, and said the blessing; then he broke the bread and gave it to them. Then their eyes were opened and they recognized him, but he disappeared from their sight. (Luk 24:30-31, GNT)

Holy Spirit and Knowledge

The Holy Spirit is given to us by God as a helper, and through praying to him, we will grow in love, holiness, and knowledge of God. He will impart his divine wisdom upon us and enrich us with knowledge and understanding of spiritual truths. Wisdom, knowledge, and understanding are gifts of the Holy Spirit (Isaiah 11). He who has recourse to God's Spirit also has access to divine truths and insights.

You gave your good spirit to instruct them. (Neh 9:20)

Areas to Examine:

- Do I seek and thirst to know God in prayer? How much quality time do I spend each day in prayer seeking and thirsting to know God?
- Do I "study" and reflect on the Word of God every day?
- Do I "meditatively reflect" on sacred Scriptures every day?

- Am I regular to the sacraments? (daily Eucharist if possible, Weekly confession, weekly fasting if healthy)
- If I am not able to go for weekday Masses, do I at least meditate on the Mass readings of the day?
- Do I make time to read good Christian literature and works of saints to grow in the knowledge of God?
- Do I spend at least an hour a week in prayer before the blessed sacrament?
- Do I show interest in Godly and spiritual activities? (Lack of interest stems from a lack of love)

Love for God

Man's love for God is a response to God's love for man. Scripture reveals that God loved us first. Man is not trying to win God's love and attention but responding to it.

God, who is rich in mercy, out of the great love with which he loved us even when we were dead through our trespasses, made us alive together with Christ. (Eph 2:4)

The sacrifice of Jesus is proof of this love. God's love for man is unconditional, eternal, everlasting, and steadfast. It does not change over time or diminish when we sin against him. Jesus died for us while we were still sinners.

In this is love, not that we loved God but that he loved us and sent his Son to be the atoning sacrifice for our sins. (1 Jn 4:10)

Man is fully able to love God with the given faculties. God is love, and he created everything in love, which includes you and me. We are created in love, for love, and to love. In our lifetime, we fall in love with many things. We are attracted, attached, and addicted to many things. Love is our primary vocation and call. We are always in love.

We are foremost called to love God, who created us and loved us. Have we fulfilled this call? The first commandment requires us and commands us to love God, above all else. And of course, God who has given us free will has left the choice to us. In love, there is freedom. Jesus, quoting from Deuteronomy, emphasizes love for God as the greatest commandment.

You shall love the Lord your God with all your heart, and with all your soul, and with all your strength, and with all your mind. (Luk 10:27)

Jesus uses some strong words about our priority of love in the Gospel of Matthew. Love for God is the primary or fundamental love upon which every other love relationship should be built.

Whoever loves father or mother more than me is not worthy of me, and whoever loves son or daughter more than me is not worthy of me. (Matt 10:37)

Let us put our love to the test and do a reality check. Take the example of a Christian who goes to church every Sunday. One may go for Sunday Mass for many reasons. Some do it out of compulsion from family, while others do it as an obligation. Some do it out of habit or as a handed down tradition while others do it out of guilt to avoid mortal sin. Some do it to impress somebody, and others do it only because their kids go to Catholic school, and Mass attendance is necessary. There are numerous reasons why one does spiritual activities. All things can be done with or without love. What is the sign that I am doing it out of love? Is love the force behind my spiritual activities? Let us look at some qualities of true love and see where we stand and whether our religious exercises flow out of love.

I Always Want to be With the One I Love

Be it an object or a person; we want to be with the one we love. As parents, we like to be with our children. People are always with their phones these days. We like to spend time with the one person or one thing we love. Similarly, God, because he loves us, wants to be with us always.

Those who love me will keep my word, and my Father will love them, and we will come to them and make our home with them. (Jn 14:23)

Do we long to be with God, the way God wants to be with us? As the Psalmist writes,

As a deer longs for a stream of cool water, so I long for you, O God. I thirst for you, the living God. (Ps 42:1-2, GNT)

Areas to Examine:

- Do I have a fixed time for personal prayer every day?
- Do I look forward to my prayer time?

- Are God and prayer the first things that come to my mind when I wake up each morning?
- Do I make it a point not to miss my personal prayer, no matter how busy or tired I am?

We Try to Please the One we Love

When we look at young lovers, we notice that they always try to please each other, sometimes by giving gifts, calling, texting, and behaving nicely. They try not to do anything displeasing. Lovers go to great lengths to find out what the other likes and attempt to please beyond measure. They value their relationship. Jesus has unconditional love for the Father, which is expressed in many places in the Gospels. He always pleased the Father in his thoughts, words, and actions.

The one who sent me is with me; he has not left me alone, for I always do what is pleasing to him. (Jn 8:29)

Areas to Examine:

- Do I try to please God by finding out and doing what he wants from me?
- Do I try to know God's laws and obey them?
- Do I hate and avoid doing what God hates?

Additional Reading: Matt 3:17

We Make Sacrifices for the One we Love

Love calls for sacrifice, and without sacrifice, love cannot be fulfilled. God proved his love for us when he sacrificed his only son for us. We too, make many sacrifices for the one we love, be it a person or an object or something of this world. We stay late to watch a movie and sacrifice a couple of hours of sleep. We stand on our feet for hours to cheer our team when we are at a stadium watching a game. At the same time, when it comes to loving God, what sacrifices have I made? Small things count, when we are in love. For example, giving up an hour of sleep and utilizing it for prayer is also a sacrifice. When our love for our God is genuine, we will be able to take the pain. Fasting and abstinence are also a kind of sacrifice to prove that God is valuable for us. Giving up certain worldly pleasures and comforts for God is also a sacrifice. God made the ultimate sacrifice on Calvary to fulfill his relationship with us.

God so loved the world that he gave his only Son, so that everyone who believes in him may not perish but may have eternal life. (Jn 3:16)

In the life of Jesus, we see his dedication and commitment to prayer. There were times when Jesus would sacrifice his sleep and spend the whole night in worship.

During those days, he went out to the mountain to pray; and he spent the night in prayer to God. (Luk 6:12)

Areas to Examine:

- Am I able to see the hindrances and obstacles to my spiritual life and make the necessary sacrifices to be with God?
- Do I willfully make sacrifices to fulfill my relationship with God?
- Does my prayer time always gets compromised because of work, rest, and family commitments?
- Do I find it hard to come out of my comfort zone?

Additional Reading: Luk 5:15

Lovers Always Talk to Each Other

One of the most beautiful aspects of being in love is the joy lovers get out of talking to each other. They can go on for hours on end without getting tired of talking.

Rejoice always, pray without ceasing, give thanks in all circumstances; for this is the will of God in Christ Jesus for you. (1 Thes 5:16-18)

When we pray, we talk to God. When we read the Scriptures, God talks back to us. Prayer and Scripture reading go hand in hand and become a two-way communication. The psalmist tells us to delight in his word. His word is a source of joy for all who meditate on it.

Their delight is in the law of the Lord, and on his law, they meditate day and night. (Ps 1:2)

Areas to Examine:

- Do I talk to God outside of my prayer time?
- Do I think about God outside of Church?

- How often do I remember God outside of Church and prayer time?

Love Strengthens Us

When a person finds prayer as boring or tiring, it is proof that he is not in love with God. Love itself provides that supernatural strength to fulfill the obligation. For example, we have heard excellent reviews about a movie or a book. It produces a desire in us to buy or possess it. Once it is in our possession, we waste no time watching the movie or reading the book in one sitting. It is love for that movie or that book that makes us go through it even if it is too late in the night. Our tiredness and boredom suddenly vanish. At the same time, if we are asked to read the Scriptures or some religious book, within about 10 minutes, we either feel sleepy or tired or bored. The real reason is a lack of love.

Areas to Examine:

- Do I feel bored at the very mention of prayer and Bible reading?
- Do I feel sleepy or tired, as soon as I start praying or reading the Bible?
- Do I get distracted in my mind and thoughts while praying or reading scripture?

Love of the World

The desire and love for this world will choke our spiritual life. The reason why most people find spiritual life hard and fruitless is because of the unhealthy desire for this material world and their unwillingness to give up certain pleasures, hobbies, and passions.

Do not love the world or the things in the world. The love of the Father is not in those who love the world. (1 Jn 2:15)

Indifference

Indifference is the lack of interest shown to God and godly matters. Our love for God should come from the depths of our heart, mind, soul, and body. Lack of concern and unwillingness to grow spiritually are sins against the first commandment. Call and vocation deserve priority than career and ambition. If we do not strive to grow in faith, little of what we have will be taken away from us. We tend to give more value and priority to our career and ambition and give little to no importance or attention to our life's call and vocation. Failure to meditate on the love and the sacrifice of God is also indifference.

Lukewarmness

Lukewarmness is similar to indifference. This is a person who shows little to no enthusiasm for God and spiritual matters. David, in the Old Testament, was a man who was devoted and passionate for God. His psalms reflect his love and zeal for God. There is an incident mentioned about him where he is bringing the Ark of the Covenant back to Israel (2 Sam 6:21). David is so excited that he dances naked on the streets. That is how much ardent his love was for his God. Let us compare our faith with his. We try to put God in a box, and prayer for us is just one of the activities of the day. We are unwilling to stretch and make sacrifices to be with God. A lukewarm soul will sooner or later lose the little passion that is left for God.

I know your works; you are neither cold nor hot. I wish that you were either cold or hot. So, because you are lukewarm, and neither cold nor hot, I am about to spit you out of my mouth. (Rev 3:15-16)

Worship of God

Love of God leads to the worship of God. Worship proceeds from a heart filled with love. The world worships and honors money because the hearts of the people are filled with the love of money. God deserves our worship, and Satan demands our worship. Worship of created things is the same as the worship of Satan. Satan derives his pleasure when we worship created things. He tempts us to offer worship to him, and every sin is an indirect worship of the devil. The entire world is under the power of the evil one

We know that we are God's children, and that the whole world lies under the power of the evil one. (1 John 5:19)

Worship of one true God leads one to blessings and fullness of life. It also frees us from sinful inclinations and evil intentions. A person who is connected with God in worship is free from sin, evil tendencies, and cravings.

You shall worship the Lord your God, and I will bless your bread and your water; and I will take sickness away from among you. No one shall miscarry or be barren in your land; I will fulfill the number of your days. (Exo 23:25-26)

God alone should be the recipient of our worship, and the worship of anything other than the one true living God is idolatry. All forms of idol worship are a sin against the first commandment.

You shall worship no other god, because the Lord, whose name is Jealous, is a jealous God. (Exo 34:14)

We, in the modern world, may not offer worship to idols, but deep inside we hold on to other Gods such as money, beauty, power, reputation, intellect, physical strength, etc. The so-called gods of this world control us and lead us to revere and honor them. Some of us are obsessed about losing weight and looking skinny. Some of us have made, becoming wealthy as the sole objective of life. Some of us put much time, effort, and value in looking young. There are still others who put their career first in line. All these material things have become our gods.

Even if our gospel is veiled, it is veiled to those who are perishing. In their case the god of this world has blinded the minds of the unbelievers, to keep them from seeing the light of the gospel of the glory of Christ, who is the image of God. (2 Cor 4:3-4)

Even prayerful people can be trapped in some way of idol worship. One may be praying a lot, but what is one seeking from the lord? If we pray only for blessings and wellbeing of our family, our health, and finances, then there is an idol there. All these material and worldly things have consumed our heart and become idols. The Prophet Isaiah writes that although people sit before God and perform all the rituals, their heart is not in it. Their God is elsewhere.

The Lord said: Because these people draw near with their mouths and honor me with their lips, while their hearts are far from me, and their worship of me is a human commandment learned by rote. (Is 29:13)

Areas to Examine:

- Is my prayer God-centered or self-centered?
- Is my relationship with God restricted to receiving blessings and getting my prayers answered?
- Am I able to freely worship God without any demands?
- Am I holding on to something in place of God?
- Is there anything in my life that I value more than God?
- Am I giving God's place in my heart to a human being?
- Do I maintain reverence and proper posture when I pray?

There is a deep thirst and search for God in every human heart. The fact that we have so many religions and denominations in this world is a sign that man has always looked for divine power above himself. In this search for a higher power, man has made a created being or object to be his God in many cultures and countries around the world. There are many variations of idol worship, and some popular ones are listed below.

Idol Worship

It is the worship of a human, animal, or any created object other than God. Idol worship is of many kinds. People worship idols of animals, reptiles, humans, mythological creatures, or it could even merely be a block of stone. God forbids all forms of idol worship. Idols are creations of humans, and they are powerless and helpless. St. Paul also says that all idol worship is worship of demons which in turn is a worship of the devil. In short, Idolatry can be summarized as

- Veneration of divinities other than the one true God
- Idolatry consists in divinizing what is not God
- Honoring and revering a creature in place of the creator
- Idolatry rejects the unique lordship of God

Do not turn to idols or make cast images for yourselves: I am the Lord your God. (Lev 19:4)

Additional Reading: Lev 26:1, Ps 115:4-8, 1 Cor 10:20-21, Deut 6:14, Deut 4:16, Deut 4:23, Deut 5:8, Wis 15:17, Wis 13:17-19, Rom 1:21, Jer 10:3-5, Is 44:9-20, 2 Chron 28:1-4

Animal Worship

Helpless animals are thought to be embodiments of the divine in some cultures. It is a scientifically known fact that they have a lower intellect and little to no reasoning ability. They are weaker than us in all respects. Yet, people have continued to seek their help and intervention in their lives. The Bible condemns this practice.

In return for their foolish and wicked thoughts, which led them astray to worship irrational serpents and worthless animals, you sent upon them a multitude of irrational creatures to punish them. (Wis 11:15)

Additional Reading: Wis 12:24, Rom 1:25, Lev 17:7, Wis 15:18-19

Human Worship

In some eastern cultures, men and women are believed to be incarnations of gods and hence elevated to divine status and worshipped. Christian teaching is clear that all human beings are created beings and do not deserve any worship. We have no special powers unless given by God.

Claiming to be wise, they became fools; and they exchanged the glory of the immortal God for images resembling a mortal human being or birds or four-footed animals or reptiles. (Rom 1:22-23)

Additional Reading: Deut 4:15-16

Nature Worship

Nature is mostly friendly to man but at times shows its fury and causes devastation on land, property, cattle, and people. In primitive times, the natural world was thought to be divine, and I have personally seen in places where people offer sacrifices to nature sometimes to calm it down or to please it. In some cultures, special prayers are offered to nature in times of drought or famine. The Bible forbids such customs. The natural world around us submits to the Almighty over which he has complete authority. When we are obedient and submissive to God, the natural world around us will also be favorable to us.

Jesus stood up and commanded the wind, "Be quiet!" and he said to the waves, "Be still!" The wind died down, and there was a great calm. Then Jesus said to his disciples, "Why are you frightened? Do you still have no faith? (Mrk 4:39-41, GNT)

Additional Reading: Ps 19:1, Gal 4:8-9, Deut 17:2-3, 2 Kgs 21:3-5, Zeph 1:4, Bar 6:60-65, Wis 13:2-3

Worship of Celestial Bodies

In addition to nature worship, all visible solar bodies are also worshipped and honored by many. People see the heavens above as something more powerful than them and hence honor and revere them. The sun, the moon, and the stars are seen as embodiments of the divine, and therefore, worship and honor are offered to them. The scientific community has proved without a doubt that all celestial bodies are lifeless and are run by energy and force.

When you look up to the heavens and see the sun, the moon, and the stars, all the host of heaven, do not be led astray and bow down to them and serve them, things that the LORD your God has allotted to all the peoples everywhere under heaven. (Deut 4:19)

Additional Reading: Deut 17:2-3

Worship of the Dead

Some see death as a means of attaining divinity. Christian teaching is clear that the dead are with God but do not themselves become gods. Worshipping the dead or summoning the deceased is a sin against the first commandment.

Additional Reading: Jer 8:1-3, Wis 14:15-16

Godmen and Cult Leaders

From time to time, history has witnessed many who have claimed to be incarnations of the divine. Some have even pronounced themselves as the second coming of Christ. Hundreds and even thousands of people have fallen victims to such bizarre and absurd claims. As a result, people have ended up venerating fellow humans and treating weak and powerless people as Gods. Jesus is the only mediator sent by God to save mankind from sin and evil, and there is no need for another one. Jesus defeated sin on the cross once and for all and those who believe in him shall not die and will attain eternal life.

Do not let the prophets and the diviners who are among you deceive you, and do not listen to the dreams that they dream, for it is a lie that they are prophesying to you in my name; I did not send them, says the Lord. (Jer 29:8)

Additional Reading: Jer 27:9

Worship of the Material World

Worship is rooted in love and fear. Fear and insecurities in finances, job, and the future have led people to worship wealth. Money has consumed the hearts of people, and everybody is busy trying to get rich. This unhealthy love for money has transformed into worship and obsession. Power, beauty, youthfulness, material possessions are other gods that people seek and go after.

Additional Reading: 1 Jn 2:15-16

Idolizing Celebrities (Movie stars, Pop Stars, Superheroes, Sports Personalities, Political Leaders)

This practice or habit is fed into a human being from an incredibly early age. Parents and the society around have a key role to play in it. Children begin to admire superheroes for their charisma and other superhuman strengths. In most cultures, it is very much encouraged. Superhero movies generate big revenue these days. Innocent children get sucked into their fantasy world. They begin to idolize these figures and wish to become like them. This kind of love is unhealthy and excessive. Adults are no better in this area. People attach strong values to ideas, movements, people, political affiliation, etc.

Work

Work can become an idol if not done in moderation and balance. The world around us is becoming more and more workaholic. Greed and emptiness within is driving people to work more than what is required. An unhealthy bond is developed which destroys family life and faith life.

Clothes, Jewels, Gadgets, etc.

We cannot do without clothes. They protect us from the harsh weather. They cover our private parts, and they also enhance our beauty. Although, we cannot do without clothes, we should be careful that they don't become the center of our lives. It also applies to shoes, handbags, gadgets, etc. All these things have a purpose, and we use them solely to make our lives better. Once, we start giving priority to these material things above other things, we are making an idol out of them.

Areas to Examine:

- Have I associated myself or joined any group whose leader claims himself to be an incarnation of God?
- Did I leave my Catholic faith at any time?
- Did I worship any gods or goddesses of other religions?
- Do I give more importance to work and money than God?
- Am I in possession of any idols to whom I offer worship and honor?
- Did I worship, fear, or pay honor to any celestial body?
- Have I worshipped or feared nature?
- Have I worshipped the dead or had an unhealthy relationship with the dead?

- Have I worshipped any animal or object?
- Do I celebrate or observe feasts and festivals of other religions?
- Am I overly concerned and worried about "what to wear"?

Serve God

Every baptized Christian is an evangelist who serves God wholeheartedly. God has a ministry for each one of us, and he anoints us with gifts and talents to carry out his mission in this life. Jesus, through his life and ministry, has modeled this mission for us.

The Son of Man came not to be served but to serve, and to give his life a ransom for many. (Mrk 10:45)

The one who serves him must follow him. To follow Jesus is to follow the path that Jesus chose. Jesus took the way of the cross and to follow Him means to carry our daily cross and deny ourselves.

Whoever serves me must follow me, and where I am, there will my servant be also. Whoever serves me, the Father will honor. (Jn 12:26)

God wants to see our faithfulness and commitment in serving him. Whatever we do for the Lord will never be in vain or useless.

Areas to Examine:

- Have I discovered my ministry of service for the Lord?
- Am I actively desiring and praying for a ministry?
- Do I make use of my natural talents, gifts, and abilities for the kingdom of God?
- Am I giving freely as I have received freely?
- In my service for the Lord, am I selfless or self-seeking?
- Do I have a deep thirst for the conversion of souls?
- Do I pray for others?
- Do I help others to find Christ?

Additional Reading: 1 Cor 15:58, Deut 11:13, 1 Sam 12:24

Praise

Praise is a forgotten and neglected prayer in Christianity today. Outside of the Holy Mass, Catholics are not familiar with praise and do not know how to practice it. Praise is a simple yet powerful exercise which can be expressed by singing, clapping, loud shouts, etc. The old testament Jews were very active in praising and glorifying God. They witnessed mighty miracles when they praised Yahweh. God is great and greatly to be praised. We praise him because he is worthy of being praised. All his works are great, and we acknowledge his creation, each time we praise him.

Praise is the form of prayer which recognizes most immediately that God is God. It lauds God for his own sake and gives him glory, quite beyond what he does, but simply because HE IS. It shares in the blessed happiness of the pure of heart who love God in faith before seeing him in glory. By praise, the Spirit is joined to our spirits to bear witness that we are children of God, testifying to the only Son in whom we are adopted and by whom we glorify the Father. Praise embraces the other forms of prayer and carries them toward him who is its source and goal: the "one God, the Father, from whom are all things, and for whom we exist. (CCC 2639)

In the excerpt given above, the Catechism gives five reasons to praise and glorify God.

- Praise recognizes God as God
- Praise spiritually unites us with those who love God
- Praise unites our spirit with the Holy Spirit
- Praise lifts all other prayers with it.
- Praise gives glory to God which he deserves

Praise Gives Glory to God

Catechism 2639 teaches that praise acknowledges God for who he is. God is omnipresent (present everywhere), omniscient (all knowing) and omnibenevolent (all good) and we recognize and proclaim all these qualities in him when we praise and thank him.

"You are worthy, our Lord and God, to receive glory and honor and power, for you created all things, and by your will they existed and were created." (Rev 4:11)

Praise Recognizes God as God

By praise, we acknowledge ourselves as a creation of God and God as the sole creator of the entire universe. We thank him and marvel at his creation each time we praise him.

Praise Unites us With God

Praise lifts us from our human level and takes us to the spiritual realm, giving us insight into many spiritual truths and mysteries that God wants to reveal to us. We are surrounded and shrouded in the glory of God and protected from the evil one, each time we sing praises to him.

Praise Lifts our Prayers to God

Praise is the sum total of all the prayers we make. All our petitions, needs, supplications, and intercessions are lifted to God when we praise. When we are in need, when we face trials or persecutions, and when we are tempted, praise is the way to see God's mighty intervention.

I will praise your name continually, and will sing hymns of thanksgiving. My prayer was heard. (Sir 51:11)

Praise Brings us into God's Presence

God is enthroned on the praises of his people. God dwells where his name is glorified and honored through praise and singing. We enter his presence by exalting and glorifying his name. The sign of God's presence is the fullness of Joy and peace in us.

You are holy, enthroned on the praises of Israel. (Ps 22:3)

Praise is a Demonstration of Faith

Praise is an act of faith. God wants us to exercise our faith and praise him when things do not go our way. Unfortunately, people find it hard to praise God during such times. There is a passage in the Old Testament, in the book of Daniel, where he and his friends are arrested and put in a heated furnace to die. The king visits to see what had happened to them. To his surprise, he sees them praising and singing to God. They are protected by divine intervention. As a result, they escape the fire without any harm. Our faith grows stronger each time we praise Him, and we will see bigger miracles.

They walked around in the midst of the flames, singing hymns to God and blessing the Lord. Then Azariah stood still in the fire and prayed aloud. (Dan 3:24-25)

Praise Frees us From Negativity

Continuous praise and having a heart and attitude of gratitude will draw us out of a life of negativity and self-centeredness. Praise brings us into the presence of God and fills us with joy and gladness. As a result, all negativity will leave immediately. There is no place for sadness, sorrow, fear, worry, or any anxiety in his presence.

Praise Delivers us From Evil

The evil forces in the spiritual realm cannot bear to hear the sound of praise. It torments them, and they are forced to flee. In the book of Samuel, there is an incident mentioned where each time King Saul was tormented by an evil spirit, he would send for David who would sing praises to God with his music. Immediately, King Saul would be freed of the oppression. Although it is an old testament verse, the method still works. Satan and evil spirits cannot tolerate Godly praise and music.

I call upon the Lord, who is worthy to be praised, so I shall be saved from my enemies. (Ps 18:3)

Praise Frees us From Sin and Addictions

Another advantage of praising God is that we receive freedom from sin and addictions. Sinful tendencies and desires leave us when we are filled with God's presence, and we are strengthened by his grace, which acts as a shield around us.

While they praised God's holy name, and the sanctuary resounded from early morning. The Lord took away his sins, and exalted his power forever. (Sir 47:10-11)

Praise Removes Obstacles in Our Lives

The wall of Jericho was the last obstacle between the people of Israel and the promised land (Joshua 6:1-7). God gave them specific instructions about how to bring down this wall and enter the land of Canaan. God instructed the people to sing and praise. When the people of Israel praised God with loud shouts and music, the wall of Jericho came tumbling down. We too are faced with many obstacles in our life, and praise is the way to bring down these mighty walls and mountains. Praise opens locked doors in our life.

Praise Anoints us With the Holy Spirit

Anointing of the Holy Spirit is another blessing we receive out of praising God as we read in CCC 2639. All evil spirits leave us, and the spirit of God takes control over us. The Holy Spirit is a sign of God's love, care, and protection. Each time we praise God, we receive a fresh anointing of the Holy Spirit. Praise expels all evil and clothes us with God's spirit.

Signs, Wonders, Miracles, and Healings

The book of the Acts of the Apostles narrates a story where Paul and Silas were in prison. They did not give in to negativity and despair. Instead, they praised God and sang hymns to God, and while they glorified God, there was a powerful earthquake, and the prison doors opened. God performs mighty wonders and miracles for his people when his name is praised and glorified.

About midnight Paul and Silas were praying and singing hymns to God, and the prisoners were listening to them. Suddenly there was an earthquake, so violent that the foundations of the prison were shaken; and immediately all the doors were opened, and everyone's chains were unfastened. (Acts 16:25-26)

Praise and Word of God

We are sometimes overly critical of people who praise aloud, and we ourselves do not take an active part in singing to God. Music and singing in the church are neither for our entertainment, nor it is solely the musician or the choir's job to praise God. Praise is immensely powerful, and it lifts the soul when we wholeheartedly participate in it. Most of our songs we sing are taken from the Bible, and as we sing praises to God, we also meditate on his Word at the same time.

Rejoice in the Lord, O you righteous. Praise befits the upright. Praise the Lord with the lyre; make melody to him with the harp of ten strings. Sing to him a new song; play skillfully on the strings, with loud shouts. (Ps 33:1-3)

Additional Reading: Col 3:16

Continuous Praise

The psalmist tells us to praise God always and for everything. Praise should not be reduced to once a week church activity. A Christian praises God even when things do not happen according to his will and desire.

I will bless the Lord at all times; his praise shall continually be in my mouth. (Ps 34:1)

Praise With all Your Strength

Powerful praise brings guaranteed results. We always give our best cheer and the loudest shout when we are watching a game where our favorite team is playing, whereas we look and sound tired in Church during praise and worship. Few people know that the way to get rid of tiredness and laziness is praise. The more we praise, the stronger we become. God deserves our best praise, and we simply cannot praise him enough.

Glorify the Lord and exalt him as much as you can, for he surpasses even that. When you exalt him, summon all your strength, and do not grow weary, for you cannot praise him enough. (Sir 43:30)

Do Not be Ashamed to Praise God

People do not praise God or give their best shout or clap because they are conscious of the world around them. Why are we ashamed to praise the one who sent his son to die for us on the cross but give our best praise and shout to movie stars and sports personalities who entertain us for money?

May your soul rejoice in God's mercy, and may you never be ashamed to praise him. (Sir 51:29)

Areas to Examine:

- Do I praise God always and in all circumstances?
- Do I get tired or weary of praising him?
- Am I ashamed of praising God in front of others?
- Do I actively and whole-heartedly take part in singing during Mass?
- Do I sing praises to God at home?
- Have I judged anyone for praising aloud?
- Have I judged anyone for lifting their hands during prayer?
- Have I judged anyone for being loud in church during praise and worship?

Additional Reading: 1 Chron 16:23-31, Deut 10:21

Thanksgiving

The next area under the first commandment is thanksgiving. It is not only sinful for being thankless for his many blessings, but it is also the reason for many problems we face in life. Are we able to see all the blessings in our lives and the hand of God in small matters? Are we able to see God's plan and purpose behind life's events and the little miracles that happen each day? Are we able to rejoice always? If we can say yes to all the above questions, then we have a thankful heart. Thanksgiving is not merely an expression of words, but a condition of the heart. God is delighted with a grateful person. God is very much at work in our lives to the smallest details. When we see God's hand in the smallest of blessings and be thankful, we will begin to see bigger miracles in life.

A person who walks with God will spend more time praising, worshiping, and thanking God than praying for his needs. Our loving Father knows what we need, and he will never forsake or abandon us. We just praise, worship, and always thank him, trusting in his goodness.

Give thanks in all circumstances; for this is the will of God in Christ Jesus for you. (1 Thes 5:18)

God's plan for our lives is always good. God never makes mistakes or does anything evil. All the things that happen to us are for our good and purification; therefore, all things except sin must be received with thanksgiving.

Everything created by God is good, and nothing is to be rejected, provided it is received with thanksgiving. (1 Tim 4:4)

Many of us are sad and gloomy because we do not see God working amidst the challenges we face right now. One should remember that all the events of the past have brought us here, and all the events of the present will take us into the future. God will not abandon or forsake his children. Many who went to bed last night did not wake up this morning. We are blessed to have one more day added to our lives. There is a need for repentance where there is ingratitude and lack of thanksgiving.

Sin of Complaining

Complaining is a serious sin which blocks the God-given blessings from flowing into a person. It is a condition where a person is unhappy about many things and is always fixated on the lack and shortages. Such a person will also find fault with everyone, including God. Every complaint is a complaint against God.

Moses said, "When the LORD *gives you meat to eat in the evening and your fill of bread in the morning because the* LORD *has heard the complaining that you utter against him – what are we? Your complaining is not against us but against the* LORD.*" (Exo 16:8)*

Below are some aspects of life where a person often tends to complain

- Lack of money
- Too much suffering
- Unhappiness with the physical body.
- Weaknesses
- Feeling unloved
- Sickness and pain
- Unhappiness with our vocation, career, or a life partner

In the gospels, when Jesus was in a situation where over five thousand people were hungry and had nothing to eat after three days, the people around him were extremely negative. One of them complained about having no money; another asked Jesus to dismiss the crowd. Jesus, upon seeing that there were only five pieces of bread and two fish, did not complain or get discouraged. He took the bread and the fish and looked at heaven and thanked God. Jesus looked at the little that he had and saw the hand of God in it. When he was thankful, God was able to perform a bigger miracle, and as a result, all of them were fed miraculously.

He ordered the crowds to sit down on the grass. Taking the five loaves and the two fish, he looked up to heaven, and blessed and broke the loaves, and gave them to the disciples, and the disciples gave them to the crowds. (Matt 14:19)

There is another example in the gospels where Jesus came to attend Lazarus' funeral. He stood in front of the tomb, and it was a hopeless situation. Jesus did not even have a body, to begin with. After four days, a dead person would have naturally decayed beyond recognition, yet Jesus was not moved. He looked up to heaven and thanked the Father, and as a result, Lazarus was restored back to life.

Jesus looked upward and said, "Father, I thank you for having heard me. I knew that you always hear me, but I have said this for the sake of the crowd standing here, so that they may believe that you sent me." (Jn 11:41-42)

St. Paul urges everyone to make all petitions with thanksgiving. For example, we complain so much about our physical pain, and we are also vocal about it. We make it a point to share it with at least one person. Have we ever thanked God for the perfect health before the agony? Pain can sometimes be a message from God to reveal our inner state to us.

Do not worry about anything, but in everything by prayer and supplication with thanksgiving let your requests be made known to God. (Phil 4:6)

Life is a gift, and everything a person has is a result of God's love and generosity. We brought nothing into this world, and we can take nothing out of it. All our gifts and talents are from God, who has blessed us out of his riches. None of us deserve anything or can take any credit for our accomplishments or achievements. One who acknowledges this fact is humble and spiritually mature.

Thanksgiving is a spiritual exercise that can be practiced every day. It may be hard at the beginning, but God, when he sees the effort, will give us a spirit of gratitude. I know a person who recites a thanksgiving Rosary each morning; fifty reasons to be thankful, one per bead. An exercise like this will please our Father, and his ears will always be open to our prayers.

Once we begin this exercise and are faithful to it every day, the Holy Spirit will show more reasons to be thankful, and we will be able to complete a whole thanksgiving Rosary with at least fifty intentions. This kind of prayer will bring in us a total change of heart. The hardheartedness and negativity will leave, and we will receive freedom from a grumpy attitude, which in turn will fill our hearts with joy and peace.

Areas to Examine:

- Do I thank God every day for all the material blessings?
- Do I thank God every day for all the people in my life beginning with my parents who brought me into this world?
- Do I thank God for all the opportunities and favors in life?
- Do I complain to God about everything?
- Do I have the attitude of always focusing on the shortages in life?
- Do I thank God for the weaknesses and failures in life?

- Am I still thankful when nothing is going right in my life?
- Do I acknowledge everything as a gift from God?
- Am I a vocally complaining and a negative person?
- Am I able to thank God for all the people who hurt and wounded me?
- Am I able to thank God for all the missed opportunities in life?

Additional Reading: Heb 12:28-29, Ps 100:4, Col 3:17, Ps 9:1

Prayer

Prayer is the link between the material and the spiritual world which connects man with God. God is the food for the soul, and we receive this food through prayer. There is a deep inner hunger and thirst in each soul which God alone can fill. Man tries to fulfill this void and emptiness by filling himself with the goods of this world. As a result, the soul is unfulfilled and spiritually sick. Prayer nourishes the soul and keeps it healthy.

My soul yearns for you in the night, my spirit within me earnestly seeks you. (Is 26:9)

Man is called to stay connected with God always. Prayer is a channel through which all blessings, mercies, and graces flow. The words such as, "come to me," "cry out to me," "seek me" are used very frequently in the Bible. Jesus gave immense value and importance to prayer. The strength and secret of Jesus' life was his commitment to prayer. He always responded to the call of the Father and stayed connected with him and never disappointed him. As a result, he was able to know and do the will of the father.

Prayer is not a skill we can master in a day. As in all other aspects of life, we also tend to make many mistakes in our prayer life. We attain maturity and growth by praying regularly and learning about God in the Bible. The Holy Spirit is the best person to teach us to pray. Given below are some mistakes we make in our prayer life.

Praying Solely for Material Things

The majority of Christians define prayer as a means of getting something from God. When our heart is fixated on the things of this world, it will also reflect in our prayers. Most people solely pray for material things. Prayer is much more than just asking or receiving something from God. St. Paul reminds us in the book of Corinthians,

If for this life only we have hoped in Christ, we are of all people most to be pitied. (1 Cor 15:19)

Praying for Spiritual Things

God saw King Solomon's heart when he prayed and how he did not pray for any material thing but prayed for wisdom. God was incredibly pleased with this prayer and as a result, blessed Solomon with wisdom and along with it, the worldly goods as well.

God answered Solomon, "Because this was in your heart, and you have not asked for possessions, wealth, honor, or the life of those who hate you, and have not even asked for long life, but have asked for wisdom and knowledge for yourself that you may rule my people over whom I have made you king, wisdom, and knowledge are granted to you. I will also give you riches, possessions, and honor, such as none of the kings had who were before you, and none after you shall have the like." (2 Chron 1:11-12)

Prayer and Surrender

Prayer calls for surrender. Surrender means to lay down the human will and submit to God's will and to give everything in God's hands. Surrender is a stage in our prayer life, which brings freedom from many worldly spirits such as worry, fear, and anxiety. Many of us, though we pray a lot, are still worried about many things. We like to be in control. Surrender gives God access and permission to work in our lives. If we do not surrender, we create a block in us, and as a result, we do not see our prayers answered, and we are controlled and tormented by many worldly spirits such as fear, worry, etc.

Lack of Desire

To be successful in anything, a passion for it and focus is necessary. It also applies to prayer and worship. If we build a strong desire to be with God, we will sooner or later be successful in our prayer life. The psalmist says,

One thing I asked of the Lord, that will I seek after to live in the house of the Lord all the days of my life. (Ps 27.4)

We have many worldly cravings, and we pursue them tirelessly. Worldly desires choke the godly desires in us, which in turn prevents us from growing closer to God. Longing for God and holiness will give us the desire to pray and spend time with God.

Wrong Priorities in Life

To know our priorities and to work toward achieving them is a task and responsibility for all of us. Each day comes with the activities that we are given to accomplish. How we start our day and how we end our day is important. A person who begins his day by giving glory to God will see the day go in his favor. A day will be blessed if it is built around God and prayer.

Strive first for the kingdom of God and his righteousness, and all these things will be given to you as well. (Matt 6:33)

Long Prayers with an Absence of Heart

Jesus, when referring to the Pharisees, said that though they prayed, their hearts were not in it. They liked to say long prayers only to be noticed by others. They were ineffective and drawing God's attention.

This people honors me with their lips, but their hearts are far from me. (Matt 15:8)

The above verse may also apply to us. Am I always told to pray by my family members? Do I still have to be reminded to pray? If this is the case, even though I am praying, my heart will not be in it. This kind of prayer is ineffective and fruitless. Do I always read prayers from books with little to no participation of the heart? Such prayers are fruitless.

Mechanical Prayers

Even prayerful people fall victim to mechanical prayers and prayers learned by rote. Prayer without the participation of the heart is useless and unproductive. Although we have many wonderful prayers in the Church, people tend to recite them without love and wholehearted participation. We are keen on finishing our daily quota of prayers without meaning any word we say.

These people draw near with their mouths and honor me with their lips, while their hearts are far from me, and their worship of me is a human commandment learned by rote. (Is 29:13)

Praying to be Noticed

There is that person who has an excellent public prayer life, always seen in church, signs up and gets involved with every ministry out there, but does not pray when he is alone. He may even lead many to pray but has no relationship with God. Jesus, in the sermon on the mount, gave detailed instructions on how to pray and how not to pray.

Whenever you pray, do not be like the hypocrites; for they love to stand and pray in the synagogues and at the street corners, so that they may be seen by others. Truly I tell you, they have received their reward. (Matt 6:5)

Praying for the Wrong Things.

Like everything else, our prayer life should also mature. The more we pray, the closer we will reach to how God wants us to pray. Most often, we do not know what is good for us. We desire for things based on what our senses tell us, and It may even be harmful to us and stray us away from the plan that God has for us. We learn how to pray effectively and what to ask for when we grow in the spirit.

You ask and do not receive, because you ask wrongly, to spend what you get on your pleasures. (Jas 4:3)

On the contrary, if our prayer is according to his will, he will hear us and answer. Surrendering our will and desires is a key factor to grow spiritually and enter into a higher level of faith.

This is the boldness we have in him, that if we ask anything according to his will, he hears us. (1 Jn 5:14)

Distractions

It is quite natural to be bombarded with distractions during prayer. We must learn to block them out. It comes with time and effort. Spiritual forces work tirelessly to distract and discourage us from having any fellowship with God. But all evil powers can be defeated if we do not give up and not lose heart.

Busyness of Life

One of the reasons people give for not praying is that they do not have time. We occupy ourselves with so many activities and at the end are left with little or no time to pray. No matter how busy we are, we always are available to eat and sleep. We understand the needs of the body but fail to understand the needs of the soul. One-tenth of our daily time belongs to God. By not praying, we deny time to the one who created time. We will always be available for all the things we love which bring us back to the question, do I love God?

Tiredness and Weariness

Tiredness and weariness are a sign of lack of love and interest. We are never tired of doing things we love. We even sacrifice our sleep and stay up late if there is a good program on television, or there is something fun to do. We feel tired at the very mention of prayer because we do not enjoy and cherish the time with God.

Do Not Give Up

Patience is a gift that goes with faith and prayer. Some prayers take longer to be answered by God, and he teaches us many things while we pray and wait. Giving up on prayers is the same as giving up on God. Jesus is specifically addressing this in the gospel of Luke, chapter 18, using a parable. He wants us not to lose heart but continue to pray and persist

Pray for Others

Most good practicing Christians who believe in God usually pray for themselves and their immediate family members. Although this is a good place to start, God looks for more than that. To pray for the conversion of sinners and those in need is more acceptable and pleasing to the Father. Praying for oneself and one's family alone is a sign of selfishness.

First of all, then, I urge that supplications, prayers, intercessions, and thanksgivings be made for everyone. (1 Tim 2:1)

We Do Not Know What to Pray

People do not pray because they do not know how to pray. We are not the only ones struggling when it comes to prayer. The apostles faced a similar crisis. They did not give up but came to Jesus, who taught them how to pray. God is willing to help when we find it hard to pray. The easiest way to pray is by beginning with the Lord's Prayer. It is a complete prayer, and one can expand on it and make it personal to one's life.

Areas to Examine:

- Do I pray solely for material needs?
- Do I long and pray for spiritual blessings?
- Have I surrendered everything in prayer?
- Do I have a desire to pray always?
- Do I pray for others?

- Do I miss or skip prayer because of busyness and overload of work?
- Have I missed prayer because of tiredness and laziness?
- Do I always seek the will of God in what I pray for?
- Do I enjoy my time with God?
- Am I always told or forced to pray by my family members?
- Am I distracted while praying?
- Do I see prayer as boring and mundane?
- Do I pray and seek God with all my heart?
- Did I give up on prayer because I did not see results?
- Do I begin each day in prayer?
- Do I end each day in prayer?
- Do I pray about all things and always?
- Do I take part in my family prayer?
- Do I have a set time each day for personal prayer?

Will of God

The majority of the people in this world are good people who strive to do good things. Although it is good to be good, we as Christians are not here to do just any good, but the good that God wants. For example, I could have been doing many good things at this moment, like feeding the poor or cleaning the streets. But the question is, what good work does God want me to engage in, at this moment? Doing the will of God is more pleasing to the Father than just doing good things. God has called each one of us with a definite call and plan. We are here to fulfill his will, and his will is always good for us and for the whole of humanity. God's will is good, acceptable, and perfect

Do not be conformed to this world, but be transformed by the renewing of your minds, so that you may discern what is the will of God – what is good and acceptable and perfect. (Rom 12:2)

Jesus did not come to this world just to heal the sick or to cast out demons, but to do the will of the Father even if it meant working as a carpenter and helping his earthly father. Jesus always obeyed the will of the Father in everything.

I have come down from heaven, not to do my own will, but the will of him who sent me. (Jn 6:38)

Doing the will of God keeps us on the path of salvation and the purpose of this life. We will not stray if we continuously seek his will and walk according to it. Where the will of God goes, there his presence, provision, and protection will follow. Everything that happens against the will of God is sinful.

We will analyze how one goes against the will of God by studying some sins we commit in our daily life.

Disobedience

We do things that God does not want us to do and do not do things that God wants us to. Many examples can be given. Take the verse from the first book of Thessalonians, chapter 5, verse 16, where St. Paul tells us to rejoice always, to pray without ceasing, and to give thanks under all circumstances. How many of us truly obey this word? We behave quite the opposite. We are not always happy, and we seldom pray. We complain and grumble about many things. Every sin we commit is an act of disobedience against God.

If you love me, you will keep my commandments. (Jn 14:15)

It is evident that many of us do not love God the way he wants us to. Our love for God is shown, foremost by obeying him and doing his will.

Areas to Examine:

- Do I obey God's word in everything?
- Do I obey the Church in all matters?
- Do I diligently seek to know what God wants from me?
- Have I surrendered my life, desires, and ambitions to God?

Stubbornness

Stubbornness is a human nature where one firmly sticks to one's purpose, opinion, etc. not yielding to argument, persuasion, or correction. According to the Bible, such people walk in their own counsel and do not make any spiritual progress.

They did not obey or incline their ear, but, in the stubbornness of their evil will, they walked in their own counsels, and looked backward rather than forward. (Jer 7:24)

Sin is also known as the stubbornness of the heart. A sinner is stubborn, and a persistent sinner is persistently stubborn. Stubbornness is a powerful force in many of us. We do not seek the truth and follow it but are stuck to our evil will and ideas which lead us to destruction. A stubborn person needs prayers and divine intervention from God.

Then you will realize that I am the Lord your God, and I will give you a desire to know and a mind with which to understand. There in the land of your exile you will praise me and remember me. You will stop being so stubborn and wicked, for you will remember what happened to your ancestors when they sinned against the Lord. (Bar 2:31-33, GNT)

Areas to Examine:

- Do I yield to the inspirations from God?
- Am I submissive to my spiritual counselor?
- Am I open to correction and discipline?

Rebelliousness

Rebelliousness, along with stubbornness, is a term frequently used in the Old Testament. Rebellion is defined as defying or resisting God's authority and as following one's own counsel or instincts. A rebellious person trusts his wisdom beyond reason and is often deceived in the end.

I held out my hands all day long to a rebellious people, who walk in a way that is not good, following their own devices. (Is 65:2)

A slave or servant does not do anything on his own. He waits for his master's instruction. Similarly, a Christian accepts God as the Lord and master of his life and submits to his authority. He allows God to have total control over him, and every aspect of his life comes under the Lordship of Jesus.

Jesus came and said to them, "All authority in heaven and on earth has been given to me." (Matt 28:18)

Hastiness

Some of us are hasty in doing things. We are quick to implement and convert our thoughts into actions without putting it in prayer and waiting on the Lord for counsel. A hasty and impatient person is an easy target of the devil. Such a one is deceived by the evil one easily and quickly. He will find himself in many traps. A godly person tests everything and waits on God for counsel.

The plans of the diligent lead surely to abundance, but everyone who is hasty comes only to want. (Pro 21:5)

The book of Acts narrates an incident about how the early Church prayed before taking a decision. They were not quick to act but waited on the Lord for direction.

While they were serving the Lord and fasting, the Holy Spirit said to them, "Set apart for me Barnabas and Saul, to do the work to which I have called them." They fasted and prayed, placed their hands on them, and sent them off. (Acts 13:2-3, GNT)

Areas to Examine:

- Do I wait on the Lord in prayer for direction?
- Do I hastily implement plans into actions?

Imprudence

Imprudence is the tendency to rush into decisions, actions, or matters without careful and diligent contemplation. A person who acts without much thinking or prayer is an imprudent person. People find themselves in sinful situations and even dangerous situations because of imprudence.

Impulsiveness

Impulsivity or impulsiveness is a habit or tendency to act on an urge, with little or no forethought or concern of the consequences or aftereffects. Making purchases or spending without analyzing the financial condition is an example of impulsive behavior.

Instinctiveness

Instinctiveness is defined as doing something without thinking. It is an animal like behavior. Animals attack other animals and humans because they are threatened, hungry, or scared. There is no ulterior motive or reason behind their actions. Humans, on the contrary, have a God-given ability to think, reason, ponder, investigate, and test; to avoid sin, evil, mistakes, and danger.

Recklessness

Recklessness is the lack of regard and concern for the consequence of one's actions and behavior. Rash decisions are another way of describing it. Some years ago, a pop star, who on a trip to Vegas, married her friend after a couple of rounds of alcohol. The next day, she divorced him. It was all over the news, and her reckless behavior and rash decision destroyed her career.

Impatience

God is patient with us, and he wants us to exercise patience in all matters. Patience is one of the nine fruits of the Holy Spirit mentioned in Galatians, chapter 5. Impatience is an ungodly quality and one of the traits of the devil. An impatient person can expect to receive nothing from the Lord. It is through patience, along with faith that we inherit the promises of God.

Ambitions in Life

Having an ambition in life is not a sin by itself if it is in line with what God wants. However, at times, ambitions, careers, worldly titles, educational qualifications have become idols for many, taking them away from the plan of God.

Areas to Examine:

- Am I ambitious about worldly titles and rewards?
- Is my ambition in line with God's will?
- Am I reckless or rash in my decision making?
- Do I act without thinking, reasoning, or contemplating?
- Do I instinctively or impulsively take decisions without calculating the consequences?
- Do I wait on God to know his will in all matters?
- Do I take decisions without consulting with the Lord?

Conclusion

All the above qualities may not be directly classified as sin but lead one to many sins and even troubles. Surrendering to the will of God will be the best choice one can make for oneself. Mother Mary gave up her self-will and submitted to the choice and plan of God for her life. Because of Mary's "yes" to God, the world has access to salvation. We too must consistently strive to say yes to him in all areas of our life, thereby striving to fulfill the first commandment of worshipping the one, true God.

Word of God

To give primary importance to the Word of God is a means of honoring and worshipping God. The words we speak come directly from the heart. The condition of our heart is always reflected in our speech and countenance. Similarly, God, out of the abundance of his heart, has spoken. He who reads the Word of God looks deeply into the heart of God. God is full of love, and his words reflect his love. The written Word of God is not a result of some human imagination, but the overflow of God's love and feelings for man. You may call it the love letter of God for man. Sadly, many of us fail to see the Father's love and even ignore his word. St. Jerome rightly said it, "Ignorance of Scripture is Ignorance of God." The Word of God is not just for the theologians, Bible scholars, and for the religious, but for every child of God. God speaks to us directly in his word. He who meditates on his word builds a deep and intimate relationship with God.

God's word heals, renews, revives, encourages, directs, corrects, and leads us. One cannot grow spiritually without meditating on his word daily. The Bible was written roughly over two thousand years, by men and women moved by the Holy Spirit. It is an all-time best seller, and no book has influenced people the way the Holy Bible has. We spend time with God when we read the Bible, and as Christians, we are called to read, study, memorize, and meditate on the Scriptures every day. Once, we put in this effort, the Word of God will become our weapon. This life is like a battle, and the mind and heart are the battlegrounds. We are all fighting many battles, whether we like it or not, and we know it or not. Some are battling sickness, some struggle with some addictions; all of us are fighting temptations, negative emotions, etc. The list is long. Now that we know that we are in a battle, how do we successfully conquer these enemies? The answer is in the Word of God. The book of Ephesians calls the Word of God as the sword of the spirit given to fight our battles.

We give many reasons as to why we do not read the Scriptures regularly. We will look at some primary reasons why the Word of God is neglected in our lives and why it is important for us to read the Bible daily.

Just Another Book

All religions and faiths have at least one religious book, and the Bible is seen by many as one of the many religious texts. Although nearly all Catholic families have at least one copy of the Sacred Scriptures at home, the amount of time they spend in reading it is not encouraging. People tend to see it as a history book or a book of rules and regulations. The purpose of the Bible is much broader, as St. Paul is writing to Timothy,

All scripture is inspired by God and is useful for teaching, for reproof, for correction, and for training in righteousness, so that everyone who belongs to God may be proficient, equipped for every good work. (2 Tim 3:16-17)

It is Dry

This is another unspoken complaint. People find it dull and boring. I completely agree with the reader. The question is; why is it dry, mundane, and boring? The answer lies in how close I am to the Holy Spirit. God's Spirit is our prayer partner, and if we invoke his presence during prayer and scripture reading, he will reveal and open the scriptures to us.

First of all you must understand this, that no prophecy of scripture is a matter of one's own interpretation, because no prophecy ever came by human will, but men and women moved by the Holy Spirit spoke from God. (2 Pet 1:20-21)

I Know the Stories

People see the Scriptures as a mythological book full of stories and myths. A story is interesting only when we read it for the first time. People do not pay attention to scripture reading because they feel that they have heard the stories before. The Bible is a lot more than merely a collection of stories. It is the Word of God, and each time we read it or listen to it being read; we listen to the voice of God.

Indeed, the Word of God is living and active, sharper than any two-edged sword, piercing until it divides soul from spirit, joints from marrow; it is able to judge the thoughts and intentions of the heart. (Heb 4:12)

Is it Relevant?

People often question the relevance of Scripture for our times and our way of life. The Bible is the love-letter of God for all humanity, and it is addressed to each one of us. It was written keeping you and me in mind making it a very personal book. The words are life-giving and nourishing.

Until heaven and earth pass away, not one letter, not one stroke of a letter, will pass from the law until all is accomplished. (Matt 5:18)

I Have Read it

"I have read it" is another excuse of people. The Bible is not just another book or novel that is read once and put on the shelf. It is a guidebook for our life. Every human character and personality are embedded within the characters of the Bible. It is a mystical and spiritual book deep in meaning and content which is unleashed when we read it over and over again. It is also the voice of God speaking to us each time we meditate on it. The psalmist, knowing and believing that it has the power to save our soul, tells us to meditate on it day and night.

Their delight is in the law of the Lord, and on his law they meditate day and night. They are like trees planted by streams of water, which yield their fruit in its season, and their leaves do not wither. In all that they do, they prosper. (Ps 1:2-3)

I Do Not Understand

"I do not understand much of it" is another excuse given for not reading the Bible. The answer again lies with one's relationship with the Holy Spirit. If his working is absent in our lives, we will find all spiritual things boring. One must begin with the Gospels, which are the easiest parts of the Bible, and as one studies the Gospels, grace will be given to read the other tougher books.

Areas to Examine:

- Do I read the Word of God every day?
- Do I prayerfully meditate on the Word every day?
- Do I write down what God is speaking to me each day through his word?
- Have I ever spoken against the Bible?
- Have I ever had doubts against the Bible being the Word of God?
- Do I share the Word with all family and friends, in person or through media?
- Have I defended the Word of God?
- Do I encourage people to read the Word of God?
- Have I treated the Bible with disrespect?

Holy Spirit

The Holy Spirit is often referred to as the forgotten member of the Trinity or the forgotten God. The Holy Spirit has played a vital role from the beginning of creation and in all the noteworthy events mentioned in the Bible. We Catholics, bless ourselves in the name of the Father, Son, and the Holy Spirit. He is "a person" like the Father and Jesus. Yet, he is ignored and does not get the reverence he deserves. He is to be worshipped with the Father and the Son. Jesus wanted all believers to be filled with the Holy Spirit.

In the last days it will be, God declares, that I will pour out my Spirit upon all flesh, and your sons and your daughters shall prophesy, and your young men shall see visions, and your old men shall dream dreams. (Acts 2:17)

The Holy Spirit is given to us as a helper, counselor, comforter, advocate, guide, and prayer partner. There are many titles to the Holy Spirit based on the role he plays in our life. All sins against the Holy Spirit are grave sins, according to Jesus (Matt 12:32). We will look at some specific areas where we fail to acknowledge the Holy Spirit as God.

Not Praying for the Holy Spirit

God wants to give us his own Spirit to be with us always. Jesus specifically told his believers to ask fervently for the Holy Spirit, and it is through this thirst and longing that a person can be filled with the Holy Spirit and grow in an intimate relationship with him.

If you then, who are evil, know how to give good gifts to your children, how much more will the heavenly Father give the Holy Spirit to those who ask him! (Luk 11:13)

Areas to Examine:

- Am I aware of the presence of the Holy Spirit in me?
- Do I thirst and long for God's Spirit in me?
- Do I actively pray for the gifts and charisms of the Holy Spirit?
- Do I take the help of the Holy Spirit during prayer and in times of temptation, dangers, trials, and decision making?

Not praying to the Holy Spirit

If asking for the Holy Spirit is the first step, then praying to the Spirit is the next step. The Holy Spirit can hear us and speaks to us, just like the Father and the Son. Pope John Paul II had a great devotion toward the Holy Spirit, which he shares in his writing.

From the time I was little, I learned to pray to the Holy Spirit. When I was 11, I was feeling sad because I was having a lot of trouble with math. My dad showed me in a little book the hymn "Veni Creator Spiritus," and he told me, "Pray this and you'll see that He'll help you to understand." I have been praying this hymn every day for more than 40 years, and I have seen how much the Divine Spirit helps us. (Pope John Paul II)[2]

Not praying with the Holy Spirit

Once we are filled with the Spirit, we learn to pray with the Holy Spirit. He is a great companion and prayer partner. He prays for us and with us, leading and guiding us. Prayer and Scripture reading will not be boring and tiring anymore but will become a source of joy when we are led by the spirit. We will also be praying the right prayers for he knows how best to pray.

The Spirit intercedes for the saints according to the will of God. (Rom 8:27)

Do Not Judge the People Who Use the Charisms

St. Paul speaks about the nine charisms of the Holy Spirit in his first letter to the Corinthians, chapter 12. These gifts are given by the Holy Spirit to believers for use in ministry. All these gifts are legitimate, and people who are granted these charisms use them for the glory of God. Some pray in tongues, while others have the gift of healing. Some get prophetic visions and dreams. We may not understand these gifts, but do we or have we judged these people who use such gifts?

Pursue love and strive for the spiritual gifts, and especially that you may prophesy. (1 Cor 14:1)

Areas to Examine:

- Am I open to the Gifts and Charisms of the Holy Spirit?
- Have I judged people/ ministries who use the gifts/ charisms?
- Do I actively pray for the gifts and charisms?
- Have I used the charisms for my own glory?

- Am I envious or jealous of another person's gifts and charisms?

Fruits of the Holy Spirit

The Fruits of the Holy Spirit are mentioned in Galatians, chapter 5. Unlike the gifts of the Holy Spirit, fruits are for our personal growth and maturity. One must seek and ask the Holy Spirit regularly for the fruits. Satan is also working hard to inject his fruits in us. The fruits of the evil one are opposite to the fruits of the Holy Spirit. Hatred in place of love, sorrow in place of joy, trouble in place of peace, etc. It is a good practice to also examine ourselves based on the fruits of the Holy Spirit.

Areas to Examine:

- Do I actively seek the fruits of the Holy Spirit and grow in them?
- Do I confess the negative fruits that are in me?
- Do I seek and pray for the fruits of the Holy Spirit that I lack?

Sexual Sins and Holy Spirit

Our Body is a temple of the Holy Spirit, and that makes us the dwelling place of God. All sexual sins we commit with our body destroy the temple of the Holy Spirit, which is holy. All sexual vices committed with the body are mortal sins, and they gravely wound our soul. It also breaks fellowship with God.

Do you not know that you are God's temple and that God's Spirit dwells in you? If anyone destroys God's temple, God will destroy that person. For God's temple is holy, and you are that temple. (1 Cor 3:16)

Additional Reading: 1 Cor 6:19-20

(A thorough examination of the sins against the body is covered under the sixth commandment)

Do Not Give Importance to People with Charisms

People who believe in charisms give too much emphasis to people with charisms and put them on a pedestal. All charisms and gifts are from God, and he alone deserves the glory for the work done by his servants. Some have the gift of healing, while others receive prophetic visions and dreams. To each one is given a gift or gifts for the upbuilding of the church and to spread the good news of the Kingdom of God. We may even cause these people to stumble by giving them importance and attention.

After all, who is Apollos? And who is Paul? We are simply God's servants, by whom you were led to believe. Each one of us does the work which the Lord gave him to do: I planted the seed, Apollos watered the plant, but it was God who made the plant grow. The one who plants and the one who waters really do not matter. It is God who matters, because he makes the plant grow. (1 Cor 3:5-7, GNT)

Areas to Examine:

- Do I see a priest or preacher as an idol?
- Do I give importance or value to a priest or lay people based on their charisms?
- Am I always trying to be friendly or contact people with specific charisms?
- Do I seek the help of people with charisms without having a relationship with God?

Misuse of Charisms and Gifts

A humble servant of God never lets himself be noticed or exalted. The attitude of John the Baptist, "he must increase, and I must decrease." must be practiced by all. We work for the kingdom of God with the gifts, charisms, and strength that God provides.

Areas to Examine:

- Do I seek attention or glory while the charisms are manifested through me?
- Do I draw people to myself or to Christ when I use the charisms and manifestations of the Holy Spirit?
- Have I sought any monetary gain or favors for the use of charisms?
- Do I, in any way, use the gifts and charisms for my personal monetary gain?

Do not Grieve the Holy Spirit

The Holy Spirit abides and communes with those who have fellowship with God. He is a person with the ability to speak to us, and he convicts us of our sinfulness, thereby giving us a chance to repent. The more we repent and forsake our sins, the more powerful and stronger he grows in us. The opposite is also true. If we do not pay attention to his promptings and warnings, his power in us decreases. He is grieved by our insensitivity and ignorance.

Do not grieve the Holy Spirit of God, with which you were marked with a seal for the day of redemption. (Eph 4:30)

Do Not Quench and Choke the Holy Spirit

A Christian is a person who is Christ-like and one who imitates Christ in everything he does. While he was on this earth, Jesus had a mission. His mission was to seek and save the lost. This mission is now carried on by his Church, making every Christian a missionary. Jesus equips the Christian with the Holy Spirit for this purpose. Therefore, every Christian is a missionary with a mission. The mission is to become the witnesses of Jesus to the people through love and holiness in personal life. The Holy Spirit makes this possible by filling the person with his fruits, gifts, and Charisms. A person who lives for himself without feeling the burden of Jesus in his heart quenches the power of the Holy Spirit within him.

Areas to Examine:

- Have I made holiness and love as the primary mission of my life?
- Do I actively use the gifts/ Charisms for the building up of the Church?
- Do I repent and confess the sins when I receive a conviction?
- Do I repent for grieving the Holy Spirit with my thoughts, words, and actions?

Faith

Faith to our Christian life is what calories is to food. However tasty, eye appealing and flavorsome our food maybe, without the calories it provides, it is of no use to our body. Similarly, however loud our worship, and however long our prayer and the beautiful words, without faith, worship and prayer is empty and meaningless. St. Paul, writing to the Hebrews, tells us,

Without faith, it is impossible to please God, for whoever would approach him must believe that he exists and that he rewards those who seek him. (Heb 11:6)

The above verse shows what God looks for when we pray. He wants to see our faith, and he also rewards our faith. A person who doubts the existence of God seldom receives anything. Apostle James also adds to this claim.

Ask in faith, never doubting, for the one who doubts is like a wave of the sea, driven and tossed by the wind; for the doubter, being double-minded and unstable in every way, must not expect to receive anything from the Lord. (Jas 1:6-7)

Apostle Paul gives an apt definition of faith, calling it an assurance of receiving things hoped for. Faith is also the conviction of things not seen.

Faith is the assurance of things hoped for, the conviction of things not seen. (Heb 11:1)

Jesus always commended people for their faith and, rebuked people for their lack of faith. The Catechism of the Catholic Church deals with the topic of faith in the very first commandment. Lack of faith manifests in us in various ways, and it is a sin against the first commandment.

Fear

Fear is the opposite of faith. Fear is a negative spirit which dominates and controls a person when faith is absent. The author of the book of Wisdom gives a simple yet profound definition of fear,

Fear is nothing but a giving up of the helps that come from reason; and hope, defeated by this inward weakness, prefers ignorance of what causes the torment. (Wis 17:12-13)

The Bible, in over 300 places, tells us not to have any fear (do not fear). Our fears need to be confessed. When God tells us not to do something, and we do it, it becomes a sin. We are called to walk by faith, not in fear.

Worry

It is said that there are two kinds of people in this world; warriors and worriers. People accept worrying as part of their personality, and they are ruled and mastered by it. A person subjected to worry cannot be at peace.

Do not worry about your life, what you will eat or what you will drink, or about your body, what you will wear. Is not life more than food, and the body more than clothing? Look at the birds of the air; they neither sow nor reap nor gather into barns, and yet your heavenly Father feeds them. Are you not of more value than they? (Matt 6:25-26)

Worry does not produce anything good in us. Instead, it harms us. It cannot solve our problems either. St. Luke adds that worry cannot add a single hour to our span of life, which means it cannot change things or solve our life's problems.

Can any of you by worrying add a single hour to your span of life? If then you are not able to do so small a thing as that, why do you worry about the rest? (Luk 12:25-26)

Anxiety

Anxiety, like fear and worry, is rooted in a lack of faith, trust, and hope in God. The Prophet Jeremiah relates anxiety with lack of trust in God.

Blessed are those who trust in the Lord, whose trust is the Lord. They shall be like a tree planted by water, sending out its roots by the stream. It shall not fear when heat comes, and its leaves shall stay green; in the year of drought it is not anxious, and it does not cease to bear fruit. (Jer 17:7-8)

The Bible connects anxiety to various bodily ailments. God does not want us to be afflicted with any unwanted sicknesses. Recent studies show that our physical health has strong connections with our emotional state. Stress and anxiety can lead to various cardiovascular diseases.

Anxiety brings on premature old age. (Sir 30.24)

Anxiety is not part of God's plan for us. The way to escape these forces is by growing in faith, hope, and trust in God.

Cast all your anxiety on him because he cares for you. (1 Pet 5:7)

Additional Reading: Eccl 11:10, Pro 12:25

Areas to Examine:

- Do I fear Satan and evil spirits?
- Do I fear sickness and death?
- Do I have any kind of phobias?
- Do I worry about my life and future?
- Do I worry about my kids and their future?
- Do I worry about my finances and health?
- Do I have any kind of insecurities, or am I too anxious about life?

Doubt

Doubt is defined as a lack of conviction or a feeling of uncertainty. The author of the book of James defines a doubter as one who is double-minded or unstable. Unbelief is the sin of the world, and as a result, there is widespread lawlessness and evil. It is not because of any animosity that people do not pray or go to church but because of lack of faith and unbelief.

For the doubter, being double-minded and unstable in every way, must not expect to receive anything from the Lord. (Jas 1:8)

Areas to Examine:

- Have I doubted the existence of God?
- Have I doubted in the real presence of Jesus in the Eucharist?
- Have I doubted that the Bible is the Word of God?
- Have I doubted in the healing and saving power of God?
- Have I doubted any of the Church's teachings?
- Have I doubted the unconditional love of God for me?
- Have I doubted the love of God in times of suffering?

Atheism

Not all baptized Catholics are believers. Some have turned away and become atheists. Atheism is the doctrine or belief that there is no God. An atheist does not believe in the existence of God or any supreme power. There are atheists within our Catholic faith who live like there is no God. Our words, actions, and thoughts sometimes prove that we are no better than atheists. We may not be termed as atheists, but we have an atheistic mindset. At times we go without prayer and scripture reading for weeks and sometimes for months and stay away from church for an extended period. In short, we live an atheistic lifestyle.

Fools say in their hearts, "There is no God." (Ps 14:1)

The growth of atheism is on the rise. 22% of the US population is religiously unaffiliated. An atheist does not believe in God for one or more reasons namely,

- Too many religions and too many gods
- Lack of empirical evidence

- Presence of evil and suffering in the world
- Bad example of people who believe in God
- Influenced by atheistic philosophers and their thinking

Additional Reading: Ps 10:4

Legalism

Legalism is the excessive adherence or dependence on the law, thereby placing little to no value on love and mercy. A legalist is full of faith but has a weak relationship with God. They also have a poor image of God in their hearts. They follow what is called a works-based religion. They are judgmental and critical of those who break the commandments of God. Such people work extremely hard to impress God by obeying the laws but without love for God and neighbor.

Additional Reading: Matt 23:23-28, Jn 6:28-29

Heresy

Heresy is defined as the belief, faith, or devotion contrary to sound Catholic teaching. Our teachings, doctrines, and belief come from the Church, which is the pillar of truth and the teaching authority on faith and morals. The Catechism calls heresy as the denial of faith.

Heresy is the obstinate post-baptismal denial of some truth which must be believed with divine and Catholic faith, or it is likewise an obstinate doubt concerning the same. (CCC 2089)

Apostacy

Apostasy is the abandonment, rejection, revolt, and renunciation of our faith in God. It is a grave sin. It is the voluntary giving up of faith. Peter is said to have committed the sin of apostasy when he denied knowing Jesus three times.

Apostasy is the total repudiation of the Christian faith. (CCC 2089)

In later times some will renounce the faith by paying attention to deceitful spirits and teachings of demons, (1 Tim 4:1)

Additional Reading: Jer 2:19

Agnosticism

Agnosticism is the belief that the existence of God is unknown. An agnostic is different from an atheist. An atheist denies the existence of God, whereas an agnostic does not know if there is a God or not. An agnostic refrains from denying God.

Agnosticism assumes a number of forms. In certain cases, the agnostic refrains from denying God; instead he postulates the existence of a transcendent being which is incapable of revealing itself, and about which nothing can be said. In other cases, the agnostic makes no judgment about God's existence, declaring it impossible to prove, or even to affirm or deny. (CCC 2127)

Incredulity

Neglect or unwillingness to believe the truth about God. Having a skepticism about God and religion. This sin goes against faith, as a person tries to understand everything with his mind and without the heart.

Incredulity is the neglect of revealed truth or the willful refusal to assent to it. (CCC 2089)

Schism

Schism is a split or division between opposed sections within an organization, or more precisely, in the Catholic Church, it means refusing to submit to the Holy Father or the Church.

Schism is the refusal of submission to the Roman Pontiff or of communion with the members of the Church subject to him (CCC 2089)

Despair

Despair is a sin against hope. It is the opposite of hope or the absence of hope. Hope is something we experience every single minute of our life. For example, we go to bed every night hoping to wake up the next morning. Without the hope of waking up, we will not be able to sleep all night. One should not let oneself be subject to despair. Even if this life holds nothing good for us, we still have the hope of eternal life.

By despair, man ceases to hope for his personal salvation from God, for help in attaining it or for the forgiveness of his sins. Despair is contrary to God's goodness, to his justice - for the Lord is faithful to his promises - and to his mercy. (CCC 2091)

Though the fig tree does not blossom, and no fruit is on the vines; yet I will rejoice in the Lord; I will exult in the God of my salvation. (Hab 3:17-18)

Presumption

A drowning man cannot save himself. He is saved by someone outside the water who can pull him out. Similarly, a sinner cannot save himself, and if it was possible, the death and resurrection of Jesus would be unnecessary. Jesus made eternal life possible for us so that there is hope for us even after we die. We cannot achieve or attain salvation with our capabilities and to think otherwise is the sin of presumption. The second kind mentioned in the Catechism is about one who keeps sinning and adds more sin presuming to be forgiven by God endlessly. Presumption is a sin against the first commandment as it gives a wrong picture of God.

There are two kinds of presumption. Either man presumes upon his own capacities, (hoping to be able to save himself without help from on high), or he presumes upon God's almighty power or his mercy (hoping to obtain his forgiveness without conversion and glory without merit). (CCC 2092)

Areas to Examine:

- Do I presume in my own capacity to attain holiness and eternal life?
- Do I take the forgiveness of God for granted and keep adding sin to sin?
- Do I give in to despair when things do not go according to my wishes and plans?
- Have I rebelled against the Holy Father or the Church in thoughts, words, and actions?
- Do I deliberately not adhere to the truth about God revealed by the Church?
- Have I ever denied the existence of God?
- Do I have a legalistic mindset or way of thinking?

Church

The Church is not merely a place of worship or a house of God. Jesus, when he first used this term in Mathew, chapter 16, did not refer to a site, or a structure, but an institution built on Peter, making it apostolic.

And I tell you, you are Peter, and on this rock, I will build my church, and the gates of Hades will not prevail against it. (Matt 16:18)

The Church is one, holy, Catholic, and apostolic in structure. In the gospel of Luke, we receive another confirmation of the authority of the Church.

Whoever listens to you listens to me, and whoever rejects you rejects me, and whoever rejects me rejects the one who sent me. (Luke 10:16)

St. Paul, in his letter to the Ephesians, further reiterates this point. It gives more clarity to the definition of our Church.

So then, you Gentiles are not foreigners or strangers any longer; you are now citizens together with God's people and members of the family of God. You, too, are built upon the foundation laid by the apostles and prophets, the cornerstone being Christ Jesus himself. He is the one who holds the whole building together and makes it grow into a sacred temple dedicated to the Lord. In union with him you too are being built together with all the others into a place where God lives through his Spirit. (Eph 2:19-22, GNT)

Jesus is the Church, and we are the members of it. When referring to the church, we are not talking about any human structure, but Jesus himself. Jesus and the Church are one. In the book of the Acts of the Apostles, when Paul is on his way to Damascus to persecute the Christians living there, he is met with an apparition of Jesus. Jesus asks this question to Paul, "*Saul, Saul, why do you persecute me?*" Jesus sees the Church as himself. He who goes to church goes to Jesus, and he who persecutes the Church persecutes Jesus. He who obeys the Church obeys Christ, and he who is faithful to the Church is faithful to Christ. Jesus and the Church are inseparable.

Jesus nourishes the Church with his Word, body, blood, and Spirit. He who comes to Christ is sustained by these things (Word, body, blood, and Spirit).

No one ever hates his own body, but he nourishes and tenderly cares for it, just as Christ does for the church. (Eph 5:29)

Any sin against the Church is a sin against Jesus. Let us look at our relationship with the Church, which is the body of Christ.

Sacramental Life

Every sacrament makes us more and more like Jesus and puts us on the path of holiness. A Catholic is faithful to the Church by living a sacramental life which nourishes, enriches, and leads him to eternal life.

Areas to Examine:

- Do I regularly attend Mass on Sundays and all Holy Days of Obligation?
- Do I attend Mass daily, if time permits?
- Do I go for my weekly confession?
- Do I examine my conscience and repent before going to confession?
- Do I set the example for all my family members in leading a sacramental life?
- Do I receive the sacraments with due respect and reverence?
- Did I ever leave the Church?

Obedience and Submission to the Church.

Jesus says in Luke 10:16, "whoever listens to you listens to me." When we submit to the Church, we do not give in to any human institution, but to Christ. What is sin and what is not, is decided not by me but by God, which is communicated to us through the Church. The Church does not act on its own but under the guidance of the Holy Spirit. A person who picks and chooses what he wants to believe cannot be Catholic. The Church is the teaching authority of God, and all teachings and instructions should be in line with what God has revealed through his Spirit, taught to us by the Church.

If I am delayed, you may know how one ought to behave in the household of God, which is the church of the living God, the pillar and bulwark of the truth. (1 Tim 3:15)

The Church reveals and shares the truth about God with us. Our knowledge of truth is almost always corrupted by the world around us. Our idea of truth is very shallow. We hold to something as right if it is followed by everybody or most around us. What we wear, what we speak, what we do, and what we believe are all influenced by the world and the media, which makes us incapable of knowing the truth by ourselves. Jesus says these words in the Gospel of John,

Jesus said to those who believed in him, "If you obey my teaching, you are really my disciples; you will know the truth, and the truth will set you free." (Jn 8:31-32, GNT)

Obedience and submission to the Church show our love for Jesus. He who disobeys or rebels against the Church wounds the heart of Jesus. Reverent submission to the Church and obedience to all the laws and precepts of the church pleases Jesus.

Areas to Examine.

- Do I pick and choose what I want to believe?
- Do I leave out that which I do not understand?
- Do I leave out that which is hard for me to follow?
- Am I faithful to the Holy Father and my parish priest?
- Do I see the church and its laws outdated and irrelevant to my way of thinking?
- Do I spend time reading the catechism and other church documents and grow in the knowledge of the Church?
- Have I spoken against the Church?
- Do I defend and uphold the teachings of the Church sincerely?

Consecrated Places

A Catholic church is unlike any other house of worship. All religions and denominations have a sanctuary to worship and pray. A Catholic church is different because it is not only a place of worship and prayer, but it is also the dwelling place of the living God. Jesus, who walked on this earth two thousand years ago, resides in every Catholic church in body and blood. This is what makes it unique and special. All who come to the church interact with Jesus the way people interacted with him two thousand years ago. Jesus is still teaching, healing, and performing signs and wonders. He is in the church, with the church, and he is the Church. As Jesus promised in Matt 28:20, "I am with you always, till the end of time."

This section of the first commandment deals with how one must conduct oneself in the Church of God. In the words of St. Paul, "...how one ought to behave in the household of God..." A church is foremost, a place where God talks to man, and man talks to God in prayer. Conversations with others should be kept to a minimum and only related to matters of faith. Proper attire must be followed by all. Reverence should be given to Jesus in the tabernacle. All cell phones and gadgets should be switched off. People should not come in with any unholy objects. People should not arrive late or leave early during the Mass. One must ensure that one is present body, mind, and soul.

- Do I have the habit of coming late or leaving early during mass?
- Do I engage in any kind of worldly conversation with other believers?
- Do I switch off all electronic gadgets that cause a distraction to myself and others?
- Am I adequately clothed and not tempting others with my attire?
- Do I genuflect when I enter and exit the sanctuary?
- Am in a state of prayer, and is my mind entirely paying attention to what is happening in the church without any distraction?
- Do I carry to Church any unholy substance with me like cigarettes, tobacco, drugs, or any secular literature?

Additional Reading: Jer 32:34, Lev 26:2, Amos 2:8,

Consecrated Times

All of us remember the days and times of all significant events in our family and celebrate it every year, thereby teaching the younger members of the family, the importance and value of these events. For example, it is customary to celebrate the birthdays of the family members each year. Families remember the death of their loved ones on their death anniversary. Couples remember their wedding day year after year. In addition to the family traditions, we also have cultural traditions like Valentine's day, Mother's Day, etc. We also commemorate national holidays depending on the country we live in.

Similarly, the family of God also has days and events to remember and honor. If we were to look at the Church calendar, we see that it is filled with events and feasts on all days. Most days, we remember a saint or a holy person. There are days of obligation and feast days recollecting some major event in the life of Jesus or Mother Mary or the apostles. This tradition shows that we are part of one big family of God. As a Catholic, I am called to observe these days and follow all Church precepts and recommendations. We have the season of Advent preparing us for Christmas, and the season of Lent preparing us for passion week and Easter. We have days of fasting and days of abstinence. We have prayers to be prayed on the first Fridays of each month. These traditions strengthen us and help us in our walk with Jesus.

The practice of attending Sunday Mass or celebrating the Lord's day can be traced back to the apostolic times.

They continued steadfastly in the apostles' teaching and fellowship, and in breaking of bread, and in prayers. (Acts 2:42)

The tradition of praying at 3 o'clock can also be traced back to the apostolic times,

One day Peter and John were going up to the temple at the hour of prayer, at three o'clock in the afternoon. (Acts 3:1)

Areas to Examine

- Do I observe Lent and Advent according to the requirements of the Church?
- Do I pray the Divine Mercy prayer at 3 o'clock every day?
- Do I fast on the days that the Church or the Holy Father is asking me to?
- Do I abstain from meat on days that the Church is asking me to?
- Do I recite the way of the cross either individually or in a community (family or church) during Lent?

Consecrated Things

Consecrated things are objects dedicated or set apart for the service of God or used in worship. We treat with utmost care and reverence, that which is consecrated to God. Examples are holy water, blessed images, rosaries, scapulars, mass utensils, etc. At the same time, all the holy objects are made holy by God; therefore, one must not put one's trust in these things without first loving and trusting God. The purpose of all holy and consecrated objects is to point us to God and lead us to him.

Areas to Examine

- Have I ever spoken against the Catholic tradition of using consecrated things?
- Am I a Catholic with all different kinds of scapulars and rosaries but with no prayer life?

Consecrated People

A religious person dedicates his or her life for the service of God and his Church. A religious person is referred to as "the anointed one" in the old testament, although this title primarily refers to Jesus. The Bible gives many references about how one must treat the servants of God. A classic example is of King David, when he gets a chance to kill Saul, does not do so, solely because Saul was anointed by God.

He said to his men, "The Lord forbid that I should do this thing to my lord, the Lord's anointed, to raise my hand against him; for he is the Lord 's anointed." (1 Sam 24:6)

Judging, slandering, gossiping, ridiculing, mocking, and speaking against God's anointed or consecrated people is a grave sin. We are called to respect and honor all servants of God.

We appeal to you, brothers and sisters, to respect those who labor among you, and have charge of you in the Lord and admonish you. (1 Thes 5:12)

Areas to Examine:

- Do I regularly pray and intercede for my parish priest?
- Do I sincerely pray for the Holy Father and all the religious?
- Have I spoken against a priest or religious?
- Have I judged a priest or a religious person?
- Have I mocked/ teased/ made fun of a religious person?
- Have I supported religious people in their missions?
- Have I gossiped or spread rumors about a religious person?
- Do I envy their lifestyle?
- Have I made unreasonable demands for receiving sacraments?
- Do I have any unforgiveness or bitterness toward the clergy?

Additional Reading: Sir 7:29, Ps 105:15

Support the Parish and the Universal Church

It is the primary duty and responsibility of a Catholic to support his or her parish financially and with the gifts and talents that God has given. A parishioner's foremost obligation is to stay involved with his parish and become part of at least one ministry. Our connection with our parish is not merely to attend Mass on Sunday. We read in the book of the Acts of the Apostles about how the early Christians worshipped as a community.

Day by day, as they spent much time together in the temple, they broke bread at home and ate their food with glad and generous hearts, praising God and having the goodwill of all the people. And day by day the Lord added to their number those who were being saved. (Acts 2:46-47)

The early Church spent much time together, and as a result, the Church was being strengthened day by day. A parish is only as good as its members. Sadly, we see around us, in the western world, so many churches closing. This is a result of a lack of unity in the hearts and minds of people. Lack of worship and intercession is also another reason. Jesus promises that he is there when we are gathered in his name.

Where two or three are gathered in my name, I am there among them. (Matt 18:20)

Areas to Examine:

- Is my relationship with my parish solely to attend the Sunday Mass?
- Have I put my God-given talents and gifts for the service of my parish and the whole Church?
- Do I financially support my parish and the evangelization efforts of the universal Church?
- Do I give my time for my parish and its missions?
- Do I participate and stay involved in any kind of prayer group within my parish?
- Do I spend time adoring Jesus in the blessed sacrament if it is exposed in the parish?

Mother Mary

Our Blessed Mother is fondly called the mother of the Church, and she is also the most revered, honored, and blessed among all human beings. She is foremost remembered for bringing Jesus into this world. She, by her "yes" to the Father, brought the Savior into our lives. Her ministry and vocation did not end with just bringing Jesus into the world but ensuring that each person receives Jesus into his heart and accepts him as his Savior. Her mission continues even today. She continuously intercedes for us, and her prayers are very powerful.

Jesus entrusted her to the Church, giving her a mission until the end of the world to save and to bring all the lost children back to God through her intercession.

When Jesus saw his mother and the disciple whom he loved standing beside her, he said to his mother, "Woman, here is your son." Then he said to the disciple, "Here is your mother." And from that hour the disciple took her into his own home. (Jn 19:26-27)

Jesus continues to honor his mother. Our Blessed Mother and her role in salvation are widely misunderstood by our protestant brothers and sisters. One of the accusations levied against Catholics is that we offer worship to mother Mary. We Catholics see her as a mother, model, and an intercessor.

Throughout her life and until her last ordeal when Jesus her son died on the cross, Mary's faith never wavered. She never ceased to believe in the fulfillment of God's word. And so the Church venerates in Mary the purest realization of faith. (CCC 149)

Mary is seen as a person of great faith who surrendered her complete will to the Father.

This motherhood of Mary in the order of grace continues uninterruptedly from the consent which she loyally gave at the Annunciation and which she sustained without wavering beneath the cross, until the eternal fulfillment of all the elect. Taken up to heaven she did not lay aside this saving office but by her manifold intercession continues to bring us the gifts of eternal salvation.... (Lumen Gentium 62)

Mary, because of her faith, became the mother of believers, through whom all nations of the earth receive him who is God's own blessing: Jesus, the "fruit of thy womb." (CCC 2676)

The role of motherhood is an eternal title given to Mary. She is also an intercessor for the whole of humanity.

Mother Mary has never sought worship from us. It is evident from all her messages and apparitions that she always points us to her son. She sees us as her own children and as the brothers and sisters of Jesus. She sacrificed her son on the cross so that we may enjoy eternity with God.

Areas to Examine:

- Do I honor the Blessed Mother as my own mother?

- Have I spoken anything against the blessed mother?
- Is my Marian devotion leading me closer to Jesus?
- Have I made mother Mary my sole mediator or an object of worship, thereby denying the power of Jesus and his work on the cross?
- Am I living by the messages of our lady given at various apparitions all over the world?
- Am I imitating Mary in virtues of humility, simplicity, obedience, and surrender?
- Have I judged anyone because of their Marian devotion?
- Do I always defend Mary's name and honor?

Saints

A saint is one who lived a holy and virtuous life while on earth, now in heaven, united with Christ and interceding for us who are still living. The catechism and the Bible call them witnesses.

The witnesses who have preceded us into the kingdom, especially those whom the Church recognizes as saints, share in the living tradition of prayer by the example of their lives, the transmission of their writings, and their prayer today. They contemplate God, praise him and constantly care for those whom they have left on earth. When they entered into the joy of their Master, they were "put in charge of many things." Their intercession is their most exalted service to God's plan. We can and should ask them to intercede for us and for the whole world. (CCC 2683)

Therefore, since we are surrounded by so great a cloud of witnesses, let us also lay aside every weight and the sin that clings so closely, and let us run with perseverance the race that is set before us. (Heb 12:1)

St. Dominic on his death bed said to his brothers,

"Do not weep, for I shall be more useful to you after my death, and I shall help you then more effectively than during my life."

A saint is very much alive like you and me, though not in the flesh but in the spirit. We, the children of God, are urged to call on the saints for prayer and protection. Saints, because of their proximity to God, have better insight into things happening in our lives and can pray in the right way for us.

The meeting of Jesus with Moses and Elijah at the transfiguration proves to show that all the holy men and women of God are still alive and active, fully involved in the affairs of this world.

He was transfigured before them, and his face shone like the sun, and his clothes became dazzling white. Suddenly there appeared to them Moses and Elijah, talking with him. (Matt 17:2-3)

We ask for the intercession of the saints, but do not worship them. There is an incident in the life of St. Peter, where Cornelius when he meets him, falls at his feet. Peter corrects him and gives an apt reply.

On Peter's arrival Cornelius met him, and falling at his feet, worshiped him. But Peter made him get up, saying, "Stand up; I am only a mortal." (Acts 10:25-26)

Areas to Examine:

- Do I treat the saints, who are the members of the household of God, with honor and dignity?
- Have I spoken against the Catholic faith of honoring the saints?
- Have I judged the saintly devotion of other Christians?
- Have I at any time given more value and importance to saints than to God?
- Have I spoken against the Catholic teaching on the intercession of saints?

Additional Reading: Acts 14:13-15

Angels

The Bible defines angels as heavenly beings sent to assist us in our salvation.

Are not all angels spirits in the divine service, sent to serve for the sake of those who are to inherit salvation? (Heb 1:14)

Angels are obedient to God the Father and carry out all his commands and purposes. The Bible is full of incidents of angelic visitation. By reading them, one can understand the role that angels play in human lives. They are also deliverers of divine messages from God. Like our blessed mother and saints, angels are to be treated with respect and at the same time, not to be worshipped.

Angels do not seek our worship or offering. They want us to worship God just as they do. They are obedient to God and carry out his purposes in heaven and on earth. On the island of Patmos, John the Apostle sees a series of visions, and in one such vision, he sees an angel, and he bows down to worship. It is interesting to see the response of the angel given in Revelation, chapter 19.

Then I fell down at his feet to worship him, but he said to me, "You must not do that! I am a fellow servant with you and your comrades who hold the testimony of Jesus. Worship God! (Rev 19:10)

Areas to Examine:

- Have I ever treated heavenly beings equal to God?
- Have I placed my trust in any of the heavenly beings without first loving God?
- Have I given more time and importance to any heavenly being other than God?

Additional Reading: Rev 22:8-9

Superstition

Superstition is the mixture of local culture and tradition with our Catholic faith. It varies from culture to culture and country to country; therefore, it is not practical to list out all the practices that are out there. Superstition is rooted in fear and guilt. It can also be defined as something not true and spiritual, or a belief that is not coming from God.

All external acts of worship without the involvement of the heart are also termed as superstition. The Catechism says that it is a deviation from the real faith which can choke or affect genuine worship.

Superstition is the deviation of religious feeling and of the practices this feeling imposes. It can even affect the worship we offer the true God, e.g., when one attributes an importance in some way magical to certain practices otherwise lawful or necessary. To attribute the efficacy of prayers or of sacramental signs to their mere external performance, apart from the interior dispositions that they demand, is to fall into superstition. (CCC 2111)

The Catechism goes on to say that some of the superstition may be rooted in the occult. It is also a perverse or wrongful excess of religion.

Superstition is a departure from the worship that we give to the true God. It is manifested in idolatry, as well as in various forms of divination and magic. (CCC 2138)

Superstition in some sense represents a perverse excess of religion. (CCC 2110)

The Bible warns of following the customs of the land which may take us away from true worship.

They worshiped other gods, followed the customs of the people whom the Lord had driven out as his people advanced, and adopted customs introduced by the kings of Israel. The Israelites did things that the Lord their God disapproved of. (2 Kgs 17:7-9, GNT)

Superstitions and false traditions were widespread during Jesus' time just as it is now, in this modern day and age. Jesus addressed this issue more than once in the gospels.

Then some Pharisees and teachers of the Law came from Jerusalem to Jesus and asked him, "Why is it that your disciples disobey the teaching handed down by our ancestors? They don't wash their hands in the proper way before they eat!" Jesus answered, "And why do you disobey God's command and follow your own teaching? (Matt 15:1-3, GNT)

We fail to understand the difference between a true doctrine that comes from God, which is handed down to us by the Church and human precepts coming from the human mind.

In vain do they worship me, teaching human precepts as doctrines. (Matt 15:9)

People see superstition as a way of pleasing God and increasing in holiness.

The Pharisees, and all the Jews, do not eat unless they thoroughly wash their hands, thus observing the tradition of the elders; and they do not eat anything from the market unless they wash it; and there are also many other traditions that they observe, the washing of cups, pots, and bronze kettles. (Mrk 7:3-4)

The problem in the above verse lies not in washing one's hands before eating, although it is necessary and good for personal hygiene, but how these things were performed as religious doctrines. St. Paul warns us in the book of Colossians to stay clear of all such traditions that do more harm than good.

See to it that no one takes you captive through philosophy and empty deceit, according to human tradition, according to the elemental spirits of the universe, and not according to Christ. (Col 2:8)

All our religious activities cannot earn us heaven. It is only by grace through faith that we are saved. At the same time, we have something called sacred tradition, which is handed down by the Church for our growth in godliness and piety. Given below are some broad examples of superstitious beliefs

Additional Reading: 1 Tim 4:7, 2 Thes 2:15, 2 Thes 3:6, Col 2:8, 1 Cor 11:2, Mrk 7:8, Is 65:3-4

Days and Times

I have personally seen many good Catholics bound by days, dates, and times wherein they believe certain days of the week to be auspicious and specific times to be inauspicious. They devotedly follow these customs giving religious value to it. These customs have been absorbed from other world religions and secular traditions, and they are not supported by the Church or the scientific community.

You are observing special days, and months, and seasons, and years. I am afraid that my work for you may have been wasted. (Gal 4:10-11)

We Categorize Animals as Either Good or Bad

Although it is a widespread practice to have a pet these days, people for some reason, categorize animals to be either good or bad. There are cultures where people see some animals to bring bad luck or omen. Bats are symbolic of evil spirits in some cultures. Some fishermen throw back the first catch believing it to bring more catch. The belief that black cats bring bad luck is a widely popular superstition. Animals are created by God, and they are inferior to us in intellect. Therefore, they cannot decide our destiny or change the course of our lives.

You appointed them rulers over everything you made; you placed them over all creation: sheep and cattle, and the wild animals too; the birds and the fish and the creatures in the seas. (Ps 8:6-8, GNT)

Guilt Attached to Missing Daily Prayers

Most practicing Catholics have certain daily prayers that they race to complete every day. They feel good about themselves if they do so and feel a sense of guilt when they are unable to complete them by the end of the day. Foremost, one should understand that our God is a loving Father, and prayer is an experience of love and not a burdensome task. There should be freedom in prayer and worship. All the prayers we make, without the participation and involvement of the heart, becomes superstition.

False Traditions Around Major Christian Feasts

Christian holidays are adulterated with many unchristian rituals and practices these days. Commercialization of Christmas and Easter has taken away the essence and purpose of these holidays. Millions of dollars are spent each year during Christmas on things that have nothing to do with Jesus or our Catholic faith.

Superstition Involving Numbers

Fear of the number thirteen is a widely known superstition that has been around for some time. Many buildings and hotels simply omit to label their thirteenth floor, and some airlines do not have a thirteenth row. Some people don't travel on the 13th day of the month if it falls on a Friday. This fear is purely connected with superstition, and this tradition originated and was made popular by Hollywood.

Objects of Luck

Some people keep certain objects with them for luck, while others believe in certain colors to bring them good fortune. All such customs fall into the realm of superstition. A Christian does not subject himself to luck and chance but trusts in God for everything.

Making Wishes

This is a category of superstition where certain events trigger people to make a wish which they believe will come to pass. People, when they notice a shooting star make a wish. Wishing on eyelashes, wishbones, dandelions, and leprechauns are some examples.

Anxiety Over the End Time

The world is sure to end someday after the second coming of Christ. Obsession, curiosity, and fear about the end time leads one to the realm of superstition. Always on the lookout for the antichrist is another distraction for some Christians. People try to connect world events with biblical prophecies and confuse themselves and others. Jesus has a good answer to all the end-time enthusiasts.

But about that day and hour no one knows, neither the angels of heaven, nor the Son, but only the Father. (Matt 24:36)

Areas to Examine:

- Do I believe in superstition?
- Do I see or treat numbers as lucky or unlucky?
- Do I see any colors to be either lucky or unlucky?
- Do I treat any days or dates to be auspicious or inauspicious?
- Do I believe in making wishes on events?
- Do I possess any objects that claim to bring me luck?
- Do I celebrate any non-Christian festivals (occult, festivals of other religions) or feasts?

Additional Reading: Col 2:16-19, Acts 28:3-6

Occult

God forbids all occult activity that tries to communicate with or control evil powers, either to bring good to oneself, or as a means of income or mere amusement, or for the harm of one's neighbor. The practice is forbidden even if it is done to restore one's health or finances or elevate one's lifestyle.

All occult practices, though many are recognized by society, are harmful and takes one away from God. Taming occult powers for whatever reason is gravely sinful and dangerous.

All practices of magic or sorcery, by which one attempts to tame occult powers, so as to place them at one's service and have a supernatural power over others - even if this were for the sake of restoring their health - are gravely contrary to the virtue of religion. (CCC 2117)

Additional Reading: CCC 2116

Why are People Attracted to the Occult?

- Some forms of it promise the healing and restoration of health

- It promises relaxation of mind and body
- It promises financial blessings
- Young people are trapped into it by curiosity and for amusement and entertainment
- To contact one's deceased loved one
- It offers to bring harm to people who have harmed us (casting spells & curses)
- It claims to give us insight into our past and future
- It claims to give us a false sense of strength and power
- Some think of it as another religion to choose
- Some who are hurt by the church may get involved with the occult to retaliate
- It promises good luck, blessings, and protection
- It is passed down as a family tradition
- To control or harm another person
- To gain prominence and power in society
- An unhealthy curiosity of the future

Deuteronomy, chapter 18, is the foundation of all teachings on the occult. God, through his prophet, makes it clear for the people not to get involved with any such practices.

When you come into the land that the LORD your God is giving you, you must not learn to imitate the abhorrent practices of those nations. No one shall be found among you who makes a son or daughter pass through fire, or who practices divination, or is a soothsayer, or an augur, or a sorcerer, or one who casts spells, or who consults ghosts or spirits, or who seeks oracles from the dead. For whoever does these things is abhorrent to the LORD; it is because of such abhorrent practices that the LORD your God is driving them out before you. You must remain completely loyal to the LORD your God. Although these nations that you are about to dispossess do give heed to soothsayers and diviners, as for you, the LORD your God does not permit you to do so. (Deut 18:9-14)

The Bible calls all such practices abhorrent and evil. Christians who have practiced any form of occult activities should renounce it and repent of all such sins. All occult activity blocks the Holy Spirit in our lives. Most of these practices are merely human inventions, although some have connections with the dark forces.

For the teraphim utter nonsense, and the diviners see lies; the dreamers tell false dreams, and give empty consolation. Therefore the people wander like sheep; they suffer for lack of a shepherd. (Zech 10:2)

Some of the widely popular practices are included in this section giving the reader some basic idea of what occult is, and what signs to look for to determine if certain practices are acceptable or not. If in doubt, always consult a priest and share your thoughts for more information. The occult practices are categorized according to the claims they make.

Communicating with the Dead

At times, people who find it hard to let go of their deceased family member or lover, resort to communicating with them through the help of the occult. There are various methods people use depending on the country and region.

Séance

Séance is a means or an attempt to communicate with the spiritual entities, either evil spirits or deceased human spirits. In Deut 18:11, the Bible forbids all communication with the dead. The below verse from the book of second Kings is proof that God hates such practices.

He made his son pass through fire; he practiced soothsaying and augury, and dealt with mediums and with wizards. He did much evil in the sight of the Lord, provoking him to anger. (2 Kgs 21:6)

Mediumship

Mediumship is the practice of purportedly mediating communication between the dead and living human beings. Practitioners are known as "mediums."

Do not turn to mediums or wizards; do not seek them out, to be defiled by them: I am the Lord your God. (Lev 19:31)

Additional Reading: Lev 20:6, Lev 20:27, Deut 18:10-12

Spirit Channeling

Spirit channeling is a means of inviting or allowing a spirit to take over a living body and communicating through it.

Necromancy

It is a practice of occult which involves communication with the deceased either by invoking or summoning their spirit or raising them bodily for the purpose of acquiring hidden knowledge or foretelling future events.

Wisdom, Knowledge, Prophecy, and Destiny

All of us are hungry for knowledge of various things happening around us. People are willing to take any route to get information about their future and destiny. From time to time, we hear people make predictions about the end of the world. People are curious to know about the type of person they are going to marry, the year of their death, their financial prospects, etc. There are many practices out there, promising people with all the information that they are seeking. Most of these methods are debunked by the scientific community, and certain methods opt to take the help of the occult. The Bible teaches that Satan is a liar and not to be believed and trusted. The most popular occult practices are listed below.

Astrology

Astrology is the study of the movements and positions of stars, planets, and other celestial objects as a means of deriving information about human affairs and terrestrial events.

Do not learn the way of the nations, or be dismayed at the signs of the heavens; for the nations are dismayed at them. (Jer 10:2)

Additional Reading: Is 47:13

Ouija Board

There are two theories behind this phenomenon. Scientists argue that it is one 's subconscious that is moving the planchette. This theory is called the ideomotor effect. Spiritualists are determined that it is the work of the spirits. Either way, it is forbidden for two mains reasons. Firstly, A child of God should never be communicating with any spirit other than the holy spirit. Secondly, the devil is a liar, and no truth should be expected of him or his agents.

Palmistry

Palmistry or palm reading is a method of telling one's character or foretelling one's future through the study of the palm.

Horoscopy

Horoscope is a chart representing the position of all visible celestial bodies like the Sun, the Moon, the planets and constellations, etc. at the time of one's birth or any major event. Horoscopy believes in the theory that the position of the celestial bodies at the time of one's birth reveals information about one's life. The scientific community has rejected all such claims.

Clairvoyance

Clairvoyance is the ability to gain insight and information about an object, person, location, or an event by extrasensory perception and ungodly means. Clairvoyance is different from receiving insight through the gifts of the Holy Spirit.

Numerology

Numerology is a belief where numbers are thought to have meaning and are related to events and people. Numerology is practiced widely in countries like India and China.

Healing Methods (Alternative Medicine)

Reiki

Reiki is a form of alternative medicine which uses a technique called palm healing through which some kind of universal energy is said to be transferred through the palms of the healer to the patient for healing. According to an article published by the US Conference of Catholic Bishops, Reiki is not compatible with sound Christian teaching.

> *Since Reiki therapy is not compatible with either Christian teaching or scientific evidence, it would be inappropriate for Catholic institutions, such as Catholic health care facilities and retreat centers, or persons representing the Church, such as Catholic chaplains, to promote or to provide support for Reiki therapy.*
> *(USCCB)*[3]

Exercise & Relaxation

This is another way evil is penetrating the lives of innocent Christians these days. Everyone is conscious about their health and weight, and people are willing to try newer methods to stay fit and relax their mind and bodies. As a result, they fall victim to rituals that have a strong connection with evil and false deities.

Yoga

Yoga is an eastern method of workout which combines exercise with meditation. Yoga is more than just physical activity. It infuses spirituality with bodily postures. Although it may sound harmless on the outset, there is a deep meaning to each position and in a way, makes one submit or pay reverence to the eastern deities. A Christian should not be performing yoga even if he were to leave out the meditation. Spirituality is rooted within the various postures. Yoga is not just exercise, but the worship of eastern deities.

Practices like yoga and meditation could 'degenerate' into a cult of the body…The love of God, the sole object of Christian contemplation, is a reality which cannot be 'mastered' by any method or technique. (Pope Benedict XVI)[4]

Transcendental Meditation

Transcendental Meditation or TM terms itself as a non-religious method for relaxation, stress reduction, and self-development. It goes against the biblical teaching which affirms Jesus as the source of all joy, peace, and rest.

Additional Reading: Matt 11:28-29, Jn 14:27, Jn 16:33, Phil 4:7

Amusement & Recreation

Occult powers can also be controlled or tamed for amusement and recreation. People take the help of occult to earn money and make a living out of it. They also see it as a gift or talent to master. The occult is used in art and entertainment to amuse others.

Magic

Magic is mainly of two kinds, black magic, and white magic. Black magic is eviler than white magic, while white magic may be performed for personal benefit or amusement. Regardless, all magic is forbidden. It is a sin to draw power from the satanic forces either for good or bad or just for entertainment. Scripture teaches that when the Gentiles accepted Jesus, many of them who practiced magic burnt all their books.

A number of those who practiced magic collected their books and burned them publicly; when the value of these books was calculated, it was found to come to fifty thousand silver coins. (Acts 19:19)

Additional Reading: Rev 21:8

Sorcery

It is a practice of using spiritual forces to influence and control the physical realm. It is a practice condemned by God. There are over ten places in the Bible where God uses strong language and warns us from getting involved with any kind of sorcery. One who performs sorcery is known as a sorcerer or wizard.

Additional Reading: Gal 5:20, 2 Chron 33:6, Wis 12:4, Nah 3:4, Rev 18:23, Rev 21:8, Exo 7:11, Exo 22:18, Deut 18:10, Jer 27:9, Mal 3:5, and Rev 22:15

Cult / False Religions

A cult is a belief system, devotion or veneration directed toward a person or object. This section solely deals with groups within Christianity that has some connection with Jesus. False beliefs and cults have always existed alongside mainstream Christian denominations. Scientology, Freemasonry, KKK, Mormonism, 7th Day Adventist, Santeria, Jehovah witness, The Unification Church, Gnosticism, etc. are examples of Christian cults. Below are the major deviations and errors you see in these groups.

- They deny the divinity of Jesus
- Some claim to have knowledge about the end time and the second coming of Christ
- They limit their membership to a certain class of people
- Jesus is seen as one among many Gods
- Some groups have a leader who may claim to be the incarnation of Jesus or have a special charisma
- The age of the group is a few hundred years old or less
- It is confined to mostly one part of the world
- They give equal or more value to a book or text other than the Bible
- Most groups have a degree of secrecy to it
- Their doctrines are not in line with sound Christian teaching
- They believe in the supremacy of their group and have hatred toward others
- Evangelism is not their priority

New Age Movement

It is a collection or range of spiritual or religious practices which came to existence in the 1970s. NAM supports the theory of organic evolution and the evolution of the spirit. It also believes that soon, humanity will evolve itself to become God. "Global Unity" is another major doctrine believed in NAM. There is no adherence to absolute truth and objective morality in their teachings.

Even if it can be admitted that New Age religiosity in some way responds to the legitimate spiritual longing of human nature, it must be acknowledged that its attempts to do so run counter to Christian revelation. (Jesus Christ the bearer of the water of life, A Christian reflection on the "New Age")[5]

Christians believe man is a union of body and soul, and that the soul is an essential form – not an energy force. The belief that one can meditate and be at one with the forces of the universe is based in pantheism, the belief that the universe, God and nature are all equivalent. ("A Catholic Response to the NEW AGE Phenomenon", The Irish Theological Commission)[6]

Satan Worship & Satanic Rituals

The highest form of the occult is the direct worship of Satan. There are people who have voluntarily consecrated their lives to Satan. There are many groups that venerate and worship Satan as God. The Satanic Church, Voodoo, Wicca, Temple of Set, human sacrifice, etc. are some examples.

Satanism is the worship of Satan, involving mocking or blaspheming God and desecrating holy objects. Satanists also have their own Bible called as the Satanic Bible, and their own version of the Holy Mass called the Black Mass.

You hated for their detestable practices, their works of sorcery and unholy rites. (Wis 12:4)

Additional Reading: Bar 2:3

Occult Ornaments / Jewelry

People around the world wear Jewelry and ornaments either to enhance their appearance or to flaunt their wealth. In addition to this, people also wear it to bring good luck and protection from evil. As Christians, we only wear objects that are blessed by a priest. Rosaries, scapulars, and crucifixes are permitted religious objects one can carry or wear. There is another set of objects worn by people that come from the occult world, which gives many false promises of healing, wellness, prosperity, and protection. These things bring only harm, and people should refrain from keeping all such evil objects in their home or from wearing.

Talisman

An object believed to have magical powers worn for good luck or protection from evil. Seal of Solomon, Swastika, Talismanic scroll, Uraniborg are some examples.

Lucky Charm

It is an amulet worn that is believed to bring good luck. It is either worn by the person or placed at home, vehicle, or workplace for luck and protection.

Additional Reading: Eze 13:18, Is 3:18-20, Deut 7:26

Control, Harm or Manipulation of People

Hexes or Spells

It refers to the process of putting an evil spell over someone or something. It goes by many terms, such as a curse, spell, Jinx, and bewitching. Deuteronomy, chapter 18, verse 11 forbids all casting of spells.

Witchcraft

Witchcraft is the practice or exercise of invoking supernatural powers or entities to control people or events using magic or sorcery.

You shall not practice augury or witchcraft. (Lev 19:26)

Additional Reading: 1 Chron 10:13, 2 Chron 33:6

Occult Holidays & Festivals

Satan and his evil kingdom demand our attention and worship. Many major holidays have its roots in the occult. We Christians are called to remember the major events in the life of our Lord Jesus, the Blessed Mother, and the saints. In addition to this, we are ignorantly celebrating other pagan festivals that honor Satan and his kingdom. One classic example is Halloween where little children are made to dress up like witches, demons, zombies, superheroes and other non-existent or imaginary figures. Commercialization and infusion of non-Christian elements in our worship is another threat we face.

When the Lord your God has cut off before you the nations whom you are about to enter to dispossess them, when you have dispossessed them and live in their land, take care that you are not snared into imitating them, (Deut 12:29-30)

Occult Literature and Media

Literature and media are ways Satan uses to spread his kingdom in the world. Young people are addicted to novels such as "Harry Potter," "Twilight series," and other materials of the occult. Books that blaspheme the name of God also get popular from time to time, such as Dan Brown's "Davinci Code." Many of the children's novels and fairy tales are filled with references to the occult. The book of the Acts of the Apostles mentions an incident (Acts 19: 18-19) where many magicians brought their occult literature and burnt them publicly, once they were convicted of the truth. Satan has infiltrated the hearts and minds of people with his teachings and doctrines through music, movies, and TV shows that people innocently watch. A Christian should be mindful of the deception and craftiness of the devil and should discern with the help of the Holy Spirit about what he should subscribe, watch, and listen.

Areas to Examine:

- Do I have an unhealthy attachment with any of my deceased family members?
- Have I communicated or contacted any dead person directly or with the help of a medium?
- Do I practice any pagan or occult exercise or workout methods?
- Do I use any non-Christian meditation technique to relax my mind and body?
- Am I wearing any non-Christian Jewelry or keeping any artifact for good luck, healing, protection or blessing?
- Have I used any occult means for the healing of sicknesses?
- Have I resorted to any occult rituals to come out of debt or financial problems?
- Have I used any occult powers to control, manipulate, or harm people?
- Have I cast any spell on people?
- Have I used any occult powers to know my future or any information?
- Am I in possession of any unholy, evil, and occult literature or media?
- Do I celebrate any pagan festivals?
- Did I participate in any Satanic ritual or worship?

- Did I have any tie or membership with any Satanic group or cult?
- Do I watch or listen to any ungodly shows, movies, or music?

Conclusion

God deserves our love and attention, whereas Satan demands it from us through forceful means, deception, and lies. Occult involvement of any kind separates us from God. Renunciation, repentance, and confession of these sins is the only way to freedom. A holy person is not ignorant of the working of the devil. We are the dwelling place of God, and we take no part in any unholy, evil, and wicked activities of this world. We renounce all occult activities and consecrate ourselves to God. The first commandment, if followed wholeheartedly, will make it easy to obey the other commandments to follow. We will move on the second commandment, which gives us more insight into how we must worship God.

The Second Commandment

You shall not take the name of the Lord your God in vain

God's Name

We invoke, begin, and do all things in the name of the Father, and of the Son and of the Holy Spirit. We Catholics, implore the name of the triune God when we make the sign of the cross. The name of Jesus is a prayer by itself, and there is power in his name. St. Paul writes in the book of Philippians,

God raised him to the highest place above and gave him the name that is greater than any other name. And so, in honor of the name of Jesus all beings in heaven, on earth, and in the world below will fall on their knees, and all will openly proclaim that Jesus Christ is Lord, to the glory of God the Father. (Phil 2:9-11, GNT)

The blind man in the Gospel of Mark repeatedly called out Jesus' name and therefore was heard by the Lord and his prayer was answered. Jesus healed him of his blindness.

"Jesus of Nazareth is passing by," they told him. He cried out, "Jesus! Son of David! Have mercy on me!" The people in front scolded him and told him to be quiet. But he shouted even more loudly, "Son of David! Have mercy on me!" (Luk 18:37-3, GNT)

We Make all Prayers in the Name of Jesus.

We have access to heaven and eternal life because of the redemptive work of Jesus, and through his mediation, our petitions are heard and answered by the Father. Jesus is giving a wonderful promise in John's Gospel about prayer,

I will do whatever you ask in my name, so that the Father may be glorified in the Son. If in my name you ask me for anything, I will do it. (Jn 14:13)

Sicknesses are Healed in the Name of Jesus

Jesus Christ came to heal the sick, and his followers today continue to heal the sick in his name. There is power in the holy name of Jesus to heal sickness and infirmities.

Peter said, "I have no silver or gold, but what I have I give you; in the name of Jesus Christ of Nazareth, stand up and walk." (Acts 3:6)

Evil Spirits are Cast Out in the Name of Jesus

If there is somebody who knows the power of Jesus' name, it is none other than Satan and the evil spirits. The kingdom of Satan is thriving because very few people know the power of Jesus' name, and still fewer people use it. All hell submits at his command, and evil spirits are cast out simply by taking his name in faith.

And these signs will accompany those who believe: by using my name they will cast out demons; they will speak in new tongues. (Mrk 16:17)

Signs and Wonders are Performed in the Name of Jesus

The apostles and the early Church performed many signs and wonders using the name of Jesus and the authority that he had given them. It did not end with the death of the apostles. It continues to this very day. In fact, Jesus said that those who believed in his name would perform greater signs.

While you stretch out your hand to heal, and signs and wonders are performed through the name of your holy servant Jesus. (Acts 4:30)

All Sins are Forgiven in the Name of Jesus

Jesus, by his death, paid the price and bought salvation for all humanity. All our sins are forgiven in the name of Jesus, provided we repent and believe. Each time a priest recites the prayer of absolution in the confessional, he is invoking the name of the triune God.

All the prophets testify about him that everyone who believes in him receives forgiveness of sins through his name. (Acts 10:43)

As children of the heavenly Father, we have the God-given right to call on his name always, and at the same time, we must use his name with utmost reverence and holiness.

Areas to Examine:

- Do I invoke the name of the Trinity each morning when I wake up?
- Do I invoke and begin all things in the name of the Trinity?
- Do I invoke the Trinity each time I drive or begin a meal?
- Do I invoke the Trinity each night, before going to bed?
- Do I call on his name when I am tempted or when I face trials?

Misuse of God's Name

In the previous section, we looked at why every believer should invoke or call on the name of God always and for everything. In this section, we will meditate on how not to misuse his name, and the most common sins we tend to commit against the second commandment.

Mocking God's Name

To mock means to tease, laugh at, or ridicule a person. The bad thief who was crucified along with Jesus, mocked and ridiculed him. The soldiers also mocked and teased Jesus.

Whom have you mocked and reviled? Against whom have you raised your voice and haughtily lifted your eyes? Against the Holy One of Israel! (Is 37:23)

Whenever we mock, ridicule, tease, or make fun of a fellow human being who is made in the image and likeness of God, we mock at God. Mocking is a sign of disrespect for the person. Mocking is a sign of pride and the spirit of haughtiness working in the person.

Those who mock the poor insult their Maker; those who are glad at calamity will not go unpunished. (Pro 17:5)

As traditional Catholics, we should be cautious not to mock, make fun or laugh at the charismatic Christians, especially for their style of worship. They may be very vocal, demonstrative, and loud. If that is how the spirit is working through them, who are we to judge?

Areas to Examine:

- Have I ever made fun of God?

- Have I ever made fun of other Christians, especially their faith and style of worship?
- Have I ever made fun of the manifestations of the charisms of the Holy Spirit in the Church or in other Christians?
- Have I ever made fun of people who approached me with the message about Jesus?
- Do I laugh at or make fun of my family members or others for their excessive faith?

Additional Reading: 2 Kgs 19:22, Luk 18:32, 2 Chron 36:15-16, Sir 23:9, Deut 5:11

Cursing

Cursing is a profane or abusive word or bad language using God's name uttered in a state of anger. Cursing God directly or cursing a neighbor using God's name is wrong and sinful. We tend to curse when we are angry or irritated inside.

Bless those who persecute you; bless and do not curse them. (Rom 12:14)

Areas to Examine:

- Do I get angry and curse when unpleasant things happen to me?
- Am I angry at God for my sufferings?
- Am I angry at God for my sickness or the sicknesses of my family members?
- Do I habitually curse or use bad language which involves the name of God?
- Do I watch or listen to any media that speaks about God in a disrespectful way?

Jokes & Humor

God is not equal to us; therefore, he must be looked at with honor and reverence. Using God's name in any kind of joke or casual talk is disrespectful and also constitutes a sin. Good and clean Christian humor is always welcome provided it does not include the Lord's holy name.

Blaming God for Life's Sufferings

Suffering is God permitted, not God-given. In times of suffering, we do not understand God's love and blame him for our miseries. Many people with a poor understanding of God blame him for everything. God is good and never does anything evil. Sin, sickness, suffering, and evil are not from God. There is an incident in the life of Job, where he loses everything he had in life. Despite this, Job is patient and accepts his condition willfully from God. Job's wife, on the other hand, finds it hard to face the situation. She is angry with Job and at God.

Then his wife said to him, "Do you still persist in your integrity? Curse God, and die." (Job 2:9)

Additional Reading: Deut 1:27

Complaints About our Weaknesses

God has given each one of us gifts, talents, and strengths. Centering on our weaknesses and being negative about it is a sin. Weaknesses are useful for our purification and should be seen as tools for our spiritual growth. We are strong when we are weak.

Additional Reading: Jer 1:6, Exo 4:10

Forgetting God's Blessings

People when they need a blessing or favor from God, are very persistent and faithful to prayer and going to church. The moment their prayer is answered, they forget all about God and move on with their lives. They show their unfaithfulness when they are blessed.

Take care that you do not forget the Lord, who led you away from the land of Egypt, from the land of slavery. (Deut 6:12)

Additional Reading: Luk 17:17, Jer 2:32

Angry with God

Anger toward God can stem from one of many reasons namely, the death of a loved one, thoughts or feeling that God is inactive and slow, suffering, pain, sickness in the family, etc. God is not biased or unjust or partial to anyone; therefore, we cannot be angry at God for life's miseries. Trusting and believing in God during such times will help us understand the purpose of life's various events.

He makes his sun rise on the evil and on the good, and sends rain on the righteous and on the unrighteous. (Matt 5:45)

Areas to Examine:

- Have I used God's name in a profane or unholy way?
- Have I joked about God?
- Have I used God's name irreverently or in a casual manner?
- Did I ever blame God for my sufferings or weaknesses?

False Claims and False Witnesses.

God, through private revelation, speaks to all of us. At the same time, one should be cautious when using phrases like "God told me," or "God spoke to me." It is important that we pray for the gift of discernment to know if a certain revelation or inspiration is from God or not. We must test every spirit to see if it is from God.

Additional Reading: Deut 18:22, Jer 23:16-17

Lying at the Confessional

Lying to the priest at the confessional is the same as lying to God because Jesus is present at every confessional, and it is he who hears our confession and forgives us.

"Ananias," Peter asked, "why has Satan filled your heart to lie to the Holy Spirit and to keep back part of the proceeds of the land? (Acts 5:3)

In the above scripture, although Ananias was lying to Peter, it is mentioned as, lying to the Holy Spirit.

Areas to Examine:

- Have I lied to the church with regards to my finances in order not to pay my tithes?
- Did I ever lie to a priest in the confessional?
- Did I confess without trying to give up sin?
- Did I confess without repenting and feeling sorry for my sins?
- Did I confess without first getting rid of the object of sin?

Making Promises and not Keeping Up

All of us are guilty of this sin. We make many promises to the Lord and forget it moments later. How many of us, after hearing an excellent sermon or reading a good Christian book or the Bible felt inspired to fast for an intention or to say an extra prayer every day? After a day or so, we cannot even remember and completely forget about making any such promises. We are forgetful of the things we must do for God and others and are calculative of the things that God or others should do for us.

Additional Reading: Matt 5:34, Ps 76:11, Ps 66:13-14

Do not Swear

To make a declaration, affirmation, or statement using God name. We make God a participant and victim to our deeds when we swear by his name. We also make him a witness to our words, actions, or thoughts. According to the book of James, we condemn ourselves and become liable to judgment when we swear.

My beloved, do not swear, either by heaven or by earth or by any other oath, but let your "Yes" be yes and your "No" be no, so that you may not fall under condemnation. (Jas 5:12)

Additional Reading: Sir 23:11, Jer 5:2

Blaspheming the Name of God

It is an act of speaking profanely, sacrilegiously, or wrong things about God or things related to God. The second commandment forbids every improper use of God's name. Blasphemy is the use of the name of God, of Jesus Christ, of the Virgin Mary, and of the saints in an offensive way. (CCC 2162)

Areas to Examine:

- Do I use the name of God in my conversations in an offensive way?
- Have I watched any movie or TV show that talks about God in an offensive way?
- Have I listened to songs, talk shows, stand-up comedy shows that openly refer to God in an offensive way?
- Have I made any promises to God and not tried to keep them?
- Did I swear using God's name?

- Did I swear falsely?
- Did I blaspheme or speak against God?

Additional Reading: CCC 2148, Matt 12:32

Judgmental Thoughts Against God

We are often guilty of judging God based on our limited insight and wisdom. To judge is to have an opinion. Although we are born and raised as Catholics, we believe and worship our own version of God. Our idea of God came from the people in our life. If we were never loved, we would find it difficult to see God as love. At the same time, we may not always understand what God is doing. We will fail to see God as good, who always does good for us.

Areas to Examine:

- Have I had negative thoughts about God?
- Have I ever spoken negatively about God, especially his love and mercy?
- Have I ever seen God as partial or biased?
- Do I see God as cruel?

Denying the Existence of Satan

We make God a liar when we deny the existence of Satan. The devil is not merely a representation of the evil in the world as thought and believed by many. He is a real person, a fallen angel, and the one cast to hell. Jesus confronted Satan directly on more than one occasion. Satan is neither to be feared nor honored. His power is limited because Jesus defeated him on the cross two thousand years ago.

We know that we are God's children, and that the whole world lies under the power of the evil one. (1 Jn 5:19)

Use of Satan's Name

Blaming Satan for all sin, sickness, and evil gives undue credit to him and undermines the power and purpose of God. Although Satan is called the tempter, one is tempted by one's own desires. Seeing the hand of Satan behind everything will bring unnecessary fear in us, which is precisely what he wants.

Areas to Examine:

- Have I ever denied the existence of Satan?
- Do I blame Satan for all evil, sickness, and suffering in my life?
- Am I always talking about Satan?
- Do I fear Satan (Satanophobia)?
- Do I blame Satan for all temptations and sin?

Additional Reading: Luk 10:17-19, CCC 395, CCC 414

Misquoting Scripture

Misquoting or tweaking Scripture to justify one's actions or belief is a sin. People who are ignorant twist the Word of God for their own destruction.

There are some things in them hard to understand, which the ignorant and unstable twist to their own destruction, as they do the other scriptures. (2 Pet 3:16)

Alcoholics are quick to quote scriptures that do not condemn the habit of drinking. People who are heavily into money-making and are business minded have their own favorite verses. One of the main reasons why we have numerous Christian denominations is because of the wrong interpretation and misquoting of scripture.

Areas to Examine:

- Do I read the Word of God in its entirety?
- Do I misquote and tweak scripture to live by my own beliefs and standards?
- Have I misled other people due to my limited understanding of God?
- Do I read any protestant Bibles?

Evangelization

All baptized Christians are called and obliged to share the good news of Jesus with others and not to keep Christ to themselves. Jesus belongs to all, and it is the duty of everyone who knows him to share Christ with others who do not know him. Evangelizing is not a call just for the select few. We are the light of the world, and we cannot stay hidden.

You are the light of the world. A city built on a hill cannot be hid. No one after lighting a lamp puts it under the bushel basket, but on the lampstand, and it gives light to all in the house. In the same way, let your light shine before others, so that they may see your good works and give glory to your Father in heaven. (Matt 5:14-16)

In his letter to the Corinthians, St. Paul is again stressing on the importance of sharing Christ with others,

if I proclaim the gospel, this gives me no ground for boasting, for an obligation is laid on me, and woe to me if I do not proclaim the gospel! (1 Cor 9:16)

The majority of Christians do not evangelize because of a weak relationship with God. Concern for reputation, fear of rejection, and lack of love for the neighbor are some reasons why we do not speak about Jesus outside of the church.

Violence and Oppression in the Name of Religion.

All human beings are created by God, and therefore inciting violence and hatred in the name of religion is a sin against God. Our God is compassionate, and we become like him when we show compassion on people of other faiths and denominations.

You have heard that it was said, 'An eye for an eye and a tooth for a tooth.' But I say to you, do not resist an evildoer. But if anyone strikes you on the right cheek, turn the other also. (Matt 5:38-39)

Areas to Examine:

- Did I ever incite any violence in the name of religion?
- Have I been part of any religious hate group or any religious supremacy groups?
- Do I look at people of other faiths with ridicule and condemnation?
- Do I have hatred and contempt for people of other faiths?

Additional Reading: Luk 6:36

Arguments in the Name of Faith.

Arguments do not work, but love does. When we take Jesus to this unbelieving world, we should begin by giving them the love of God. Arguments and debates cannot bring a person to conversion. Jesus used a godly way when he approached sinners and gentiles. Through his love and mercy, he was able to bring them closer to God.

Have nothing to do with stupid and senseless controversies; you know that they breed quarrels. And the Lord's servant must not be quarrelsome but kindly to everyone, an apt teacher, patient, correcting opponents with gentleness. God may perhaps grant that they will repent and come to know the truth. (2 Tim 2:23-25)

Additional Reading: 1 Tim 1:3-7

Do not be Ashamed of Being a Christian

Light should not stay hidden, and we, the light of Christ should also not be hidden, but shine in this unbelieving world. We are the voice, hands, and legs of Christ. If we are ashamed to live our Christian life and proclaim Jesus, we do not love him enough.

Those who are ashamed of me and of my words in this adulterous and sinful generation, of them the Son of Man will also be ashamed when he comes in the glory of his Father with the holy angels. (Mrk 8:38)

Areas to Examine:

- Am I embarrassed or ashamed to pray in public?
- Am I open about my Christian faith and beliefs?
- Have I at any time failed to testify my faith in Jesus?
- Can people see Jesus in me?
- Have I made my Catholic faith attractive to others?

Additional Reading: Rom 1:16

Promises Made in the Name of God.

All of us, married people, when we took our marriage vows, made this promise at the altar that we will be one and united till death. Yet, so many marriages fail for the silliest reasons sometimes. A marriage vow is a promise made to God and to each other in the name of God, and one must be willing to sacrifice one's life to fulfill this commitment. We make many such promises to God and in the name of God but seldom try to keep up or follow. The prayer of the act of contrition is one such promise we make, each time we go to confession. We are quick to tell God that we will avoid the near occasion of sin, yet we continue to compromise with sin. God just wants to see the effort from us, and he will provide the results.

Let your word be 'Yes, Yes' or 'No, No'; anything more than this comes from the evil one. (Matt 5:37)

Areas to Examine:

- Do I fulfill all the promises that I make to God?
- Do I abide by the promises I make to others, in the name of God?
- Do I keep the promises I make to God when I repent and confess my sins?

Perjury

Perjury is the sin of lying under oath. An oath we take makes God a witness, and any false or insincere oath makes God a participant of our sin.

Do not devise evil in your hearts against one another, and love no false oath; for all these are things that I hate, says the Lord. (Zech 8:17)

Additional Reading: CCC 2152

Areas to Examine:

- Have I lied in a court under oath?
- Did I make any false claims or lie to immigration officials or to any authority?
- Am I honest when I speak about myself?
- Have I lied about my qualification or experience when seeking a job?

Additional Reading: Hos 10:4, Pro 14:5

False Teachings

There is no shortage of false teachings in this world and it is true to Christian teachings as well. There is no shortage of false teachers either. As Catholics, we must guard ourselves from all false teachings by staying close to the Church and adhering to the teachings of Christ taught to us by the Church. St. Paul repeatedly warned his followers to be cautious about false teachers and teachings. This warning applies to today's generation as well. Listening to non-Catholic speakers and reading non-Catholic literature can put doubts about our faith and the traditions that the Church is trying to instill in us.

Additional Reading: Gal 5:7-10

Falsely claiming to have a charism or gift of the Holy Spirit

There is no shortage of people who claim to receive revelation and prophecies from God. They are misguided and they deceive others with lies. We should be careful not to mislead people with our own opinions and lies claiming it to be coming from God.

Jeremiah the prophet said to Hananiah the prophet: "Listen, Hananiah! The Lord has not sent you, and so you have caused this people to trust in a lie. (Jer 28:15)

Do not allow your prophets and your diviners, who are in your midst, to deceive you. And you should pay no attention to their dreams, which they are dreaming. For they prophesy falsely to you in my name, and I have not sent them, says the Lord. (Jer 29:8-9)

Conclusion

In this commandment, we looked at how we must use our speech when we address God or speak about God. God has given us the gift of speech to praise his name and proclaim his good works to the whole world. We will move on the third commandment, which deals with yet another important area with regards to our relationship with God.

The Third Commandment

Remember the sabbath day, to keep it holy

Importance of The Lord's Day

From the beginning of time, God has commanded man to give the first day of the week back to him. God worked for six days, completed the work of creation, and rested on the seventh day. The seventh day for God is the first day for man. God through his Word and the Church gives us specific guidelines as to how one must honor and spend this day. Sunday is unlike any other day. It has special graces attached to it, and we tap into these graces and blessing when we are faithful in obeying this commandment.

A Day of Rest

God, after completing the works of creation, rested on the seventh day and he calls man also to rest.

By the seventh day God finished what he had been doing and stopped working. He blessed the seventh day and set it apart as a special day, because by that day he had completed his creation and stopped working. (Gen 2:2-3, GNT)

Six days we work, trying to support our family and contribute to the society around us. It is also natural that our body needs its rest. Not everyone can follow this commandment because of their nature of work or the country they live in. If they sincerely desire to rest on Sunday, the Lord will find a way for them. In the meantime, they may offer it as a cross.

A day of rest does not mean a day to sleep all day. So many people are addicted to a party culture where they stay up late on Saturdays by drinking and merrymaking and spend the Sunday in bed completely drained out. God is not talking merely about bodily rest, but the rest of the whole being. Our soul and mind also need the strength to function, which we receive from resting and spending time with God. God strengthens us and fills us with his rest when we spend time with him.

Come to me, all you that are weary and are carrying heavy burdens, and I will give you rest. (Matt 11:28)

Additional Reading: Num 28:25

A Day Holy to the Lord

The word "holy" means set apart or consecrated. The Lord's day has a special blessing on it. It is different from other days of the week. It is a day where God meets man in a unique way. A Christian dedicates this day to the Lord and his mission of evangelization and service to others.

For in six days the Lord made heaven and earth, the sea, and all that is in them, but rested the seventh day; therefore the Lord blessed the sabbath day and consecrated it. (Exo 20:11)

People have a wrong idea that Sunday is a day of recreation and worldliness. People indulge in all kinds of worldly activities like movies, sports, parties, vacation, etc. It is wrong and sinful to fill the Lord's day with all carnal activities. The day is to be spent in holiness filled with spiritual exercises.

Lord's Day

It is evident and clear from the scriptures that Sunday is the most important day of the week and St. Paul refers to it as the Lord's day. It is not my day, but the Lord's. It is a day where I give myself to the Lord surrendering all my desires, plans, and self-interests.

A Day of Praise

God finished all creation in six days, and on the seventh day rested and saw that all he had made was good. He marveled at his works. We too, participate with God and give praise to Him for his marvel on this day. A Jew remembers the Sabbath as a day when God freed his people from slavery.

The Sabbath is for the Lord, holy and set apart for the praise of God, his work of creation, and his saving actions on behalf of Israel. (CCC 2171)

A Day of Refreshment, Renewal, Revival, and Retreat

When we rest in his presence and sing praises to Him, we feel refreshed, renewed, and revived. It is a day of withdrawal from our weekly activities. We are ready to take on life's challenges with the strength that God gives us.

Many of us are burned out and fatigued because of lack of rest. We have become greedy and selfish and are exerting ourselves too much to get wealthy. When we obey his commandments, blessings will follow. Weekend, especially Sunday, is not a day to work from home.

Additional Reading: Exo 23:12

A day of Charity and of Expressing our Love

In the gospel of Mark, when Jesus was confronted with breaking the Sabbath law, he uses the opportunity to teach them the value and the need for charity on the Sabbath. Reaching out to our brothers and sisters and sharing the love of God and his mercy with them is the godly way of spending the Lord's day.

Additional Reading: Mrk 2:27

Day of Resurrection

Sunday is also the day of the resurrection of our Lord. Each time we come together as a church on Sunday, we remember the great event of the resurrection. It is a way of proclaiming Jesus to the world.

Additional Reading: Luk 24:1-12, 1 Cor 16:2

A Day of Thanksgiving

The word 'Eucharist' means thanksgiving. Each time we attend Mass, we offer our gratitude for the many blessings, spiritual and material, that God has showered on us. We are thanking God for the sacrifice on Calvary by which we are saved from sin and death.

A Day with the Family

Modern life is demanding and puts undue pressure on families. The advent of technology has made it even harder. People are traveling farther and farther to find jobs and earn money. There are families where the earning member is forced to live and work in a different city or country to make money, and family life is being ripped apart in many cases. If you are a person away from your family due to work, pray to God for a solution. God values our time with our family more than we do, and if he sees our desire to be with our loved ones, he will make a way.

A Day of obligation

The church teaches that Sunday is the foremost holy day of obligation. Attending Mass is our first and foremost duty on the Lord's day. Missing Mass on Sunday is a mortal sin.

The Sunday celebration of the Lord's Day and his Eucharist is at the heart of the Church's life. "Sunday is the day on which the paschal mystery is celebrated in light of the apostolic tradition and is to be observed as the foremost holy day of obligation in the universal Church." (CCC 2177)

The practice of coming together to break bread can be traced back to the apostolic times. The early Christians gathered together as a community to break bread (Eucharist) and pray.

On the first day of the week, when we met to break bread, Paul was holding a discussion with them; since he intended to leave the next day, he continued speaking until midnight. (Acts 20:7)

Areas to Examine:

- Do I treat Sunday as a "work from home" day?
- Do I occupy myself with worldly activities on the Lord's day?
- Do I stay awake Saturday nights and sleep through Sunday?
- Do I occupy myself with work that takes me away from my family and church?
- Have I missed Mass on Sunday since my last confession?

Employers and Businesspeople

Employers with people working under them should give them a day off on Sundays so that they can be with their families and go to church. Business owners should not expect or demand employees to work on Sundays or send them home with work to be completed on Sundays.

Areas to Examine:

- Do I force or make it mandatory for my employees to work on Sundays?
- Do I send work with employees to be completed on Sundays?

Addition Reading: CCC 2187

Holy Mass

The Holy Mass is the highest form of worship, and every Catholic is obligated to take part in the Sunday worship wholeheartedly. All holy days of obligation are also to be observed by attending Mass. The more we receive Jesus, the more we will become like him. The Sacraments, especially the Holy Mass, has the power to transform our lives and make us like Jesus.

Preparation for Holy Mass

An hour of Fasting Before Holy Mass (Communion)

Catholics should refrain from eating and drinking anything one hour before communion except for water and medicine. It is a way of demonstrating one's hunger and desire for Jesus in the Eucharist. This law is not applicable to the elderly and sick.

Additional Reading: Canon 919

Confession and Repentance

It is a good practice to go for confession once every week, preferably a day before receiving communion on Sunday. The more we receive Jesus in a state of grace, the more we can experience the Lord's power in us.

It follows that if one of you eats the Lord's bread or drinks from his cup in a way that dishonors him, you are guilty of sin against the Lord's body and blood. So then, you should each examine yourself first, and then eat the bread and drink from the cup. For if you do not recognize the meaning of the Lord's body when you eat the bread and drink from the cup, you bring judgment on yourself as you eat and drink. That is why many of you are sick and weak, and several have died. (1 Cor 11:27-30, GNT)

Meditate on the Mass Readings

Spending enough time meditating on the Mass readings of the day either at home or by coming early for Mass will help us experience the power of the Holy Mass. God has something to say to us each day through his word, and reflecting on the readings is an effective way of listening to God.

Areas to Examine:

- Have I ever attended Mass without fasting for an hour?

- Have I attended Mass in a drunken state or under the influence of drugs?
- Do I meditate on the day's readings before and after Mass?

During Mass

Arrive on Time

We often see people coming late for Mass well after the opening hymn or even during the readings and the homily. If this is a pattern, one should repent for it and rectify one's habit. There are some of us who want to rush out after the final blessing or soon after communion. We want to be the first one out of the parking lot. This is a sign that our heart and mind are not fully participating. All these practices account to irreverence for God.

Attend Mass Together

Families should try and attend Holy Mass together. It is the responsibility of the head of the family to ensure that everyone attends Mass.

Switch off all Cell Phones and Gadgets

One thing that can be most distracting to us and others around us during the Mass is the phones we carry. Phones act as windows to the world. One can easily be distracted by alerts, notifications, and messages on the phone. Jesus uses the words, "go into your room and shut the door" when he talks about prayer. We will reach and attain intimacy with God only if we shut out the world around us.

Whenever you pray, go into your room and shut the door and pray to your Father who is in secret; and your Father who sees in secret will reward you. (Matt 6:6)

Do not Indulge in Worldly Conversation

A church is not a club or a gathering area. It is the house of God, and Jesus dwells tangibly in every Catholic Church. Reverence for Jesus includes not involving or engaging in any worldly conversation in the sanctuary. Jesus is the sole reason for us to be in Church. Therefore it is important that we give our full attention to Christ and be open to listening to him.

Participate by Singing and Praying Aloud

There are many benefits of singing and praying out loud. Firstly, Mass is community worship, and we are more powerful and effective when we pray together. Singing and loud worship will bring our body, mind, and soul to focus on God.

Listen Attentively to the Readings, Homily, and Prayers

Faith comes from hearing the Word of God, and hearers will become doers. The Word of God has the power to transform us, and the more we are open to his word, the more it will change our lives. One should remember the readings at least for the entire day and meditate on it.

Control of Thoughts (distractions)

Distractions can come from many sources like fear, worries, anxieties, worldliness, and desires. Whatever the heart is occupied with, can cause disturbances in us and can take us away from the present moment. It is a struggle for many of us to keep our attention on God during Mass; nevertheless, we should keep trying.

Release Forgiveness and Pray for Them

Mass is also a time to show our love for our neighbor through forgiveness and intercession. God's pardon for us is conditional. Each time we pray the Lord's Prayer and do not forgive our enemies, we hold back God's forgiveness from our own lives.

Whenever you stand praying, forgive, if you have anything against anyone; so that your Father in heaven may also forgive you your trespasses. (Mrk 11:25)

Pray for all who Need Prayers

All of us, from time to time, receive prayer requests from others. Sometimes, Christians and unbelievers who need a favor from God, cross our path. We who are close to God have a responsibility to lift these people in prayer during the Holy Mass. Their faith or religious affiliation should not hinder us from praying for them. God is the God of all.

Have a Longing for the Body and Blood of Jesus

Mass is not merely a worship service or a prayer meeting. It is a banquet, where our Lord Jesus is broken and given to us. We have not understood the full meaning of Mass unless we believe in the real presence of Jesus in the host. Any unbelief or doubt must be repented and confessed. At the same time, one should pray earnestly to experience Jesus in the Eucharist.

Additional Reading: Ezra 6:22

Mass Attire

It is important that we dress appropriately and decently for Mass because it is a banquet hosted by Jesus, the king of kings, and we are invited to take part in it. There are many good practices we learn from people of other faiths. Take the Jehovah Witnesses, for example. They always dress up to their best when they go to their place of worship. Men are always in their suits. Even when they come knocking on our doors, they are well-dressed and presentable. They take pride in their faith. We tend to dress down and wear clothes that are revealing, and it is an insult to Jesus, our host. Skimpy outfits also cause a distraction to other believers.

Proper Posture

A person, when entering or exiting a chapel, must genuflect and show reverence to the Lord in the tabernacle. It is essential that we always act and behave in a dignified manner remembering that the church is the household of God. Consecration is the most important moment in the Mass, and all who are healthy should kneel. Mass norms and rules must be followed by all, as God looks for obedience in small matters.

Holy Day Obligation

In addition to Sundays, it is also obligatory for Catholics to attend Mass on all holy days of obligation.

Areas to Examine:

- Do I deliberately/ habitually come to Mass late and leave early?
- Do I fail or forget to attend Mass on holy days of obligation?
- Do I fail to show reverence to God by not genuflecting, standing, and kneeling whenever needed?
- Do I dress indecently and immodestly?
- Do I doubt in the real presence of Jesus in the Eucharist?
- Do I pray for people who have asked for my intercession?
- Do I unconditionally forgive and love my enemies and pray for them during Mass?
- Am I able to concentrate on the Mass proceedings without any distractions?
- Do I listen attentively to the Mass readings, sermon, and prayers, or do I easily get distracted?

- Do I actively take part in the Mass prayers and worship?
- Do I keep the conversation with other believers to the minimum and not talk about worldly things?
- Do I switch off all my gadgets or put them on silent mode before entering the sanctuary?
- Do I attend Mass with all my family members?
- Have I received communion in a state of mortal sin?
- Do I distract others during Mass?
- Do I listen attentively and respond to all the prayers?

Conclusion

This concludes our study on the first part of the commandments, which primarily dealt with our relationship with God. Beginning with the fourth commandment, we will look at man's relationship with man. The cross is made up of two wooden bars; a horizontal bar and a vertical bar implying the two relationships, man to God and man to man. We cannot fulfill one without the other. We will begin the next chapter discussing about the first people we came across in this world; our parents.

The Fourth Commandment

Honor your father and your mother, so that your days may be long in the land that the Lord your God is giving you.

God's love for us is primarily shown to us through our parents. It is they who brought us into this world. They chose to give us life, nurtured us, raised us, gave us everything we needed, and helped us get on our feet. We owe our everything to our parents since through them we are who we are today. The fourth commandment is about how one must treat one's parents and how parents must raise their children. It also covers marital relations.

The First section is about how children must honor their parents. This part of the commandment is divided into two sections; for children under the age of 18 living with their parents and adults' relationship with their aged parents.

Children (Under 18) Living with Their Parents

Children who live with their parents come under their direct authority and care. God has placed the parents above the child. A home is the primary learning center for the child. It is a place where character, attitude, and behavior are developed in a child during the growing years. It is important how a child treats his or her parents, as it is the first relationship that the child builds. This section covers the qualities and traits that a child should develop and shows us how sin finds its way even in little children.

Obedience

Obedience is the foremost quality that is expected of one's children, and it leads a child to all other virtues in life. Obedience and submission to parents bring blessings and good in life. Jesus was obedient to his earthly parents, and he continues to honor his mother and her wishes. St. Paul, writing to the Ephesians and Colossians, stresses the virtue of obedience to parents and the blessings that follow.

Children, it is your Christian duty to obey your parents, for this is the right thing to do. "Respect your father and mother" is the first commandment that has a promise added: "so that all may go well with you, and you may live a long time in the land."(Eph 6:1-3, GNT)

Areas to Examine:

- Do I always have to be rewarded for doing anything?
- Have I ever disobeyed my parents or elders?
- Have I ever ignored the commands or directions of my parents?
- Do I have to be repeatedly reminded or told to do things that are expected of me?

Additional Reading: Col 3:20

Do not Provoke your Parents to Anger

Children, by their words, actions, attitude, and behavior, should not provoke their parents to anger. They should learn to please their parents and always avoid action and speech that will irritate them. In the book of Sirach, chapter 3, we read that, one who angers the mother also angers God. Sirach, chapter 3, verses 1 to 16, is a good passage to meditate on how to treat one's parents.

Areas to Examine:

- Do I manipulate my parents with my tantrums?
- Do I deliberately do or say things that will cause my parents to lose their temper?
- Have I ever grieved my parents?
- Do I complain about education and homework?
- Do I cooperate when my parents ask me to pray?
- Do I talk back to my parents?

Honor your Parents

What brings honor and dishonor to parents? If a parent receives a complaint from school that the child is unruly, it brings disgrace and dishonor to them. It is through our words, actions, and behavior outside of the home that we bring either honor or shame to our parents. It is a proud moment for the parents to see their child excel in everything and be successful in life. We honor our parents when we make them happy.

With all your heart honor your father, and do not forget the birth pangs of your mother. (Sir 7:27)

Areas to Examine:

- Have I brought dishonor to my parents by my actions in school or outside of the home?
- Have I shown disrespect to elders?
- Am I kind and gentle with other children?
- Do I fail or forget to pray for my parents?
- Have I been unkind or rude to others?

Submit to Discipline

Discipline is always hard at that moment, but the fruits are lasting and rewarding. Parental control should not be seen as a punishment rather something that builds character and prepares a child for adulthood. A parent always wishes the best for the child; therefore, a child should submit to parental discipline and not rebel against them. Many things we see as good are harmful to us, and there is a valid reason why our parents do not allow us to watch television for too long or why they make us study so much. We may not understand when we are young, but God has entrusted us to our mother and father to mold and shape us.

A wise child loves discipline, but a scoffer does not listen to rebuke. (Pro 13:1)

Areas to Examine:

- Am I continuously told to do my daily chores and duties?
- Do I feel unloved at home?
- Do I see discipline as something that goes against my freedom?
- Have I had thoughts of leaving home or running away?
- Do I see my parents as my enemies?
- Do I rebel against elders in the family?

Additional Reading: Pro 10:17, Pro 12:1

Focus and Priority in Life

Our whole life is a learning process, and we never cease to learn newer things. The first eighteen years of a person's life is primarily spent on education. The priority during this time is to learn, and children should be fully focused on their learning and education. A child learns about God, people, the world around, and life itself. Parents spend a great amount of time and money in providing education to their children. A child should cooperate with all his educators, starting with the parents and schoolteachers. A child's time with the parents is not merely a time of fun and enjoyment but a time of preparation for adult life.

Areas to Examine:

- Do I watch too much TV or internet that hinders my education?
- Do I put my heart in education and learning, or do I see it as a burden?
- Am I prompt in doing all my schoolwork on time?
- Do I deliberately make excuses to stay away from school and learning?
- Do I show a lack of interest in learning about God?
- Do I fail to prepare well for tests and exams?
- Do I seek God's help every day for my education?
- Am I addicted to toys, video games, and gadgets?
- Do I spend too much time talking/ chatting with my friends?
- Do I give more importance to games, sports, and entertainment than education?

Share Everything with Parents

Sharing is vital in a relationship, and it is no exception between a child and the parent. A child's world has many surprises and needs an adult who can guide and counsel, and the parent is the best person who can play this role. A child should not keep secrets from a parent, and both, good and bad, need to be disclosed to the parent. A parent acts as a protector, guide, and counselor for the child.

Areas to Examine:

- Do I share everything with my parents?
- Do I make my parents part of everything in my life?
- Am I hiding any grave sin/ habit from my parents?
- Do I watch anything on television or the internet without my parent's knowledge and consent?
- Do my parents know all my friends?
- Did I talk to any adult without my parent's knowledge either on the internet or in person?
- Is there any incident in my life (e.g., sexual abuse) that I am hiding from my parents?

Play an Active Role Around the House

Parents are not the servants of children. Although they do most things, children should slowly take responsibility around the house. Running the family is a collective task. Children should look for things that need to be done and assist the elders.

Areas to Examine:

- Do I resist to help my parents with household chores?
- Do I always have to be told to clean my room?
- Does somebody have to always clean up after me?
- Do I have to be told repeatedly to do things around the house?

Relationship with God

A good Christian begins his day with the sign of the cross and does everything in Jesus' name. One who has a healthy relationship with God will call on Him for everything. Secondly, sharing everything in prayer is a sign of a good relationship with God. Little children have their fears, worries, and anxieties and they should learn to offer these to God every day. Challenges in school and at home should be brought before God as well.

Areas to Examine:

- Do I share everything with God?
- Do I pray for my parents and siblings?

- Do I begin everything with a prayer?
- Do I pray for wisdom in studies/academics?
- Do I pray for protection every day?
- Do I, in faith, lift the needs of the family in prayer?

Relationship with Sibling

Families with more than one child should instruct the children to love and respect their siblings from an early age. Children learn to share when they have a sibling. A brother or sister should not be seen as a rival or competitor, and the stronger, older child should be compassionate to the weaker, younger one.

Areas to Examine:

- Do I see my sibling as a competitor or a rival?
- Do I get these thoughts that my parents love my sibling more than they like me?
- Do I feel that my parents spend more time with my sibling than with me?
- Do I ack unkindly toward my sibling and fail to love them?
- Do I have trouble sharing things with my sibling?
- Do I fail to pray for my sibling?

Adult's Relationship with Parents

Marriage, higher studies, adulthood, and life's commitments do not take away the honor and respect that a parent deserves from the child. The role they play changes from one phase to the next, but their value does not. Jesus continues to honor and revere his mother showing us an example of how to treat one's parents.

Thankfulness for the Gift of Life

We should always be thankful to our parents for the gift of life because we owe our lives to them. Remembering our parents in prayer every day is our way of showing gratitude. We will never be able to fully understand the pain that our parents went through to bring us into this world and to raise us.

Remember that it was of your parents you were born; how can you repay what they have given to you? (Sir 7:28)

Areas to Examine:

- Do I forget to remember my parents every day in prayer?
- Do I look at my parents with gratitude?
- Have I ever blamed my parents for giving birth to me?
- Have I ever blamed my parents for the hardships in life?
- Have I ever blamed my parents for the missed opportunities in life?
- Have I ever blamed my parents for the decisions they took in my life?

Additional Reading: Sir 23:14

Love and Forgive Them

Although life's priorities may have taken a person away from his parents, his love for them should never cease or decrease. All bitterness, hatred, and anger against them should be sorted out through repentance and confession. There should never be any darkness in the relationship between parents and children. A child should not hold on to any unforgiveness against the parents as this will only lead to godly blessings getting blocked from his life. A person needs his parent's blessings throughout his life.

Patience

Our parents may not be up to date with the technology or the fast pace of our lives. Add to that; old age takes away one's physical strength. It is during these times that grownup children must show utmost patience and compassion toward their parents.

Even if his mind fails, be patient with him; because you have all your faculties do not despise him. (Sir 3:13)

Violence / Abuse Toward Parents

There are many cases where old parents are verbally and sometimes even physically abused by their children. People see their parents as a burden and treat them in an inhuman way. It is a grave sin, and it hurts God. We are called not only to love, but also to take loving care of them.

Those who do violence to their father and chase away their mother are children who cause shame and bring reproach. (Pro 19:26)

Areas to Examine:

- Did I ever verbally abuse my parents?
- Did I ever physically abuse my parents?
- Did I insult my parents in front of others?
- Did I yell or raise my voice against my parents?
- Have I ever cursed my parents?

Additional Reading: Mic 7:6

Hatred Toward Parents

A child who is now an adult can hate his parent for one of the many reasons. Divorce in the family can bring hatred toward one or both parents. Sexual/ verbal or physical abuse by the parent can cause deep anger and hatred for them. Whatever the case, one should forgive and love one's parents deeply from the heart. The blessings of a parent are important for the well-being of a child.

Caring for Aged / Sick Parents

It is the responsibility of the children to care and provide for aged parents. In some developed countries, the state takes care of its senior citizens by providing subsidized health care and other benefits. It may not be the case in most third world countries, and parents are at the mercy of the children. Children do not want to attend to their parents; therefore, they send them to old age homes. There are many such parents abandoned by their children. It is cruel and a grave injustice to the parents who sacrificed their everything to raise their children.

Areas to Examine:

- Do I care for my aged and weak parents without complaining?
- Do I take them for their hospital visits if there is a need?
- Do I attend to their basic needs if they are disabled and sick?
- Do I see my weak parents as a burden?
- Have I ever wished that they should die?

Communication with Parents

Elderly adults are often lonely. Their children have moved on with their lives, and there is no one even to visit them. The children see them only when there is a major holiday like Christmas or Thanksgiving. Some are too busy even to call and talk to them. It is not a good sign when basic communication is lacking between family members.

Areas to Examine:

- Do I stay in touch with my elderly parents?
- Do I inquire or am I aware of their present health condition and wellbeing?
- Do I visit them often if they are not living with me?

Provide for the Parents

Elderly parents, having spent most of their life's earnings, may not have much left after retirement. Children's education and other expenses may have nearly emptied their savings. Additionally, they are now old, weak, and unable to work. It becomes the responsibility of the children to look after the aged parents financially and by providing accommodation if they need one. Sickness and disability are realities of old age. Children should be around their parents during their tough times.

Areas to Examine:

- Am I aware of the financial needs of my aged parents and help them if they are in need?
- Am I willing to accommodate them if they have no place to go?
- Do I care for and visit my sick and disabled parents?
- Did I ever kicked out my parents from home?

Parents with Children (Under 18)

Parenting does not come with any manual or guidebook. Each child is unique and different, and we learn the art of parenting as we go. Parenting is a great responsibility and requires one hundred percent attention and dedication that cannot be delegated or neglected. Nobody other than the father can fulfill the role of a father in a child's life. Mistakes in parenting can cause lifelong damage to a child. Parenting a child without the help of God is the biggest mistake we make. Looking at some basic areas of parenting will show us how and where we have deviated from the law of God.

Love

A parent should foremost see a child as God's gift. Every child deserves a loving parent. A child who is loved and accepted at home will be mentally, spiritually, and emotionally healthy. Thus, loving the child unconditionally is the foremost duty of the parent. A child should be accepted the way he or she is. A parent expresses his love for the child in ways such as touch, eye contact, by spending time, teaching, disciplining, and so on. A child not loved at home will be vulnerable to many inner wounds. The psalmist writes that every child is a blessing from God.

Children are a gift from the Lord; they are a real blessing. The sons a man has when he is young are like arrows in a soldier's hand. (Ps 127:3-4, GNT)

Areas to Examine:

- Have I loved and accepted my child from the moment of its conception?
- Did I expectantly look forward to the birth of my child?
- Did I at any time see my child as a burden?
- Was I at any time physically unavailable for the child during his/her growing years?
- Did I express my love through touch and eye contact during the initial infancy/toddler years of my child?
- Do I spend enough time with my child?
- Have I at any time rejected my children due to some weakness or disability in them?
- Have I ever compared my child with other children?
- Have I ever physically, verbally, or sexually abused my child?
- Do I have unjust and unrealistic demands and expectations from my children?
- Am I compassionate and considerate to my children in their weaknesses?
- Have I ever criticized, condemned, or ridiculed my child?
- Do I pray for my child?

Discipline

Discipline always goes with love, and where there is love, there will also be discipline. Love without discipline is dangerous and harmful for the child, and they will end up being spoilt and pampered. A well-disciplined child will easily discern good from bad and stay clear of evil. A balanced and mature parent will show love and discipline in equal proportions. A child who is corrected often will develop good character and moral values.

Train children in the right way, and when old, they will not stray. (Pro 22:6)

A parent who does not love or discipline a child is a neglectful parent. A child who is neglected will find it exceedingly difficult to coexist with society and family.

Do you have children? Discipline them, and make them obedient from their youth. (Sir 7:23)

At the same time, discipline without love can wound the child. Such a child will grow up to be a disciplinarian himself and will find it hard to express love to his loved ones.

Fathers, do not provoke your children, or they may lose heart. (Col 3:21)

Areas to Examine:

- Do I correct my child often?
- Have I neglected correction at any time?
- Does my discipline come from a love for the child or out of my negative character or personality?

Additional Reading: Pro 13:24, Pro 22:6, Pro 23:13-15, Eph 6:4, Pro 22:15, Pro 29:17, Sir 22:3

Do not Pamper / Spoil

Parenting is not an easy task, and all parents make mistakes in raising their kids. One of the areas parents feel pressured these days is when they are dealing with the demands of the child. Add to that; parents feel that giving what the child wants is a way to express their love. They end up giving more of everything, and the child is still not satisfied. The child has a room full of toys and asks for more. Children face peer pressure from the world around them, which also contributes to their behavior. Pampering destroys the child. Children these days are unwilling to accept a "NO" for an answer, and they patiently exercise their stubbornness until they receive what they are seeking. Parents give in easily trying to find a temporary solution. This causes long term damage to the behavior and character of the child.

Make yourselves bald and cut off your hair for your pampered children; make yourselves as bald as the eagle, for they have gone from you into exile. (Micah 1:16)

God does not want any of us to cut off our hair but repent and seek a solution from God if we have pampered our children.

Areas to Examine:

- Do I give excess love to my child without discipline?
- Do I let my child get away with unruly behavior?
- Do I sometimes find it too hard or tiring to discipline my child?
- Do I yield to my children's tantrums to quiet them?
- Do I spoil my children with too many toys?
- Do I let them have their way with television/ video games?

Teacher

The primary teacher of a child is the parent. A parent plays an active role in the learning process of the child, much before the child enrolls in a school. Home is a place of learning, and a parent should not neglect his role as a mentor. The learning process can start as early as the time when the child is still in the womb. Instructing a child can be categorized into five principal areas; faith teaching, love of neighbor, morals, and values, academics, and responsibilities.

Faith Teaching

It is important for us to introduce God to our children through family prayer, Bible reading, visiting the church, watching good Christian movies, and talking about God. A parent with a close relationship with God will find it easy to teach his faith to his children. Most people delegate this responsibility to the Catholic schools and CCD because they do not have a personal relationship with God. It is always easy to preach what we live and practice. God is the best teacher because it is he who can instruct the child effectively.

Never forget these commands that I am giving you today. Teach them to your children. Repeat them when you are at home and when you are away, when you are resting and when you are working. Tie them on your arms and wear them on your foreheads as a reminder. Write them on the doorposts of your houses and on your gates. (Deut 6:6-9, GNT)

Areas to Examine:

- Do I, as a parent, have a poor personal relationship with God?
- Do I see the area of faith as the sole responsibility of the Church and not my own?
- Do I introduce Bible stories and saint's lives to my children through books and movies?
- Do I read the Bible to my children and make them read when they are ready?
- Do I take time to pray with the children?
- Do I talk to my children about God?
- Do I instruct my children about our Catholic faith?
- Do I take my children to mass regularly?

Additional Reading: Ps 78:4-7

Love of Neighbor

The second area of teaching is about how to love one's neighbor. A child's world begins with the father and the mother. Through this interaction, the child learns to love others in the family and outside. A parent, through example and counseling, instills in the child, the qualities of love, mercy, forgiveness, compassion, gentleness, kindness, patience, and other positive qualities. A child should be corrected right away if he or she is misbehaving with peers and elders. A child can demonstrate selfishness and self-centeredness as this is a consequence of original sin. We are all in some way selfish and seeking our own interests. It should not be a surprise to see these qualities in the children as well.

Areas to Examine:

- Do I correct my child when he or she has trouble behaving well or interacting with people?
- Do I teach my child to respect all elders?

- Do I instruct my child about reaching out to others in their need?
- Do I teach my child to forgive and to love all?
- Do I lead my child in praying for others?

Morals and Values

The third area involves teaching what is good and what is bad. What is acceptable and what is not. What is morally right and morally wrong. Children can easily be influenced by the world around them. The language they hear, the dress culture, and various worldly beliefs can penetrate their minds and hearts. A parent should teach the child good Christian values. We human beings are not lawmakers but created by God and called to live by His law and commandments. We do not dictate what is right and wrong but follow and obey what God has commanded us. Sexuality, for example, is not invented by man but is a gift given to us by God and comes with its set of rules.

Academics

In addition to the above areas, we have a responsibility to give them access to education that will make them financially independent, knowledgeable, and wise. Education helps one understand and discover one's talents and gifts. A parent should be fully involved in the child's education.

Responsibilities

The final topic under this section is about teaching children the importance of taking responsibilities. Children should not be merely given jobs and tasks to do but be taught how to be responsible with everything they are given to do. With responsibility comes accountability.

Areas to Examine:

- Am I patient with my child?
- Do I teach good morals and godly values to my child?
- Do I stay involved with my child's academics?
- Do I take time to tutor my child?
- Do I give responsibilities to my child and make them accountable?

Provider of the Family

One or both parents play the role of the provider for the family. Every parent has a role to play and a contribution to make. There are families where both parents are forced to work to meet the needs of the family. There are cases when one of the parents becomes sick, and there is an additional responsibility on the other. St. Paul, in his letter to Timothy, writes about how one must contribute to one's household.

Whoever does not provide for relatives, and especially for family members, has denied the faith and is worse than an unbeliever. (1 Tim 5:8)

Areas to Examine:

- Do I feel used when I am asked to provide for my family?
- Do I feel like a servant at home?
- Do I take charge and responsibility for the financial needs of the family?
- Do I instruct my children, the importance of money management?
- Have I ever seen family life as a burden?

Protector of the Family

The parent is the primary protector of a child. Nobody can love and care for the child the way a parent does. It is the duty of the parents to make sure that their little ones are safe. We see and hear about many cases of child abuse, which brings us to the question, where were the parents? Parents should not trust anyone with their child. Sadly, there are people, who despite becoming parents, still live like single people. They leave their children with babysitters and with friends so that they can enjoy themselves. Marriage and parenting call for sacrifice. Many of the things we did when we were single may have to stop once we get married or have become parents.

Areas to Examine:

- Am I aware of the whereabouts of my children, where and with whom they are?
- Have I given up my hobbies and interests in life that keep me away from my children and family?
- Do I habitually leave my child with others to indulge in my hobbies and passions?
- Have I put my child in any kind of danger?

Model and Example

What are we modeling to our children and what kind of example are we to the next generation? A father, through his life, is showing a child how a father and husband should be. A mother is showing her children how a mother and wife should be. Both the parents should reflect godly qualities in them. A son should be taught how to treat his wife and other women in general. Similarly, a daughter should be taught how to treat her husband and men in general. A child should be able to see Jesus in the parent. For example, a father who smokes and drinks in front of his children is going to pass on these habits to them. A father who is abusive to his wife can cause the children to lose faith in the sacredness of marriage. Only a godly parent can raise a godly child. Given below are some primary areas where parental modeling is necessary.

- Clothes worn by parents
- The language used around kids
- Treating one's spouse
- Cleanliness
- Relationship with God
- Priorities and work ethics
- Discipline
- Love of neighbor

Areas to Examine:

- Do I sin in front of my children?
- Do I treat my spouse with respect and dignity in front of my children?
- Am I a good model for my children?
- Do I preach anything to my children that I do not practice?
- Can my children see in me a strong parent?
- Are my weaknesses affecting the children?
- Do I value God and family more than anything else?

Parents of Adult Children

Stay Involved

A parent, even after the children have grown up and left the nest, should stay involved in their lives. All of us need counsel and guidance from time to time. Our parents love us and want the best for us. There is a fine line between involvement and interference. A parent should not interfere in a person's life once he or she is married because parental interference can cause rifts and divisions in a marriage. A parent becomes a guide, mentor, and friend after a person has reached adulthood.

Areas to Examine:

- Am I guiding my adult children in their decisions?
- Am I interfering in my children's marriage and life?
- Am I available for them when they need advice?

Freedom to Choose

A parent plays an important role in a child's choices regarding career and vocation, but at the same time should train the child to make choices of his own. A parent should not curb the freedom of an adult child or force his opinions on him.

When they become adults, children have the right and duty to choose their profession and state of life. They should assume their new responsibilities within a trusting relationship with their parents, willingly asking and receiving their advice and counsel. Parents should be careful not to exert pressure on their children either in the choice of a profession or in that of a spouse. This necessary restraint does not prevent them - quite the contrary from giving their children judicious advice, particularly when they are planning to start a family. (CCC 2230)

Marriage Partners

Marriage is a covenantal relationship between God, man, and woman. It is an institution established by God. Every other relationship is a byproduct of marriage. It gives birth to a family, and the family grows into a society. Marriage is always under the radar of Satan. A marriage destroyed is a family destroyed, which in turn will destroy the society. Therefore, Satan works overtime for the downfall of marriage and its values.

Then the LORD God said, "It is not good that the man should be alone; I will make him a helper as his partner." (Gen 2:18)

A Christian marriage comes with a set of rules given by God. The best way to live a happy married life is by following God's law. We are not alone in fulfilling this commitment. God is with us through and through. Let us look at some areas where marriage partners tend to go against God's law concerning marriage.

Love

As we have seen in many other places in this book, love is the binding agent of any relationship, be it, between man and God or man and man. Marriage is no exception. In fact, the purest form of love amongst humans is primarily expressed in marriage. Marriage is a sacrament, and going by the definition of a sacrament; it should make us holy like Jesus and unite us with Jesus. There is exclusivity in love between a husband and wife. One ought to love one's spouse the way Jesus loves the church.

Husbands, love your wives, just as Christ loved the church and gave himself up for her (Eph 5:25)

St. Paul goes further and deeper into the meaning and purpose of marriage and tells us how one ought to love one's spouse.

In the same way, husbands should love their wives as they do their own bodies. He who loves his wife loves himself. (Eph 5:28)

Areas to Examine:

- Do I unconditionally love my spouse?
- Have I accepted all the imperfections and weaknesses of my spouse unconditionally?
- Are the weaknesses and imperfections causing a burden in loving my spouse?
- Have the physical and personality changes of my spouse over time hindered my love?
- Do I joyfully make sacrifices for my marriage and spouse?
- Has my selfishness and self-centeredness ever caused a rift in the marriage?
- Have I ever had thoughts of separating or divorcing my spouse?

- Have I ever been unjustly angry toward my spouse?
- Have I ever physically or verbally abused my spouse?
- Do I complain about my spouse to other people?
- Do I put my self-interest above the interest of the family?
- Do I talk disrespectfully about my spouse?
- Am I compassionate and merciful to my spouse?
- Am I forgiving?
- Do I give more importance to my children than my spouse?
- Do I ignore or neglect my spouse?

Holiness Through Marriage

Marriage is one of the seven sacraments of the Church through which the members grow in love and holiness. Marriage draws spouses close to each other and to Jesus. Each member, by his or her life, should draw the spouse closer to Christ. The question is, how much closer have I and my spouse gotten to Jesus after marriage?

Areas to Examine:

- Has my spouse gotten closer to Jesus after marriage?
- Does my spouse see godly qualities in me?
- Do I behave like the devil, manifesting his qualities and fruits?
- Have I made Jesus and the Catholic faith appealing to my spouse through my words and actions?
- Do I pray with my spouse?

Freedom

Marriage should by no means take away the freedom of its members, and it also does not give one, ownership of one's spouse. Whatever is done should be done in love. We cannot cage a person and expect that person to love us. God, when he gave free will to man, knew very well what he was getting into. Without freedom, love cannot be expressed. A table or a chair is more obedient than a husband or a child, but sadly, it cannot love the way a human being can. Repression and oppression cannot earn love. Husbands should give wives their full freedom, and wives should likewise give total freedom to their husbands.

A coin always has two sides. While freedom ought to be given to a life partner, there is also abuse and misuse that takes place. For example, a wife who is addicted to shopping and overspending may have some of her privileges taken away. We all come with some character flaws and weaknesses, and God for our purification chooses the right spouse. Submission to correction will bring the best out of us. Withholding freedom in order to discipline is the right thing to do but curbing the freedom to earn love is not right and may also account to sin.

Areas to Examine:

- Do I treat my spouse as a slave?
- Am I withholding any of my spouse's basic rights?
- Have I or do I see marriage or family life as a prison?
- Do I give due respect to my spouse?

Sacrifice

Marriage, like every other relationship, calls for sacrifice from its members. Without the willingness to sacrifice, there will always be conflicts and heartaches amongst the partners. God fulfilled his side of love when he made the ultimate sacrifice of his only son, thereby showing us its value and importance. Selfishness, self-centeredness, and self-interests can ruin a marriage.

Areas to Examine:

- Am I still living like a single person after marriage?
- Are there conflicts in my marriage because I like to do the things I want?
- Have I given up friendships, hobbies, passions that conflict with my marriage?
- Have I given up all friendships with the opposite sex (ex-girlfriends, etc.) after marriage?

Faithfulness

Faithfulness is a fruit of love. It means being committed, loyal, reliable, and devoted. Fidelity and allegiance are some of the synonyms. Faithfulness is shown not just on the outside or by merely living in the same house, but deeper from the heart.

Areas to Examine:

- Am I faithful to my spouse when he or she is not around?
- Is my spouse the only person in my mind, or do I secretly think or fantasize about being with somebody else?
- Do I compare my spouse with others?
- Do I have any addictions that my spouse is not aware of?

Trust

A person wounded and hurt in a relationship finds it hard to trust others. Such people, when they get married, will also begin to doubt their life partner. Lack of trust can open doors to spirits of doubt, suspicion, and distrust.

Transparency and Sharing

Marriage is much more than merely living in a house, raising kids, paying bills, and sharing the bed. It is different from every relationship that we form in this world. A marriage partner is one with whom we share everything without inhibitions or reservations. Sharing multiplies joy and minimizes the pain. If one is hurt by the actions or words of the spouse, the best way to deal with it is by sharing. Communication is key in a marriage. Communication is not merely the exchange of information. It reveals our heart to the other person and draws us closer to each other. There should be no place for any secret friends or dealings without the knowledge of the spouse. Talking to people of the opposite sex, either on social media or in person should be avoided if it is without the consent of the spouse.

Areas to Examine:

- Do I share everything with my spouse?
- Am I able to freely communicate with my spouse?
- Am I always available for my spouse?
- Do I enjoy my spouse's company?
- Do I have friends that my spouse is not aware of?
- Do I have any kind of financial or business dealings without the knowledge of my spouse?
- Do I have contacts with people of the opposite sex without the knowledge and consent of my spouse?

Oneness

When the Bible speaks about marriage, it is talking about two people becoming one. It is a unique bond not just on the physical level, but on a spiritual and emotional level. Although in the body, they are still two people, the soul is united with the other and forms a soul tie. Any unhealthy attachments with other people can wound the marriage. Once a person gets married, his or her parents only have a secondary role to play. Interference from parents can cause rift and wounds in the marriage. It is important that a person who enters into marriage cuts of all ties with past boyfriends and girlfriends. There is exclusivity in marriage, which should be respected and honored by members. People today, due to the internet and social media, have reconnected with all the people of their past, and this is not healthy for the marriage.

A man leaves his father and his mother and clings to his wife, and they become one flesh. (Gen 2:24)

Areas to Examine:

- Do I still entertain thoughts about my past romantic relationships?
- Am I in contact with my ex-girl/boyfriends?
- Am I in contact with people with whom I have had sexual relations?

Additional Reading: Matt 19:4-5

Sexuality in Marriage

The only place to express our sexuality is within the institution of marriage. Only married people have this freedom. Sex is not just a mingling of bodies, but a union of the heart. It is sacred within marriage and sin outside of it. Sex is an expression of love within marriage. It unites one partner to the other in the physical, emotional, and spiritual level. It is a gift from God which brings forth life. Therefore, a husband and wife coming together should always be open to the possibility of a child. Sex outside of marriage will be covered under the sixth commandment.

- Sex is an act of giving oneself to one's partner without any selfishness in it.
- It is a known fact that sex brings pleasure. One should not only seek one's pleasure but be willing to give it to the partner as well.
- A spouse should not be seen or used as an object of sex. One should be considerate and yield to one's partner.

- One should not deprive the other in sexuality. (conjugal rights)
- Both partners, upon mutual agreement, may abstain from sex for a period for prayer.
- Public display of sexual affection is a sin.
- Spacing out the number of children is not a sin if natural family planning (NFP) is practiced.
- Use of any artificial methods of contraception is a sin.

Authority of the Husband

A husband/ father is the spiritual head of a family. This authority is not an invention of the male-dominant society but dictated by God through his word. This does not give the man the right to abuse or treat his family members with disrespect. A husband should treat his wife with love, respect, and dignity. With authority comes responsibility. Jesus exercised authority and at the same time, served his Church. The man in the family should have an attitude to serve. Authority does not mean yelling, screaming, and using force. Jesus cared for his church and tenderly nourished it, and likewise, we the men of the family are called to be the leaders of the domestic church. This authority can be enforced in a godly way only when one has a strong connection with the Lord.

I want you to understand that Christ is the head of every man, and the husband is the head of his wife, and God is the head of Christ. (1 Cor 11:3)

Areas to Examine:

- Do I, as a husband, use the God-given authority to lead my family in holiness?
- Have I ever abused the God-given authority?
- Do I fail to use my God-given authority in leading my family?

Additional Reading: Tit 2:4-5, 1 Pet 3:1, Eph 5:23-24

Wives, Submit to your Husbands

A wife does not lose her dignity by submitting to her husband. In the previous section, we saw how Jesus used his authority and showed us how a husband should treat his wife. Jesus once again can be a model to the wives in the way he submitted to human beings who are weaker than him. He submitted to his parents, the Jewish authorities, and everybody that God put over him. Submission and obedience did not make Jesus lose his glory or position. He humbled himself before a mere human being from his birth and up until his death. There is beauty in submission, and the grace and blessings that flow through marriage are lost when the wife refuses to submit to her husband.

Wives, be subject to your husbands, as is fitting in the Lord. (Col 3:18)

Areas to Examine:

- Do I resist to submit to my husband's authority?
- Have I ever rejected my husband's authority?
- Do I see myself superior to my husband?
- Do I do things or take decisions without my husband's knowledge or consent?
- Do I see and recognize my husband as the head of the family?

Additional Reading: Eph 5:22

Husbands, Love Your Wives

The Husband, the primary and sole head of the household, is called to be loving and caring toward all family members. With authority comes great responsibility and accountability. The book of Ephesians (Eph 5:25) talks about how a husband should love his wife. Love calls for sacrifice, without which, it cannot be fulfilled. The husband must be willing to give himself up for the wife. It goes on to say that he who loves his wife loves himself. A man should love his wife the way he loves his own body.

Husbands, in the same way, show consideration for your wives in your life together, paying honor to the woman as the weaker sex, since they too are also heirs of the gracious gift of life – so that nothing may hinder your prayers. (1 Peter 3:7)

Areas to Examine:

- Am I considerate and understanding toward my wife?
- Do I listen to my wife and take suggestions from her?
- Do I give time to my spouse and her needs?
- Am I patient with my wife?

Areas to Examine: Col 3:19

Sharing Family Responsibilities

A family cannot be effectively run by a single person. All the members must do their part and share the burdens and responsibilities. Maintaining a household is a collective responsibility of the husband, wife, and the children if they are old enough. Earning money, cleaning the house, helping with the children's education and needs, and running errands are some basic household jobs. As the family increases and multiplies, activities, burdens, and responsibilities will also increase. Therefore, each one should see what is needed and how to contribute accordingly. There are several factors that can cause an undue burden on any one family member.

Areas to Examine:

- Do I spend a lot of time outside the home with friends or at the gym and not pay attention to the needs of the family?
- Am I a lazy person not helping my spouse and children?
- Do I have passions and hobbies that conflict with my family time and responsibilities?
- Do I complain about the responsibilities at home?
- Do I financially support my family if there is a need?
- Is my unhealthy lifestyle causing undue burdens on my family members?

Togetherness

Modern families have many distractions. Children, especially after reaching teenage years, tend to spend increased time with their friends and gadgets. Even parents these days are so preoccupied doing their own activities that the time of togetherness is lost somewhere between busyness and commitments. Families spend less and less time together, even if all of them are present at home. Within the house, there are many temptations that keep members away from each other. Praying together and eating together are some basic activities that strengthen family ties. Friends will come and go, but family time and commitments are to be given more value and attention.

Areas to Examine:

- Do I always make plans with my friends and absent myself from my family?

- Do I spend too much time on media and gadgets?
- Do I eat at least one meal a day together with my family?
- Do I make myself available for the family prayer?

Friendships

When it comes to friendships and fellowships, the Bible gives us some basic guidelines to follow. Foremost, we must not associate with a sinner who can pose a threat to our spiritual life. Secondly, we must be careful not to destroy the spiritual life of another person. A Christian is called to form a godly fellowship with his friends. Similar to marriage and family, friendships must also be centered on Christ and Christian values.

Among stupid people limit your time, but among thoughtful people linger on. (Sir 27:12)

Who will take pity on an enchanter struck by a serpent, or on someone who draws near to wild beasts? And so it is with one who keeps company with an iniquitous man and is involved in his sins. (Sir 12:14)

Additional Reading: 2 Cor 6:14-16, 1 Tim 5:22

Civic Responsibilities

Duties

The fourth commandment, in addition to dealing with our relationship with our family members, also talks about our civic responsibilities. A good Christian obeys all civic and social laws as long as they do not contradict God's laws. We have a responsibility toward our neighbor and the land we live in. While we are on this earth, we are dependent on the society around us and the society, in turn, is dependent on us. Our contribution begins with following the laws of the land.

For the sake of the Lord submit yourselves to every human authority: to the Emperor, who is the supreme authority, and to the governors, who have been appointed by him to punish the evildoers and to praise those who do good. (1 pet 2:13-14, GNT)

Areas to Examine:

- Am I a law-abiding citizen?
- Do I follow all traffic rules?
- Do I obey the authority that God has put over me; namely at work, school, and church?
- Do I participate and vote in all elections for the candidates who stand for and uphold good Christian values?
- Do I follow the laws about cleanliness in public places?

Rights

Every individual has rights in a democratic society. The rights must be used and used with caution. Rights and freedom should not be misused or abused. Exercising our rights are important. It is my responsibility to vote in an election, and it also is my right. We have a right to voice out our concerns if the country and the leaders are headed in the wrong direction and have the right to express our opinion if laws go against our faith and values.

Areas to Examine:

- Do I exercise my rights in all civic matters?
- Am I a silent spectator when evil, lawlessness, and wickedness is increasing around me?
- Do I stand up and support those who do not have rights or whose rights are being taken away?

People in Authority

A person in authority should first submit to the authority of God and follow the laws of God. He or she should not act in any way contrary to God's law and bring dishonor to the name of God. A Christian should not shy away from politics or any public office. The more we engage or get involved with the lawmaking and governance, the easier it will be for the kingdom of God to expand and operate smoothly.

An unwise king shall be the ruin of his people: and cities shall be inhabited through the prudence of the rulers. (Sir 10:3, DRA)

Areas to Examine:

- Have I, a man of authority, ever brought dishonor to the name of God?
- Have I with my full conscience, represented the Christian faith in voicing my opinions?
- Do I sincerely work for the cause of the poor and the minority?
- Have I supported or endorsed any law that goes against Christian teaching?
- Am I a good Christian to all those who are under me?
- Did I ever hide my Christian faith or identity in front of others?

Conclusion

The fourth commandment being the first commandment focusing on the love of neighbor, we looked at how families should love and treat each member. We will look at more areas in the fifth commandment and see how deep sin has penetrated each one of us. Every sin that is discerned and brought to light will lose its power over us.

The Fifth Commandment

Thou shall not Kill

To kill is to murder or to take a life, be it our own or the life of another. Killing is a mortal sin in most cases. Most people reading this book would never have murdered someone or will commit a murder in the direct sense. People break this commandment often without knowing or in ignorance. Life is one of the masterpieces in God's creation. We see life around us everywhere, namely; plants, animals, and humans. No scientist has figured out how life enters and leaves a body. Christianity has all the answers about the origin, meaning, and destination of human life. We are not the owners of our life. Life still belongs to God, and he chooses when to give and when to take it away. This commandment is divided into two sections; Killing others and killing of self.

Pro-Life

The issue of pro-life is very dear to Christians because it is close to God's heart. God has always stood for life, and he hates the murder of unborn children. Every child from the moment of conception is a life of its own. The life of the unborn must be protected at any cost, and anyone who undergoes or supports abortion commits a grave sin. We receive life from God at the moment of conception. A child is not a property, but a gift from God and should be received with gratitude. God made us participants in his creative work when he gave us the gift of procreation, and his first words to man is a blessing.

God blessed them, and he said, "Increase and multiply, and fill the earth, and subdue it." (Gen 1:28)

God's view on pro-life and abortion is revealed to us through his Word and the Church. God has known us and thought about us even before the foundations of this world. Every soul is precious in the eyes of God.

Whatever the reason people give about committing abortion, does not justify taking an innocent life.

Your eyes beheld my unformed substance. In your book were written all the days that were formed for me, when none of them as yet existed. (Ps 139:16)

Sex-Selective Abortion (Female Feticide)

In some cultures and communities, a girl child is not seen as a blessing and hence aborted. It is what is known as sex-selective abortion. It is generally targeted toward the female sex. It is not just a modern practice but an age-old one. Termination of a child based on sex is mentioned in the beginning chapters of the Bible. There was a decree around the time when the Israelites were slaves in Egypt. The Pharaoh ordered every male child who was born, to be killed. The midwives somehow protected these boy children and God, in turn, blessed their families.

Because the midwives were God-fearing, God was good to them and gave them families of their own. And the Israelites continued to increase and become strong. (Exo 1:20-21, GNT)

Abortion Due to Deformity

A child with congenital disabilities is also valuable in the eyes of God, and no one has the right to terminate any life for any reason. Speaking to the prophet Jeremiah, God reveals that he has a plan and purpose for every child. He tells Jeremiah not to be troubled by weaknesses but to focus on the mission of life. Jeremiah considered himself weak and gave excuses for not taking up the ministry given to him. God encourages and strengthens him with his promise.

Before I formed you in the womb I knew you, and before you were born I consecrated you; I appointed you a prophet to the nations. (Jer 1:5)

Birth Regulation and Contraception

Regulation of birth within marriage using natural family planning methods is not a sin. It is a responsible act of parenthood.

The regulation of births represents one of the aspects of responsible fatherhood and motherhood. (CCC 2399)

Use of artificial methods of contraception is intrinsically wrong and constitutes a sin. Birth control pills, condoms, diaphragm, cervical cap, intrauterine device (IUD), etc., are some common examples. These methods inhibit a complete openness to life.

Additional Reading: CCC 2377

Areas to Examine:

- Have I committed abortion and not confessed the sin? (If the sin was confessed, parents should let go and not live in guilt, but believe that the child is with God)
- Have I been part of any pro-choice group such as planned parenthood etc.?
- Have I advised or suggested anyone to get an abortion?
- Do I actively fight for the rights of the unborn?
- Have I performed an abortion or assisted in the procedure of abortion to anyone? *(for medical professionals)*
- Have I voted for or supported any pro-choice candidates to public office?
- Have I contributed to any pro-choice organization or institution?
- Have I formally cooperated in an abortion?

Euthanasia (Mercy Killing)

Euthanasia is the killing of a patient who is afflicted with an incurable disease, to relieve pain and suffering. It is illegal in most countries. Like abortion, euthanasia is a grave sin in the eyes of God. No amount of reasoning can justify the killing of a human being, be it in the early stages of life or toward the end of the journey.

No one has power over the wind to restrain the wind, or power over the day of death. (Eccl 8:8)

Whatever its motives and means, direct euthanasia consists in putting an end to the lives of handicapped, sick, or dying persons. It is morally unacceptable. (CCC 2277)

Capital Punishment

Capital punishment is the legally authorized or state-sponsored killing of someone as punishment for a crime. The church has always stood against capital punishment. In extreme cases, it does not exclude the execution of death penalty if it is the only way to defend human life. Every sinner should get a chance to repent for his sins and amend his ways. The death penalty does not put an end to evil. It can only be defeated by love and mercy. Many countries around the world have put an end to this practice. We believe that every sinner has the potential to become a saint one day.

In his hand is the life of every living thing and the breath of every human being. (Job 12:10)

Additional Reading: CCC 2267

Embryonic Stem Cell Research

The secular world and media often make this statement that the Catholic Church vehemently opposes or is against all types of stem cell research. This is not true. In fact, the Church supports and encourages ethically responsible stem cell research, while opposing any research that destroys human embryos. One can never destroy human life for therapeutic reasons, no matter how good the reason or result is. Any research that seeks to alter the embryo is morally unacceptable and should be banned. Man should not play God.

Additional Reading: CCC 2323

Murder

The sin of murder is first mentioned in the fourth chapter of Genesis. Abel and Cain are the two sons of Adam and Eve. Cain murders Abel out of jealousy, and this act does not please God. Throughout time, people have committed murders for several reasons. Although the act of genocide may have many underlying reasons, it is a grave sin because it takes the life of another person.

The Lord said to him: "What have you done? The voice of your brother's blood cries out to me from the ground." (Gen 4:10)

Unintentional killing is not a sin. I remember a person tell me that he had met with an accident once, and the other driver died succumbing to injuries. I suggested him to keep the deceased family members in prayer and reach out to them. Guilt can easily overtake us and make us miserable if we do not take some positive steps.

Areas to Examine:

- Have I murdered someone?

- Have I had murderous thoughts toward someone?
- Have I encouraged anyone to commit murder?
- Do I possess any illegal weapons (guns, arms) that is dangerous to the lives of people who live with me?
- Do I watch or have an interest in watching movies and shows filled with violence?
- Have I indirectly cooperated in a murder?
- Have I refused assistance to a person in danger?

Additional Reading: 1 Jn 3:12

War

What about war? One may ask. A nation must avoid a battle at all costs; nevertheless, all negotiations may fail, and war becomes inevitable. There have been wars where oppressed people were liberated from tyranny and persecution within their land. War is not an easy topic to discuss as there is a loss of life and property. Civilians are called to represent their country in a battle, and it is up to the leaders to see if the fight is justified. At times, war is an act of self-defense.

Additional Reading: CCC 2314

Hatred

We hear about murder and violence often in the media. However, it is unlikely that we will ever come across a murderer or be one. We feel pity for the murder victims when we read about them or watch them on television or the internet. According to the Bible, we are all in some way murderers. If this puzzles you, read the verse below from the first letter of John.

Everyone who hates his brother or sister is a murderer. And you know that no murderer has eternal life abiding within him. (1 Jn 3:15)

God sees hatred as equivalent to murder. Scripture goes on to say that we cannot love God without first loving our neighbor.

If anyone says that he loves God, but hates his brother or sister, then he is a liar. For he who does not love his brother or sister, whom he does see, in what way can he love God, whom he does not see? (1 Jn 4:20)

There are people who, in the name of religion, commit hate crimes. Our faith cannot be lived out by killing others, but by dying for others, which is what our Lord and master Jesus Christ showed us.

Discrimination

Discrimination is another evil which is prevalent during our times and throughout history. God has created all people in his image and likeness, and this is our identity. Sadly, there is widespread discrimination based on color, race, religion, gender, caste, wealth, literacy, physique (looks), etc.

There is neither Jew nor Greek; there is neither servant nor free; there is neither male nor female. For you are all one in Christ Jesus. (Gal 3:28)

With the advancement of technology, religious persecution, job prospects, and various other factors, people are migrating to various parts of the world in large numbers. People of different countries live amongst us, and everyone deserves love, respect, and a right to live.

Let the alien who resides with you be like the citizen among you. And you shall love him as yourselves. For you were also aliens in the land of Egypt. I am the Lord your God. (Lev 19:34)

Additional Reading: Jas 2:2-4, Rom 12:18, Deut 10:19

Terrorism

Terrorism is defined as the use of intentional violence and force for political or religious purposes against countries, regimes, or non-combatant civilians.

They will put you out of the synagogues. But the hour is coming when everyone who puts you to death will consider that he is offering an excellent service to God. (Jn 16:2)

Favoritism & Partiality

We come out of a job interview thinking that we have met all the requirements of the company and are also qualified and experienced for the job, only to find that somebody else took up the job. We have all been victims of favoritism and partiality at least once in our lifetime. At the same time, we may have also committed this sin to others. We may be biased to attractive and beautiful people, or if we are a person of authority, we may have been partial to our kin (nepotism).

My brothers, within the glorious faith of our Lord Jesus Christ, do not choose to show favoritism toward persons. (Jas 2:1)

Additional Reading: Acts 10:34-35, Lev 19:15, Jas 2:9

Areas to Examine:

- Have I been partial to people with good looks?
- Have I ever been partial to my friends and family members acting as a person of authority?
- Have I received favors from people by misusing God-given qualities such as good looks?
- Have I discriminated anybody based on their color, political affiliation, caste, race, religion, etc.?
- Am I cruel to people who have immigrated from other countries or places?

Suicide

Suicide is the intentional taking of one's own life. Around the world, nearly 800,000 people die by suicide each year, which is roughly one death every 40 seconds. People with suicidal thoughts and tendencies need help and counseling. A person with such thoughts must foremost understand that he or she belongs to God, and he rightfully owns them. None of us have any right over our lives. We did not have a choice of when we were born or into what family we were born. We did not choose our parents, our color, and many important details of who we are. Therefore, we also do not have the right to end our life whenever we want to. There are many reasons why one resorts to ending one's life. Hopelessness and despair are the leading causes of suicide. Our God is a God of hope. Suicidal tendencies can be conquered through prayer and counseling. Our God is a divine healer, and there is no situation impossible for him. He can heal all our inner wounds and fill us with his love, joy, and peace. Living for God and glorifying his name gives meaning to our life. We should not yield to hopelessness and despair but rather live for God and glorify his name, which will give meaning to our life.

I shall not die, but I shall live, and recount the deeds of the Lord. (Psalm 118:17)

Additional Reading: 2 Sam 17:23, Ps 119:175, CCC 2280, 2283

Areas to Examine:

- Have I ever attempted to take my life?
- Have I had suicidal thoughts?
- Have I encouraged, suggested, or assisted anyone in committing suicide?
- Have I, by my words, actions, and behavior caused anyone to attempt suicide?

Substance Addictions

Substance addiction of any kind is harmful and destructive to us. We are the temple of the Holy Spirit, and to desecrate this bodily temple with sin and evil is a dishonor to God. Excess of anything of this world will kill us. We are allowed to use the things of this world but never let it master or control us. An addict is not a free person. He has sold his soul to what he is addicted to and ultimately has given Satan control over his life.

Know you not, that your body is the temple of the Holy Ghost, who is in you, whom you have from God; and you are not your own? (1 Cor 6:19)

Any habit or addiction that causes harm or known to cause damage to the body is a mortal sin. One must do everything possible to come out of such cravings and pray for deliverance. Habits can be very overpowering, but with the help of God, it is breakable. God has created us for freedom and wants us to walk in freedom.

If therefore the son shall make you free, you shall be free indeed. (Jn 8:36)

Some common types of substance addictions are listed below. Sexual sins are covered under the sixth commandment.

Additional Reading: Gal 5:1, 1 Cor 3:17

Tobacco

Smoking is one of the most common addictions. It is believed that there are over four thousand chemicals in a single cigarette. It destroys the body and causes health defects in people inhaling the smoke (passive smoking). Smoking causes cancer, heart disease, stroke, lung diseases, diabetes, and chronic obstructive pulmonary disease (COPD), which includes emphysema and chronic bronchitis. The World Health Organization estimates that tobacco kills more than 7 million people each year. More than 6 million of those deaths are the result of direct tobacco use while around 890,000 are the result of non-smokers being exposed to second-hand smoke.

Behold all you that kindle a fire, encompassed with flames, walk in the light of your fire, and in the flames which you have kindled: this is what you shall have from my hand, you shall sleep in torment. (Is 50:11)

Chewing Tobacco

Chewing tobacco is another nicotine related addiction that leads to many oral health problems. Tobacco in all forms is addictive due to the presence of nicotine and other harmful chemicals. Chewing tobacco causes gum disease, tooth decay, tooth loss, oral cancer, cardiovascular disease, and other sicknesses. And it results in more than 250,000 deaths each year.

Invite not death by the error of your life, neither bring on destruction by the works of your hands. (Wis 1:12)

Alcohol

Alcohol is widely consumed all over the world and generally thought to be harmless, which is not the case. Overconsumption of alcohol has many adverse effects on us. Firstly, it is addictive, and it affects one's mood and thoughts. It also leads to other sins and crimes. Research shows that over-consumption of alcohol is harmful to our internal organs, and it also affects our decision making and reasoning. A person who belongs to the Lord will abstain from alcohol altogether.

Do not choose to be inebriated by wine, for this is self-indulgence. Instead, be filled with the Holy Spirit. (Eph 5:18)

Additional Reading: Pro 20:1, Pro 23:31-33, Hos 4:11

Areas to Examine:

- Do I smoke at home, thereby exposing my family members' health to various sicknesses?
- Do I sincerely pray and try to get freedom from smoking and alcohol?
- Do I educate myself about the harm and side effects of alcohol and tobacco?

- Do I have the habit of driving a vehicle or operating machinery after the consumption of alcohol?
- Have I consumed alcohol while being pregnant, thereby affecting the health of the unborn baby?
- Have I consumed alcohol and taken prescribed medication thereby putting my life at risk?
- Have I misbehaved with others in a state of drunkenness?
- Do I make a sincere effort to flee from people or company/ friendships whose primary hobby is to drink and have fun?
- Have I violated somebody sexually, verbally, or physically after consuming alcohol?
- Did I ever commit any grave sin under the influence of alcohol?
- Did I introduce alcohol or tobacco to others and cause them to sin?

Drugs

The production, sale, and consumption of drugs is a large illegal industry operating in most parts of the world. Drugs are dangerous to our body as it affects our brain directly. Our brain is the command center of our thoughts, behavior, judgment, reasoning, learning, and decision making. Consumption of drugs debilitates us and affects our necessary functional capabilities. It also affects the people around us and the whole community. Drugs are addictive, harmful, and self-destructive.

The use of drugs inflicts very grave damage on human health and life. Their use, except on strictly therapeutic grounds, is a grave offense. Clandestine production of and trafficking in drugs are scandalous practices. They constitute direct co-operation in evil, since they encourage people to practices gravely contrary to the moral law. (CCC 2291)

Medicines

Medicines can also be addictive and life-threatening if not used as per prescription. There are people addicted to prescription drugs and over the counter medicines. Medications must be consumed only under the direction of the physician and solely for the betterment of health.

Food Addiction

Food addiction is also real addiction, although food is a must for our body and survival. Processed food, foods high in sugar, and deep-fried foods are hard to resist. There is a saying which goes, "there are those who eat to live, and there are those who live to eat." Excess of anything is dangerous to the body, which also applies to food and our eating habits. Food should sustain us and not be our obsession. A detailed description on food addiction is given in the section covering gluttony under capital sins.

The virtue of temperance disposes us to avoid every kind of excess: the abuse of food, alcohol, tobacco, or medicine. (CCC 2290)

Caffeine and Soft Drinks

Consuming a cup of tea or coffee a day or twice or even thrice a day is not a sin. People who cannot live without caffeine have become an addict to it. It is no longer a daily habit but an addiction that controls them. Caffeine is an addictive ingredient, and their system is so used to this ingredient that they experience withdrawal daily and must run for the caffeinated drink so often. One should not mistake a regular coffee/ tea drinker with a caffeine addict. Has your daily habit turned into an addiction?

Media / Smartphone / Gadget Addiction

There are nearly 2.5 billion smartphone users in the world, and 36 percent of the global population has a smartphone. Americans use smartphones for an average of seven hours per day. It is a useful tool for one who uses it wisely. For the rest of us, it is a source of addiction. There are a variety of things that people are addicted to, within the phone. Some may be into news/politics, and there are those who are addicted to sports. Some may be into movies and movie related news. Some spend most of their time on social media apps interacting with other people, reading about them, and posting information and status about themselves. Gaming and porn are other reasons why people are addicted to their devices. The question is, doing all this, how much time have I spent looking at the screen? Media addiction has become a global epidemic. There is a psychological dependence on these devices. Ask yourself these questions; Do I find it hard to put my phone down? Do I get annoyed if the battery charge is low? Do I get irritated if there is poor internet connectivity? Do I get angry or violent if the gadget is taken away from me? If you can say yes to one of the questions, you are addicted to your device.

People, especially children and teens, show behavioral change when their phone is taken away. They become angry, irritated, and agitated. This is an unhealthy love for a machine which is only going to get worse.

Areas to Examine:

- Do I browse/ text while driving?

- Has my media addiction affected the people who live with me?
- Has my media addiction affected my work at any time?
- Do I go through chronic impulses to look at the screen (signs of addiction)?
- Do I feel uneasy, agitated, and sad when I am away from my phone or if it is turned off or there is no signal or connectivity?
- Do I experience behavioral change when the phone is taken away from me?
- Do I put my health at risk by my addiction?
- Am I addicted to or do I use any banned substances classified as drugs?
- Am I addicted to any medication that is prescribed to me?
- Have I abused medicines at any time?
- Am I addicted to unhealthy junk food?
- Am I addicted to caffeinated drinks or soft drinks?

Destructive Habits

Speeding

Under the fourth commandment, we focused on our commitment and obedience to the law of the land. All laws of the land are good for its citizens provided they do not contradict the law of God. Following the traffic rules not only makes me a good citizen but also saves lives and property. Speeding and rash driving is not just a breaking of the law, but dangerous to the driver, the people in the vehicle, the other cars on the road, and pedestrians.

Let every person be subject to the governing authorities; for there is no authority except from God, and those authorities that exist have been instituted by God. (Rom 13:1)

Adventure Sports

In the name of adventure and extreme sports, people put their own lives and others' lives in danger. We are in this world not to break some records or create history, but to do the will of God and become holy. Holiness with love is our call. It is important that we use our time, talents, and gifts for God's kingdom and seeking and saving the lost souls.

Obey Your Doctor

The medical profession and their services for humanity is a gift from God. A doctor cares for the wellbeing of the patient. Hence, one should obey the doctor and take the medicines as prescribed. Medications should not be abused or taken as per one's wish and convenience. People who do not complete the dosage prescribed, fall sick again.

Additional Reading: Sir 38:1-2

Care for Nature

Our wellbeing and health directly depend on the wellbeing of the natural world around us; hence, it is important that we treat it with care and invest in it. Deforestation, excessive hunting, use and improper disposal of non-biodegradable waste, and the release of harmful chemicals into the atmosphere are some ways we destroy the nature and the ecosystem around us. As an individual, am I doing my part to preserve the world around me?

The Lord God took the man and put him in the garden of Eden to till it and keep it. (Gen 2:15)

Additional Reading: Ps 24:1-2

Areas to Examine:

- Do I overspeed or drive negligently, thereby putting myself and other's lives at risk?
- Am I involved in any kind of game, sport, passion, or hobby that is life-threatening and dangerous?
- Do I obey my doctor to a reasonable level?
- Do I willfully destroy or bring harm to nature and the world around me?
- Do I promptly recycle products as per the law of the land?
- Do I engage in excessive hunting of animals or illegal hunting of endangered animals?

Conclusion

In this commandment, we looked at three basic areas where we tend to commit a sin; killing oneself, killing others, and killing or destroying the natural world around us. In the next commandment, we will focus on the sin of the flesh.

The Sixth Commandment

You shall not commit adultery

Sexual Sins

Sex, according to God, is a sacred and holy act. Because of the sinful nature in us, our sexuality tends to deviate from its original purpose, and therefore, we have many wrongful sexual desires in us. Our Christian call is to achieve holiness in us by offering our bodies to God as a spiritual sacrifice.

I appeal to you, therefore, brothers and sisters, by the mercies of God, to present your bodies as a living sacrifice, holy and acceptable to God, which is your spiritual worship. (Rom 12:1)

Man has reduced sex and sexuality to something sinful and evil. There is an elevated level of curiosity in some and repulsion in others. Some see it as the epitome of creation, while others see it as a social evil that ruins people and destroys families. The sixth commandment deals with all sins related to our sexuality. Because of our sexual nature, it affects all of us in some way or another. Sexuality, by itself, is not a sin; rather, it is a gift from God with a purpose.

These are some of the laws of sexuality taught by God through his word.

- Sexual acts are permissible only between a husband and wife.
- Sexual acts are permissible only between a man and a woman.
- Couples should be open to life and procreation
- Sex is holy and sacred in the eyes of God
- All those who are not married must commit to a life of chastity.

- Sexual purity must be attained and perfected at the highest level of the being, namely, the mind and soul.
- Love calls for giving oneself to the lover, and this applies to sexuality as well. While enjoying the pleasures of sex, one should also be willing to give this pleasure to the partner.
- A marriage partner should be treated with love, respect, and dignity and not as an object of sexual pleasure and gratification.
- One should be aware of the sexual needs of the other in marriage.
- Marriage should not be lived out in lust. Sex should not become the primary aim in life.
- Sexual satisfaction should not be a condition for a happy married life.
- Sex is a private matter, and couples should refrain from public display of sexual affection.

Sexuality Within Marriage

Sexuality is a means of expression of love between a husband and wife. Outside of the sacrament of marriage, it is a sin. Man is a sexual being. In addition to the mental faculties and senses, we also have sexual cravings built in us. God gives his first blessing/command in the area of marriage and sexuality.

God blessed them, and he said, "Increase and multiply, and fill the earth, and subdue it." (Gen 1:28)

The above verse clearly shows the purpose of sexuality in us. It comes with two conditions. Firstly, it must be expressed within marriage and secondly; marriage partners must be open to having children. It also reserves a sexual act between a man and a woman.

Sex is not merely a mingling of the bodies in the biological level, but the union of the whole being with the other. When we commit a sexual act, we are united not just on the physical level, but in the spiritual, emotional, and mental level as well.

Sexuality affects all aspects of the human person in the unity of his body and soul. It especially concerns affectivity, the capacity to love and to procreate, and in a more general way the aptitude for forming bonds of communion with others. (CCC 2332)

Sex Outside of Marriage

All sexual acts and practices outside of marriage is a grave mortal sin. Some see pleasure in it, while others see it as a commodity and a way to earn a livelihood. Some are enslaved by it while some others forcefully satisfy their lust. There are a small number of people who would go any lengths to satisfy their sexual hunger, and they resort to abnormal or unconventional methods of sex.

Because of fornication, let each man have his own wife, and let each woman have her own husband. (1 Cor 7:2)

Some of the sinful sexual practices outside of marriage are mentioned in this chapter.

Fornication or Premarital Sex

Fornication is defined as consensual sexual intercourse or relations between people not married. Sex before marriage is prohibited by most world religions and cultures. The Bible forbids all forms of premarital sex. This sin is mentioned in over 25 places in Scripture and has a negative connotation to it.

The body is not for fornication, but rather for the Lord; and the Lord is for the body. (1 Cor 6:13)

Fornication is carnal union between an unmarried man and an unmarried woman. It is gravely contrary to the dignity of persons and of human sexuality which is naturally ordered to the good of spouses and the generation and education of children. Moreover, it is a grave scandal when there is corruption of the young. (CCC 2353)

Additional Reading: 1 Cor 6:18, Eph 5:3, Tob 4:12, Acts 15:29, Sir 23:17

Engaged to Marry

Engaged to marry is different from marriage, and the people involved are still considered single and therefore must abstain from sexual activity until marriage.

Those who are engaged to marry are called to live chastity in continence. They should see in this time of testing a discovery of mutual respect, an apprenticeship in fidelity, and the hope of receiving one another from God. They should reserve for marriage the expressions of affection that belong to married love. They will help each other grow in chastity. (CCC 2350)

Adultery

Adultery is defined as the voluntary sexual act or relationship of a married person with someone other than his or her lawful spouse. It is the gravest sin against marriage. Marriage calls for exclusivity and, adultery gravely wounds the marital relationship. It is a great injustice to the partner.

Adultery refers to marital infidelity. When two partners, of whom at least one is married to another party, have sexual relations - even transient ones - they commit adultery. Christ condemns even adultery of mere desire. The sixth commandment and the New Testament forbid adultery absolutely. The prophets denounce the gravity of adultery; they see it as an image of the sin of idolatry. (CCC 2380)

Whoever is an adulterer, because of the emptiness of his heart, will destroy his own soul. He gets wounds and dishonor to himself, and his disgrace will not be wiped away. (Pro 6:32-33)

Additional Reading: Sir 23:18

Divorce

Marriage is a covenant for life, and a spouse is a life partner, and no man has the power to separate what God has joined together. Divorce is not an easy topic to discuss. It cannot be seen only as a sin, but also an injustice. There are so many people who are victimized by this evil. It is also very cruel on the children if there are any, and it destroys the family and home. God hates divorce, and it is never his will that families be broken.

What God has joined together, let no man separate. (Matt 19:6)

Additional Reading: Matt 5:31-32, Mrk 10:11, Luk 16:18, Mal 2:16

Relationship with a Married Person

A single person may associate himself or herself with any single person of the opposite sex non-sexually if one can control oneself and remain chaste until marriage. At the same time, a single person should not associate with any married person of the opposite sex unless it is related to work (with caution) or they are family. A married person should distance himself or herself from people of the opposite sex, either single or married unless related to work or family.

You should not dine at all with another man's wife. And you should not revel with her over wine, lest perhaps your heart may turn toward her, and by your emotion, you would be toppled into destruction. (Sir 9:9)

Areas to Examine:

- Have I knowingly associated with any married person of the opposite sex without any valid reason?
- Have I committed the sin of divorce or separated from my spouse?
- Have I committed adultery?
- Have I had sexual relations with my fiancé'/fiancée?
- Have I committed fornication?

Sex as a Commodity

Sex from the beginning of times is seen as a commodity by many. Sex and its pleasures are bought and sold in the form of pornography, striptease, webcam shows, phone sex, chat rooms, prostitution, sex toys, sex-enhancing drugs, and so on. It has become a global industry where many practices are legal and some illegal in many societies. Sex has been manipulated according to man's selfish appetites and cravings. Some are in it for money, and many are in it for pleasure.

Pornography

Pornography consists of sexually explicit videos, photographs, writings, or the like, whose purpose is to elicit sexual arousal. (Dictionary.com). Pornographic and sexually explicit videos and images affect and wound our sexuality. The pleasure derived from watching it is not real, and it injures our ability to see people as people. A woman is seen as an object of sexual gratification. Pornography is a billion-dollar industry where both the viewer and the actors are victims who need help.

Pornography consists in removing real or simulated sexual acts from the intimacy of the partners, in order to display them deliberately to third parties. It offends against chastity because it perverts the conjugal act, the intimate giving of spouses to each other. It does grave injury to the dignity of its participants (actors, vendors, the public) since each one becomes an object of base pleasure and illicit profit for others. It immerses all who are involved in the illusion of a fantasy world. It is a grave offense. Civil authorities should prevent the production and distribution of pornographic materials. (CCC 2354)

The more porn a person watches, the more he or she becomes dependent on the videos and images to maintain sexual arousal. Porn can become an addiction if not dealt with. More than 30 percent of internet searches are porn related, and according to an Alexa rating, there is at least one porn website among the world's top 10 most viewed sites.

Adult Rated Movies or R Rated Movies

Movies are categorized and rated based on the content in it. People watch R-rated movies knowing fully well what is in it. R rated and sexually explicit movies are made because there is a huge demand for it. There will be providers as long as there are subscribers. Christians, when they stop watching and endorsing such movies, will see a decrease in the production of such content.

Actors

Porn stars, both men and women, use pornography as a means of income. They sell their bodies to support themselves and their families. Some are trapped in it out of poverty. God knows the needs of every person and the one involved in such acts must say no to this form of livelihood and look for other avenues to earn money and support their families. Our bodies are sacred, as it is the dwelling place of God. Nude modeling and movie stars who perform sexually explicit scenes also come under this category. Our private parts are meant to be closed and private, and they should not be revealed to the world or made available for sale.

Prostitution

Prostitution is different from porn. In porn, the actor and the buyer seldom come in contact. Prostitution is a graver sin than watching porn. A prostitute makes her body available for intercourse and other pleasures for a fee. The sin of prostitution or whoredom is mentioned in the very first book of the Bible, taking its origin to the early days of humanity (Genesis 38:15). Prostitution is the primary cause of STD (sexually transmitted disease). Going to prostitutes and being in the business of prostitution are both grave sins.

Do not give yourself to prostitutes, or you may lose your inheritance. (Sir 9:6)

Additional Reading: 1 Cor 6:16, Sir 19:2-3

Webcam Live Shows

This is a way of livelihood or making money where people take off their clothes and perform sexual activities live through webcams in front of a remote audience who could be anywhere in the world. Striptease, nudist clubs, exotic dancing, and nude/ topless bars are some examples of live nude shows.

Sex Enhancing Drugs

People who have lost their sexual drive or people who seek additional pleasure in sex, resort to using sex-enhancing drugs. There are many varieties of such drugs that cater to the sexually hungry people. These potentially harmful drugs can damage one's health and sexuality. All sexual hunger, appetites, and cravings should be channeled toward true love.

Sex Toys and Adult Entertainment Material

Sex is neither a game nor a child's play. The sacredness of conjugal love must be respected, and couples should refrain from using artificial means to enhance pleasure. These are unhealthy and unholy and can become addictive. The dildo is an example of a sex toy.

Chatrooms

There are chatrooms discreetly operating around the world where people come together to seek sexual pleasure by engaging in obscene talks.

Entirely out of place is obscene, silly, and vulgar talk; but instead, let there be thanksgiving. (Eph 5:4)

Phone Sex

Phone sex is another way of sexual gratification where people dial a number and chat with a person. It is a paid service where calls are priced higher than regular calls. It is a legitimate business in some developed countries, and many innocent people lose their hard-earned savings because of such addictions.

Avoid profane chatter, for it will lead people into increased impiety. (2 Tim 2:16)

Areas to Examine:

- Have I engaged in any kind of phone sex?
- Do I spend time in chatrooms engaging in profane conversations?

- Have I used any kind of sex toys, foreplay toys, or adult magazines?
- Have I used sex enhancing drugs?
- Have I viewed any webcam or live-sex videos?
- Have I been part of any webcam shows (sexual)?
- Have I used sex to earn money?
- Have I visited a prostitute?
- Have I watched any porn or adult movie?
- Have I acted in any porn or adult movie?
- Have I sold or exchanged any adult movie or materials?

Conclusion

Though sexual acts may be consensual, any activity that takes place outside of marriage is a grave sin. So far, we looked at some normal or straight sexual practices existing between a man and a woman. We will now study about sexual practices which are illegal or intrinsically disordered.

Masturbation

Masturbation is defined as the stimulation or manipulation of one's own genitals to experience the pleasure of ejaculation and/or orgasm. It is also called sexual self-gratification (Dictionary.com). It does not require a partner, and it is widely thought to be a harmless habit. Therefore, the secular world does not forbid this act. In reality, it wounds our soul, and it is a grave sin. Given below are some truths about masturbation.

- Masturbation is a selfish act focused on self-gratification.
- Masturbation is an addictive habit and if not addressed, can bring discontentment in one's married life.
- Like every other addiction, masturbation also will increase in frequency and will make us a slave of it.
- Masturbation can lead to other sexual sins. Most people addicted to masturbation are also addicted to pornography.
- Watching porn almost always leads to or ends in masturbation.
- Sexual fantasies and imaginations lead or tempt one to masturbate.
- Masturbation is a guilt-driven habit

- Masturbation wounds marriage and can become a serious obstacle to healthy marital intimacy.

Porn and sexual fantasies develop an unhealthy connection with male ejaculation that, one will end up depending on these during intercourse with the marriage partner.

By masturbation is to be understood the deliberate stimulation of the genital organs in order to derive sexual pleasure. "Both the Magisterium of the Church, in the course of a constant tradition, and the moral sense of the faithful have been in no doubt and have firmly maintained that masturbation is an intrinsically and gravely disordered action." "The deliberate use of the sexual faculty, for whatever reason, outside of marriage is essentially contrary to its purpose." For here sexual pleasure is sought outside of "the sexual relationship which is demanded by the moral order and in which the total meaning of mutual self-giving and human procreation in the context of true love is achieved." (CCC 2352)

Incest

Incest is defined as the sexual relations between family members or close relatives not married to each other. This evil is universally forbidden at least in relationships such as parent-child and siblings etc. The Bible mentions incest at least 2 times where it was not mutually consensual; Lot sleeping with his daughters (Gen 19:32-35) and Ammon raping his half-sister. (2 Sam 13). The Bible forbids all incestuous relationships.

None of you shall approach anyone near of kin to uncover nakedness: I am the Lord. (Lev 18:6)

The Catechism states that incest is a regression toward animality (CCC 2388). Animals have no restraints as to whom they have relations with. We are above them in creation, and God has given us specific laws about sexuality.

Areas to Examine:

- Have I had sexual thoughts toward my family members other than my spouse?
- Have I ever tempted any of my family members by my conversation or the way I dress or behave?
- Did I make any advances or force any of my family members to sexual activities?

Additional Reading: Lev 20:11, Lev 20:12, Lev 20:17, Lev 20:21, Sir 23:16, Deut 27:20, Deut 27:22, Deut 27:23, Lev 20:14, Deut 22:30, Lev 18:17, 1 Cor 5:1, 2 Sam 16:22, 2 Sam 13:1-4

Bestiality and Zoophilia

It involves sexual fixation or sexual acts with animals. It is grave depravity and morally disordered. One who is sexually attracted to animals needs help because it is a result of wounded sexuality.

You shall not have sexual relations with any animal and defile yourself with it, nor shall any woman give herself to an animal to have sexual relations with it: it is perversion. (Lev 18:23)

Areas to Examine:

- Did I ever sexually abuse an animal?
- Did I ever have any unhealthy relationships with animals?

Additional Reading: Lev 20:15, Deut 27:21, Jude 1:7

Homosexuality

Homosexuality, though acceptable by many developed countries, is sinful in the eyes of God. The Bible, both in the old and new testament, forbids this union. It is important we draw a line or distinction between a person with homosexual tendencies and the act of homosexuality. Homosexual tendencies are a result of multiple reasons which are beyond the scope of this book to discuss. The Bible calls homosexual acts as unnatural (Rom 1:26) and abominable (Lev 18:22). The Catechism calls it intrinsically disordered.

In the same way also the men, giving up natural intercourse with women, were consumed with passion for one another. Men committed shameless acts with men and received in their own persons the due penalty for their error. (Rom 1:27)

Homosexuality refers to relations between men or between women who experience an exclusive or predominant sexual attraction toward persons of the same sex. It has taken a great variety of forms through the centuries and in different cultures. Its psychological genesis remains largely unexplained. Basing itself on Sacred Scripture, which presents homosexual acts as acts of grave depravity, tradition has always declared that "homosexual acts are intrinsically disordered." They are contrary to the natural law. They close the sexual act to the gift of life. They do not proceed from a genuine affective and sexual complementarity. Under no circumstances can they be approved. (CCC 2357)

All sexual desires, homosexual and heterosexual, outside of marriage is sinful. A person with homosexual tendencies should pray to God and offer it as a cross.

Areas to Examine:

- Have I ever indulged in same-sex acts with anyone?
- Have I watched same-sex videos and media?
- Did I ever support the legalizing of the homosexual union?
- Have I or do I entertain homosexual thoughts or desires within me?

Additional Reading: CCC 2396, CCC 2359, CCC 2358, Lev 20:13, Lev 18:22

Same-Sex Marriage

Marriage, from the beginning of creation, is the union of a man and a woman. Marriage, in addition to the joy and pleasure it gives to the partners, has a definite and divine purpose. The purpose of God is not fulfilled in same-sex marriages. God through his word and the Church, condemns and forbids all same-sex unions.

He answered, "Have you not read that the one who made them at the beginning 'made them male and female.' (Matt 19:4)

Areas to Examine:

- Have I ever attended a same-sex marriage ceremony?
- Have I endorsed or supported same-sex marriage either online or in a conversation?

Additional Reading: Sir 33:15, Sir 42:24, Matt 10:6-7

Polygamy

Polygamy is the custom of having more than one spouse at the same time. It is illegal in most countries and punishable by law. Although it was a union permitted by God in the Old Testament, by the time we enter the New Testament, we have clear teaching that it goes against the dignity of marriage. All Christian denominations are against polygamy. It is still followed amongst the Mormons and in some Islamic countries.

Additional Reading: CCC 2387, CCC 1664, CCC 1610, CCC 1645

Cohabitation

Cohabitation is an arrangement or agreement where two people who are not married live together. There is no agreement or plans to marry. It should not be confused with living as roommates. It is a sexual relationship which may or may not blossom into romance or even marriage. Cohabitation goes against our Christian teaching as it promotes fornication and sex outside of marriage. It is mentioned in the Bible in the fourth chapter of John, where Jesus meets with a Samaritan woman. This woman is cohabiting with a man after being married and divorced five times. Jesus reveals this to the woman implying that God does not approve of it.

"Go and call your husband," Jesus told her, "and come back. "I don't have a husband," she answered. Jesus replied, "You are right when you say you don't have a husband. You have been married to five men, and the man you live with now is not really your husband. You have told me the truth."(Jn 4:16-18, GNT)

Trial Marriage

An arrangement by which a couple lives together for some time to see if they are compatible for marriage. Trial marriage goes against the Church's teaching about marriage and family. A man should enter into marriage with a woman with the intention of becoming one flesh. Marriage is sacred and permanent.

Some today claim a "right to a trial marriage" where there is an intention of getting married later. However firm the purpose of those who engage in premature sexual relations may be, "the fact is that such liaisons can scarcely ensure mutual sincerity and fidelity in a relationship between a man and a woman, nor, especially, can they protect it from inconstancy of desires or whim." Carnal union is morally legitimate only when a definitive community of life between a man and woman has been established. Human love does not tolerate "trial marriages." It demands a total and definitive gift of persons to one another. (CCC 2391)

Let marriage be held in honor by all, and let the marriage bed be kept undefiled; for God will judge fornicators and adulterers. (Heb 13:4)

Open Relationship

A marriage relationship where the partners agree that each can or each one is permitted to have sexual relations with others. This form of agreement is nothing but legalized adultery and breaks the oneness and sanctity of marriage. The husband's body belongs to the wife, and the wife's body belongs to the husband alone.

For the wife does not have authority over her own body, but the husband does; likewise the husband does not have authority over his own body, but the wife does. (1 Cor 7:4)

Swinging or Partner Swapping

An agreement between two or more married couples where partners are swapped with mutual consent. This form of relationship or understanding between couples corrupts the sanctity of marriage. A sexual act is called to be a monogamous experience between one man and a woman who are married to each other.

Fetishes

Sexual fetishes are defined as unhealthy fixation, gratification, or attraction to a particular part of the body, clothing, ornament, or object. It is a result of wounded sexuality. One can attain freedom by repentance, confession, and prayer.

Sexual Violence / Sex by Force

Pedophilia

A pedophile is a person who is sexually attracted to a child, whereas an ephebophile is a person attracted to a teenager. Sexual attraction toward a minor is a sin and a crime punishable by law in most or all countries. Even if the minor has consented to the act, he is she is not mature enough to decide on sexual matters, and therefore it is treated as an abuse of a child. It is a grave injustice to the victim.

Rape/ Sex Abuse & Harassment/ Me Too Movement

Rape is a type of sexual assault, usually involving sexual intercourse or other forms of sexual penetration against a person without consent. The Catechism gives a similar definition and describes the gravity and consequence of the sin.

Rape is the forcible violation of the sexual intimacy of another person. It does injury to justice and charity. Rape deeply wounds the respect, freedom, and physical and moral integrity to which every person has a right. It causes grave damage that can mark the victim for life. It is always an intrinsically evil act.

Graver still is the rape of children committed by parents (incest) or those responsible for the education of the children entrusted to them. (CCC 2356)

The Bible speaks about rape in more than one place. There are three incidents of this horrific crime mentioned in the Scriptures; the rape of Dinah (Gen 34), the rape of an unnamed concubine (Judg 19), and the rape of Tamar (2 Sam 13). All these incidents result in widespread violence and destruction.

Sexual harassment, abuse, bullying, coercion, and molestation are equally evil that many of us face at our workplace, public places, schools, and colleges, and even at homes.

Areas to Examine:

- Have I raped someone?
- Did I sexually violate, abuse, or molest another person?
- Did I make any forceful sexual advances toward another person?
- Did I demand sexual favors for any reason?
- Have I committed the sin of pedophilia?

Revenge Porn

Revenge porn is the distribution or transmission of sexually explicit images or video of individuals over digital media without their permission. The explicit images or video may be made with the knowledge and consent of the individual, or it may be made without his or her consent and knowledge. The content or footage may be used to blackmail the individual for favors, to coerce them into continuing the relationship, or to punish them for ending the relationship.

Sexual Promiscuity

It is a behavior of having sex frequently with different partners on a casual basis without any emotional attachment.

Now, to the unmarried and to the widows I say that it would be better for you to continue to live alone as I do. But if you cannot restrain your desires, go ahead and marry – it is better to marry than to burn with passion. (1 Cor 7:8-9, GNT)

Additional Readings: Eze 23:19-21, Eze 16:27

Virginity

We live in a culture where losing one's virginity is seen as an accomplishment and a virtue to boast about. It is even considered shameful to be an adult and still be a virgin. God's word strongly teaches the importance of staying a virgin until marriage. Virginity is a God-given gift that needs to be guarded and kept safe until marriage.

For this is the will of God, your sanctification: that you abstain from fornication; that each one of you know how to control your own body in holiness and honor. (1 Thes 4:3-4)

Luring Others to Sex / Sexually Immoral Person

Seducing others to sex or intimacy is also a serious sin. The sin of causing another brother or sister to stumble or participate in our sin is mentioned in the gospel of Mathew.

If any of you put a stumbling block before one of these little ones who believe in me, it would be better for you if a great millstone were fastened around your neck and you were drowned in the depth of the sea. (Matt 18:6)

Additional Reading: 1 Thes 4:6

Areas to Examine:

- Did I touch others or let others touch me in an impure manner?
- Did I lure or tempt others to commit any sexual sin?
- Did I yield to another person's sexual advances?
- Did I make any uninvited or unwelcomed sexual advances toward another?

Conclusion

This completes our study on the sixth commandment. We looked at some of the deadly or grave sins, and some frequently committed sins within this commandment. We will advancee to the seventh commandment, which also deals with a kind of lust; lust for wealth.

The Seventh Commandment

Thou shall not steal

The seventh commandment is about honoring and respecting the goods of others and the topic of money and finances in general. We cannot claim ownership of anything in this life. We have something because it has been given to us by God, and we merely act as managers and caretakers of what has been entrusted to us.

What do you have that you did not receive? And if you received it, why do you boast as if it were not a gift? (1 Cor 4:7)

Everyone is guilty of breaking this commandment to some extent. There are four major areas to focus; stealing from God, stealing from our neighbor, stealing from oneself and stealing from the world around us.

Stealing from God

Tithing

Tithing is the giving of part of our income for God's work. One who does not tithe steals from God because the money we tithe does not belong to us, but it is God's money. It is he who gives us the power to get wealth. Tithing brings financial blessings in our lives, and holding back our tithe only leads to financial problems. We have clear and detailed teaching about the importance of tithing in the Scriptures. We will look at some biblical verses on tithing and its spiritual significance.

Tithing Brings Financial Blessings

When we open our heart to God and our neighbor, God opens his heart for us. If you are a Christian going through financial debt or inadequacy, unable to pay your bills and make ends meet, this is the first area to check. Sincerity and faithfulness in giving to God will draw us out of our financial mess and struggles.

Bring the full tithe into the storehouse, so that there may be food in my house, and thus put me to the test, says the Lord of hosts; see if I will not open the windows of heaven for you and pour down for you an overflowing blessing. (Mal 3:10)

We Rob God When we Do Not Tithe

Tithe money does not belong to us, and holding onto it is equivalent to robbing God. Tithing is not about how much of our money we give to God, but it is how much of God-given money am I going to keep for myself. Giving is never easy for one who is selfish and greedy.

Will anyone rob God? Yet you are robbing me! But you say, "How are we robbing you?" In your tithes and offerings. (Mal 3:8)

Additional Reading: 1 Chron 29:14, Hag 1:9

Give to God Cheerfully

God loves a cheerful and happy giver. A miser or a greedy person will feel the pain when it comes to share or give his money to God and others. It is a sign of greed and love of money. One should not be calculative when giving to God. Giving is a way of investing in one's own wellbeing. What we give will come back to us as God's blessings.

Give to the Most High as he has given to you, just as generously as you can. The Lord always repays and will do it many times over. (Sir 35:10-11, GNT)

Tithing is a God-Given Law

Tithing and supporting God's work is a biblical law, and those who do not give to God block their own blessings and are also committing a sin.

All tithes from the land, whether the seed from the ground or the fruit from the tree, are the Lord's; they are holy to the Lord. (Lev 27:30)

Give Your Best to God

People generally tend to keep the best to themselves and give the leftovers to the poor and needy. God also receives the same treatment from us. There is a promise given in the book of Proverbs, chapter 3 for those who give their best for the Lord, be it time, money, or talents.

Honor the Lord by making him an offering from the best of all that your land produces. If you do, your barns will be filled with grain, and you will have too much wine to store it all. (Pro 3:9-10, GNT)

Areas to Examine:

- Do I tithe regularly?
- Do I financially support my local parish?
- Have I denied anyone who sought help from me for doing God's work?
- Do I tithe cheerfully, or do I give under compulsion or is it guilt-driven?
- Am I generous in giving?
- Do I give the best of everything or give leftovers for God's kingdom?

Additional Reading: 2 Cor 9:7, Exo 34:26, Hag 1:7-10, Lev 27:32, Num 15:19

Stealing God's Money

This section deals with taking money that is intended for God's work, and this may not apply to everyone. Some of us, who are part of a ministry or handling the finances of a parish or community may relate to this. Judas Iscariot, the disciple of Jesus, oversaw the tithe money, and he used to steal from it (Jn 12:4). Stealing directly, unwise spending of Church money, using the money for personal wants are some examples.

Areas to Examine:

- Have I ever stolen tithe money?
- Have I ever misused tithe money?
- Have I used tithe money for personal reasons?
- Do I constantly pray for direction in using tithe money?

Additional Reading: 1 Sam 2:12

Stealing from Neighbor

Man is a social animal, and he is always interacting and transacting with his neighbor. We give what we have and take what we need from others. There are laws to follow during this interaction and transaction. There are the laws set by the land, and there are God-given divine laws regarding giving and taking.

If God's law were to be strictly followed, there would not be any poverty in this world. Man's selfish nature and greed have resulted in widespread poverty and shortage around the world.

All who believed were together, and they held all things in common. They were selling their possessions and belongings, and distributing them to all, just as any of them had need. (Acts 2:44-45)

From the least of them to the greatest, all of them are greedy for unjust gain. (Jer 6:13)

God did not plan or bring about poverty, famine, lack, or sickness in this world. The devil's envy and man's cooperation with him brought illness, suffering, and death into this world. (Wisdom 2:23-24)

Some steal directly from others, and some take discreetly. There are others who steal without their own knowledge and are ignorant about it. If you have reached this far into this book, you may not be a person robbing banks and people's houses and property. We will look at some smart ways we steal from others. And of course, if you are the bank robbing kind, here are some Scriptures for you,

Whoever is a thief, let him now not steal, but rather let him labor, working with his hands, doing what is good, so that he may have something to share with those who suffer need. (Eph 4:28)

Areas to Examine:

- Have I ever shoplifted?
- Have I stolen anything from any institution I am part of (Example: school, college, library, church, workplace, etc.)?
- Have I stolen money from my parents when living with them?
- Have I been involved in any theft or robbery?

Additional Reading: Is 61:8

Accidental Damage to Personal or Public Property

Every person has rights to the property he has acquired lawfully and legally. We must respect the property of other people. Accidental damages to others property may happen due to our negligence or ignorance, but the damage is real. It is important that we do everything in our power to restore the loss suffered by the other person. Exodus, chapter 22 speaks about restitution.

Areas to Examine:

- Have I caused damage to another's property due to my negligence and have not taken responsibility for it?
- Have I tried to restore or make restitution for the damage caused by me?
- If the damage is not repairable or not restorable, do I at least pray for the victims?

Vandalism

Vandalism is a deliberate act of destruction or damage to public or private property. People vandalize to avenge the loss done to them. It is a way of retaliation. Vandalizing is also done to express one's viewpoint. Whatever be the cause, damaging public or private property is a sin. In addition to repentance and confession, a person must make every effort to restore the damages causes to the other person.

Scoffers enflame the city, but the wise turn away wrath. (Pro 29:8)

Areas to Examine:

- Have I vandalized any public or private property as an act of revenge?
- Have I vandalized any public or private property to make a statement or to express my views?
- Have I vandalized public or private property under the influence of alcohol or drugs?

Additional Reading: Rom 12:17, Matt 5:38-39

Wages and Salary

If you are a business owner and people work under you, this may apply to you. There are some biblical guidelines to follow.

Listen! The wages of the laborers who mowed your fields, which you kept back by fraud, cry out, and the cries of the harvesters have reached the ears of the Lord of hosts. (James 5:4)

Areas to Examine:

- Have I, as an employer, unjustly withheld the wages of my employees?
- Do I pay my employees promptly (timely manner)?
- Do I pay what I have promised and agreed?
- Do I pay what everyone deserves?

Additional Reading: Deut 24:15, Mal 3:5, Jer 22:13, Tob 4:14, Lev 19:13, Eph 6:9

Taxes and Dues

Taxes are never easy to pay. People come with many justifications when it is time to pay their taxes. High taxes, wastage, and misuse of public money are reasons given for not paying the taxes. We are partially right in these matters, but it is still our duty and civic obligation to pay the taxes promptly without covering up.

Render to all whatever is owed. Taxes, to whom taxes is due; revenue, to whom revenue is due; respect, to whom respect is due; honor, to whom honor is due. (Rom 13:7)

Additional Reading: Matt 22:17-21

Bills and Debts

We incur bills for the services or material provided to us. Paying our bills and debts on time is a sign of sincerity in us. A good Christian is one who can manage his household and finances well. It is a sin to hold on to the money that does not belong to us. The Word of God teaches us that the love of money is the root of all evil.

The sinner will borrow and not give back, but the just one is generous and keeps on giving. (Ps 37:21)

Collecting taxes

Some of us may be in a position of levying and collecting tax from others. One should ensure that one is only imposing and collecting what is necessary. Some of us, working under authority, are required to impose fines and late fees on others. In which case, we must be compassionate toward our brothers and sisters. I remember, once when a police officer stopped me for a traffic violation. The cop had all the rights to serve me a ticket. Instead, he was compassionate toward me and let me go with a warning.

He said to them, "You should collect nothing more than what has been prescribed for you." (Luk 3:13)

Areas to Examine:

- Am I compassionate to the one who owes me money?
- Am I considerate to people when I use my authority to collect any debt or interest?

Bribe

To give or take a bribe is sinful because it takes away the rights of the poor and the deserving. A bribe blinds the eye of the one who receives it and compromises justice. It also compromises on the quality of service or product exchanged and makes people greedy.

You shall not accept bribes, which blind even the prudent and perverts the cause of the just. (Exo 23:8)

Additional Reading: Deut 16:19, Eccl 7:7, Ps 15:5, Is 5:23, Mic 7:3, Pro 15:27, Deut 10:17, 2 Chron 19:7

Charging Interest

The practice of charging interest has been around for an exceedingly long time. The rich have exploited the poor in the name of heavy and exorbitant interests. In developed countries, people get loans directly from the financial institutions, and if they are unable to pay, the banks may confiscate their property. In most developing countries, people themselves act as money lenders and charge interest, which leads to abuse and injustice to the poor. Money blinds people, makes them greedy, and leads them to other sins.

One who augments wealth by exorbitant interest gathers it for another who is kind to the poor. (Pro 28:8)

Additional Reading: Eze 22:12, Deut 23:19-20, Lev 25:35-37, Exo 22:25-27

Dishonesty in Business Dealings

Greed and the desire to get rich makes one a dishonest person in one's business dealings. The primary motive of any business should not be earning money, although which is why many of us start a business. Contribution to the world around us and customer satisfaction should be given importance, and it should be the driving force. God wants his people to be honest in all their dealings, be it work, church, or at home. People who cheat others cheat themselves. We may have earned some quick money, but nothing happens outside of God's view. God sees everything.

Do not depend on dishonest wealth, for it will not benefit you on the day of calamity. (Sir 5:8)

Areas to Examine:

- Am I open and honest with all my business partners about the business activities and profits (and losses)?
- Do I provide quality products to my customers?
- Do I deliver the products in the quality that I advertised it?
- Do I make unmerited and false claims of the product or the services I provide?
- Am I prompt and timely in delivering my products and services?

Additional Reading: Deut 25:14-16, Mic 6:11, Lev 19:35-36, Sir 26:29, Sir 13, 24

Extortion of Money

Extortion is a way of obtaining something, especially money, through force, blackmail, or threats. Patience and compassion should be shown to the one who owes money. God is patient and merciful toward all humanity. Therefore, a Christian must also be patient and compassionate toward his debtors. Use of force, threats, and blackmail is ungodly.

Soldiers also asked him, "And we, what should we do?" He said to them, "Do not extort money from anyone by threats or false accusation and be satisfied with your wages." (Luk 3:14)

Areas to Examine:

- Have I unjustly used force, blackmail, or threats to recover money?
- Do I give reasonable time to my debtors to pay back what they owe me?
- Am I patient, considerate, and compassionate to the one who owes me anything?

Additional Reading: Eze 18:18

Plagiarism

Plagiarism is the practice of stealing and using another person's literary work without authorization. One who plagiarizes also tells lies claiming the work to be his own.

See. Therefore, I am against the prophets, says the Lord, who steal my words from one another. (Jer 23:30)

Piracy (Copyright Infringement)

Piracy is the practice of selling, transmitting, downloading, and viewing digital media content without crediting the producer of the material. There are many websites out there that stream movies, music, sports, and shows for free. One must check to see if these providers are legitimate, and the content is legal. We support piracy and participate in the sin if we watch such content.

Areas to Examine:

- Have I stolen others' work and claimed it as my own?
- Have I used others' work without permission?
- Have I used others' work without crediting or compensating them?
- Have I patented something which was not my creation?
- Have I knowingly downloaded media from illegal websites?
- Have I knowingly uploaded or transmitted content over the internet without permission?
- Do I watch movies or shows from pirated or illegal websites?

Kidnapping

Holding a person against his will for a ransom or favor. Abduction and kidnapping are grave sins mentioned in Exo 21:16 and in Deut 24:7.

Slavery

Slavery is the extraction of labor from a person against his will. Slavery is a great evil from the early days of humanity up until now. Slavery still exists in some parts of the world discreetly. There are places where children are forced to work. The old testament is full of stories of slavery and bondage. The Israelites were under slavery in Egypt for over 400 years. Slavery can be termed as the stealing of one's free will.

Additional Reading: CCC 2414

Encroachment

Encroachment is a situation where a property owner violates the property rights of his neighbor by building on or extending a structure or altering the boundary to the neighbor's land. Encroachment is also the occupying and claiming ownership of property that does not belong to the person. It is a sin against the person who rightfully owns the property.

You must not move your neighbor's boundary marker, set up by former generations, on the property that will be allotted to you in the land that the Lord your God is giving you to possess. (Deut 19:14)

Additional Reading: Pro 23:9-10

Areas to Examine:

- Did I ever kidnap or hold a person captive?
- Did I assist in any kidnapping activity?
- Did I extract labor from a person against his will?
- Did I encroach another person's property by legal or illegal means?
- Did I claim ownership of property that did not belong to me?

Forgery

Forgery is a white-collar crime that generally refers to the false making or material alteration of a legal instrument with the specific intent to defraud anyone (other than himself or herself) (*Wikipedia*). Forging educational documents, medical records, financial records, people's signatures are some examples.

Adulteration

Adulteration is an illegal business practice where the quality of a product is compromised to cut costs and make profits. It is sinful and also a crime. Adulteration is one of the major causes of food poisoning and deaths related to food. People are greedy to make quick money and add non-edible ingredients to food products.

When you make a sale to your neighbor or buy from your neighbor, you shall not cheat one another. (Lev 25:14)

Counterfeiting

To counterfeit means to imitate or produce fake replicas of something valuable. We often hear about counterfeit money, electronics, or brand name products. It may apply to anything of value. People produce counterfeit products and make illegal money. Buying and selling counterfeit goods is a sin because it steals the livelihood of the person or people who are behind the real product.

Additional Reading: Wisdom 15:9

Areas to Examine:

- Did I ever buy (with knowledge) or sell counterfeit goods and services?
- Did I sell an adulterated product to customers?
- Did I forge any documents for personal gain?

Partiality/ Favoritism

A deserving and capable individual is often rejected and left out due to partiality and favoritism. Generally, people are partial toward their own kind. For example, people from the same country or state, people of the same race or religion, people of the same sex, etc.

My brothers and sisters, do you with your acts of favoritism really believe in our glorious Lord Jesus Christ? (Jas 2:1)

Additional Reading: Rom 2:11, Gal 3:28, 1 Tim 5:21, Acts 10:34, Jas 2:4

Identity Theft

We live in a cyber world where most of us have our personal information stored online, and there have been instances where we have been victims of identity theft. It is a serious crime where a victim's personal and vital information is compromised and stolen. To rob and misuse a person's identity is a sin and crime. Cybercriminals do it to earn money illegally. Cybercrimes are on the rise, and identity theft is one of the kinds. A case of identity theft is mentioned in the book of Genesis, where Jacob steals the identity of Esau and eventually steals the father's blessing that was reserved for Esau.

Bread gained by deceit is sweet, but afterward the mouth will be full of gravel. (Pro 20:17)

Hacking

Hacking is the practice of gaining unauthorized access to a computer system to steal or corrupt data. The motives are many. Some do it merely to show their computer skills, while others do it for monetary gains, and nations may do it to other countries simply to remain superior. Hacking for any reason is a sin because some degree of robbery takes place, be it just data.

Ponzi Schemes / Pyramid Schemes

There are many financial schemes available out there attracting people to invest, and it promises them high returns for very little investment and still less labor. Some may be legitimate, but most of them end up being fraud companies. They go by many names, and it is one way of robbing the hard-earned money of innocent people.

False Claims

People make false claims or misrepresent facts to receive some compensation or monetary benefit. Examples are; fraudulent insurance claims related to vehicle, health, and property. Paying our insurance premium and claiming in time of need is legitimate and legal. Misuse is a sin. Falsifying information to receive a benefit is also a sin.

Areas to Examine:

- Have I made any false claims to receive coverage or benefits?
- Have I stolen people's money through any kind of Ponzi or investment schemes?
- Did I hack any network or computer system to steal data or spread a virus?
- Did I steal or misuse another person's identity?
- Do I treat people unfairly, or am I partial to people whom I like?

Stealing / Wasting People's Time / Misuse of Time

Misuse of time is a sin against the first commandment. We are accountable not only for the words we have spoken but also for the time we have wasted. Take, for example, a person who goes to work but does not complete his work in the given time. He wastes the company's time, and it is also a way of stealing. Doing personal work at the company's expense is a sin against the employer.

Areas to Examine:

- Do I or waste my time at work?
- Have I misused or wasted office supplies (stationary)?
- Have I misused work amenities like car, travel allowance, and other benefits?
- Have I ever underperformed at work resulting in a loss to the company?
- Do I put my best effort in contributing to my company and its goals?
- Do I use my office hours to do my personal work?
- Do I cheat on reporting my work hours?

Help the Poor / Generosity / Charity

One who neglects the poor shuts the doors of heaven upon oneself. Jesus, from the time of his birth, chose poverty as a way of life. He was not intimidated by it. He was always glad to be identified with the poor, and he always cared for them. Christianity is not about receiving blessings after blessings from God and living in palaces and driving a Benz. A Christian does not close his eyes to the hunger and poverty around him. The early Christians shared everything they had.

The bread you store up belongs to the hungry; the cloak that lies in your chest belongs to the naked; the gold you have hidden in the ground belongs to the poor. - St. Basil the Great

Whoever is kind to the poor lends to the Lord,
and will be repaid in full. (Pro 19:17)

Additional Reading: Amos 5:12, Gal 2:10

Do Not Exploit the Poor

The poor and the underprivileged do not know their rights, and hence, they are exploited by the rich and powerful. There is an imbalance in this world where the rich are becoming richer, and the poor continue to remain in their condition. The poor often get robbed or get less than what they deserve.

Oppressing the poor to enrich oneself, and giving to the rich, will lead only to loss. (Pro 22:16)

Stealing from Self

Love of Money

Money is a good servant but a bad master. God is not against us having money if it stays within our wallet and bank account. Trouble arises when it finds its way into the heart, which is called the love of money.

No one can serve two masters; for a slave will either hate the one and love the other or be devoted to the one and despise the other. You cannot serve God and wealth. (Matt 6:24)

The above verse from the gospel of Mathew makes it obvious that we cannot love God and money at the same time. A worldly Christian cannot be a godly Christian because the love of money and the material world will choke his spiritual growth. An unhealthy love of wealth in us manifests itself in numerous ways.

Additional Reading: 1 Tim 6:10, Sir 14:3-4

Obsession and Preoccupied with Money Matters

People who love money deeply from the heart are also obsessed with talking about it. They mostly watch television channels or read the news that pertains to finances, investment, and the stock market. They can only speak about money and nothing else. Jesus rightly said that the mouth speaks out of the abundance of the heart. They see rich people as successful and want their children also to be productive and successful. They have no time for God and godly matters.

Sin of Discontentment

Financial discontentment leads us to many worries and robs our peace. Finding happiness with what God has given us is contentment. Discontentment is also a sign of unhealthy desires in us. Money cannot satisfy us; it leads to more emptiness in life. God alone can fulfill and satisfy the deepest cravings of the heart.

Keep your lives free from the love of money and be content with what you have; for he has said, "I will never leave you or forsake you." (Heb 13:5)

Areas to Examine:

- Am I able to see myself as financially blessed?

- Are my prayers restricted to the desires and needs of this life?
- Am I content and happy with what I have?

Additional Reading: 1 Tim 6:6-8, Eccl 5:10, Phil 4:11

The Desire to Become Rich

Many of us have only one goal in life; to become rich. We associate riches and wealth with joy and peace. In the process of becoming wealthy, we have compromised on life's priorities and are living a life of stress and fatigue. We have not fully understood the meaning and purpose of life, and therefore, we are running a race set by ourselves.

Do not wear yourself out to get rich; be wise enough to desist. (Pro 23:4)

Wealth and Power

Wealth gives us a false sense of power and authority, and it can make us feel independent and self-sufficient; therefore, we buy into the idea that acquiring wealth is true success. It is the wealthy who rule this world. Money is uncertain and unpredictable, and it changes people for good or for worse. Some can handle it well, but others let money change them. Those who misuse money and the power that comes with it will not enjoy its fruit for long.

He said to them, "Take care! Be on your guard against all kinds of greed; for one's life does not consist in the abundance of possessions." (Luk 12:15)

The Desire to Earn Money Quickly

Greed combined with sloth can be extremely dangerous. Our heart is not just set on riches, but we are desperate to get there as soon as possible. We look for ways to get rich with the least amount of time and investment and maximum returns. As a result, we commit many sins and find ourselves in unwanted trouble.

Those who want to be rich fall into temptation and are trapped by many senseless and harmful desires that plunge people into ruin and destruction. (1 Tim 6:9)

Additional Reading: Pro 28:22, Pro 28:20

Illegal ways of earning money, gambling, lottery, overworking, stock market are some ways we occupy ourselves because of the unhealthy love for money and the desire to get rich quickly.

Illegal Ways of Earning Money

Selling drugs, selling our body, not paying our taxes, selling banned substances, selling stolen goods, trafficking, abducting, and killing people are some illegal ways of making money. All illegal means are criminal activities punishable by law. Love of money makes us blind and chokes our conscience. We resort to illegal means because of desperation to get rich, laziness to work, poverty, and attraction to easy money.

Bread gained by deceit is sweet, but afterward the mouth will be full of gravel. (Pro 20:17)

Additional Reading: Jer 17:11, Jer 22:17, Pro 16:8, Jer 8:10

Gambling

Gambling is the wagering or betting of money or something valuable on an event or a game with an uncertain and unpredictable outcome, with the primary intent of winning money or goods of value. Gambling is legal or illegal, depending on the country. Gambling is a global industry with yields running into the billions. Some are in it for recreation, while others are in it for livelihood and still others are addicted to it. All gambling is sinful.

Let us assume; there are two players at a gambling table. Player 1 is not a regular gambler. He is an occasional gambler and a good Christian. Player 2 is addicted to gambling to the point he wastes all his hard-earned money on gambling. For this game, player 2 comes with all his savings. By the end of the game, player 2 loses it all and player 1 gets to take home all the winnings. Although player 1 is an occasional gambler, he has taken every penny of player 2. Player 2 is broke with no money even to eat.

Every time we gamble and every time we win, somebody else incurs a loss. Secondly, no labor is involved in earning this kind of money. Money is made through chance and luck. Gambling money is not earned money but stolen money. Gambling leads to greed, broken families, etc. A good Christian should completely stay out of it.

Stock Market

The stock market is another sensitive area. Millions and millions of people have some form of connection with the stock market these days. There are some questions one must ask oneself. Am I working for this money? Is anyone losing money for me to make a profit? Am I relying on luck and chance to make an earning? What am I giving or contributing to receive this money? Why am I trading? Finding an answer to these questions will help us understand the truth. Stock trading is a kind of legalized gambling. Stock trading is an addictive habit.

Wealth hastily gotten will dwindle, but those who gather little by little will increase it. (Pro 13:11)

Additional Reading: 2 Thes 3:10

Lottery

A lottery is a type of gambling that involves the drawing of numbers for a prize. It is mostly legal round the world. If something is legal does not mean it is acceptable for Christians. It is not a godly way of earning money. Lottery depends on chance and luck, and many people are addicted to this habit, hoping to get rich and, in the process, lose their hard-earned money.

When an inheritance is obtained hastily in the beginning, in the end it will be without a blessing. (Pro 20:21)

Additional Reading: 2 Thes 3:11-12

In this section, we looked at the laws of earning money. In the next section, we will cover the biblical teaching on how to use or handle money.

Do Not Trust in Wealth

If we were to look at an American bill (currency), the words "In God we Trust" is printed on it, which tells all its users not to trust in money, but in God. Money is very uncertain. We may be sitting on an enormous amount of wealth, but all of it can vanish very quickly. A person who loves money and puts his faith in it cannot be joyful and peaceful. He is always restless and trying harder and harder to make more money. With money comes insecurities, worries, and anxieties of all kind.

Command the wealthy of this age not to be haughty, nor to hope in the uncertainty of riches, but in the living God, who provides us everything in abundance to enjoy. (1 Tim 6:17)

Whoever trusts in his riches will fall. But the righteous shall spring up like a green leaf. (Pro 11:28)

Additional Reading: Matt 6:25, Sir 5:1

Wisdom and Prudence in Spending

People end up in financial problems because of the lack of wisdom in money related matters. Earning money is just half of the job; saving it and using it wisely is also important. A good Christian will spend enough time in prayer before, during, and after making any financial decisions. He will also take the help of the Holy Spirit, who is always willing to assist in all matters, including money and finances.

The intentions of the diligent continually bring forth abundance. But all the hasty are continually in need. (Pro 21:5)

Additional Reading: Luk 14:28, Pro 21:20

Areas to Examine:

- Am I hasty in making financial decisions?
- Do I pray long enough before I take any significant or long-term financial decisions?

Pay all Outstanding Debts

A Christian, if he has incurred any debt or loan due to unforeseen circumstances, should primarily work on coming out of the debt. God does not want his beloved children to be in any financial bondage. A borrower is always the slave of the lender. We are called to walk in freedom, which also includes financial and economic freedom. It is better to be poor and live with integrity than to desire for riches and become a slave.

The rich rule over the poor. And the borrower is servant to the lender. (Pro 22:7)

Areas to Examine:

- Do I sincerely try to come out of debt and pray about it?
- Have I identified the areas in my family that has led us to this situation (debt) and resolve not to repeat it?

Credit Cards

Credit cards are a blessing to those who can handle their finances well. It is not evil by itself. For the rest of us, it can be a trap. It is important that we use caution while using credit cards and not fall into any debt. Paying interest for the goods we buy is not a wise financial decision.

There are some who buy much for a small price, and who pay it back sevenfold. (Sir 20:12)

Additional Reading: Sir 18:33, Sir 21:8

Overspending and Lavish Lifestyle

One of the reasons why we opt for illegal means or quicker means of earning money is because of our behavior and pattern of overspending and lavish lifestyle. A good and wise Christian will live within his means and limit his buying and spending to the needs of life.

Do not revel in great luxury, or you may become impoverished by its expense. (Sir 18:32)

Money Can Change Us

A classic example to mention here is Judas Iscariot. He was picked by Jesus to be his witness. Judas was also given many charisms like the other apostles. The problem with Judas started when he was handed the collections bag. Money changed Judas (Jn 12:4), and he slowly began to steal from the collection purse. All of us are aware of what happened to Judas in the end. His greed destroyed him. One should be cautious when one is financially blessed. Money, if it consumes our heart, will also influence our thinking, behavior, attitude, and actions as well.

Another example is Ananias and Sapphira, who were sincere until they sold their property. Upon receiving the sale money, their heart changed, and they kept back part of the money (Acts 5:1-11).

If riches increase, do not be willing to set your heart on them. (Ps 62:10)

Needs Vs. Wants

A person who fully understands the difference between his needs and wants is less likely to make bad financial decisions. Jesus, speaking about our needs, said that our heavenly Father knows everything we need even before we ask him, and he will provide in his time. When it comes to wants and desires, there is a clause included; If it is the will of God, then our wishes and desires will be fulfilled as well. A need is a necessity for us, which God also understands. Our wants and desires can sometimes be harmful to us or take us away from the plan of God. Let us apply this to some practical areas. Daily food and water are needs, whereas going on an annual vacation is a want. Can we live without a vacation? Surely, we can. Unhealthy wants and desires can rob our financial blessings and land us in debt.

You should not pursue, in your strength, the desires of your heart. (Sir 5:2)

Give to the Needy

The secret to financial success lies in giving. One who is generous to God and his neighbor will not suffer want. Money grows when it is shared. Besides, it is our Christian call to ensure that all our brothers and sisters are blessed along with us. God blesses us so that we will be a blessing to others. Take the example of Mother (Saint) Teresa of Calcutta. She neither had a bank account, nor was there any property under her name. She did not invest in stocks or gamble or buy lottery tickets or even have a regular job. Yet, how many thousands of people were fed. Today, hundreds of thousands of poor children and sick people are taken care of by the Missionaries of Charity sisters. Where did they get their resources? The secret is generosity. She did not refuse anyone who came to her for help. When she did not deny help to others, relief and aid came to her from all directions, and this can be our reality too. Giving is the godly and biblical way of investing our wealth.

I have been young, and now I am old; and I have not seen the righteous forsaken, nor his offspring begging for bread. He gives freely and lends, at all times, and his offspring become a blessing. (Ps 37:25-26)

The sign of godliness and his presence in us is our longing and desire to love our neighbor through prayer and support.

How does God's love abide in anyone who has the world's goods and sees a brother or sister in need and yet refuses help? (1 Jn 3:17)

Areas to Examine:

- Do I make people who come to me for help, to wait?
- Do I refuse to help others even when I have the money?
- Do I see the people in need and not help them?

Additional Reading: Heb 13:16, Luk 6:38, Matt 5:42, Pro 19:17, Pro 22:9, Acts 20:35, Deut 15:11

Interest and Borrowed Money

Why do we pay interest on purchases? The reason is; we need something, and we do not have the money to buy it. We exert ourselves and fall for the trap. "Buy now and pay later" always catches our attention. These days, anything and everything can be purchased for an additional interest which gives us the freedom to pay overtime. Although this temptation cannot be completely avoided, one should be cautious when one purchases beyond one's capacity. And there are the impoverished people who, sometimes, must pawn their belongings to get a loan to meet their basic needs. We put undue stress upon ourselves when we go for things that we do not need; with the money, we do not have.

Wastage of Money

Money seldom stays with one who wastes it. Wastage and misuse of wealth is a sin. One who wastes money tests God. In this day and age, money is a need for all of us. Therefore, a Christian should pray for wisdom and prudence in handling money. All expenditures, financial plans, and plans for the future must be surrendered to God, and one must learn to wait on God in prayer before making any financial decisions. Hastiness and imprudence in spending can lead to poverty and debt. God does not want anyone to be in debt. He wants his children to be financially independent.

Save Money

The Bible makes an analogy to ants when talking about financial planning. Ants work when it is summer and save up for winter. The money we waste on our lavish lifestyle is our savings that will come to our aid when we are old and weak.

Go to the ant, you lazy one, and consider its ways, and so learn wisdom. For though it has no ruler, nor instructor, nor leader, it provides meals for itself in the summer, and gathers at the harvest what it may eat. (Pro 6:6-8)

Stinginess / Miserly Attitude

Stinginess or a miserly attitude is the unwillingness to give or spend for the most basic needs in life. Lavishness and stinginess are extremes, and both are sinful. There are people who find it hard to part with their money. They even keep large sums of money within their homes merely because they do not trust the banks, and they love to be around their money. People who do put their money in the bank are obsessed about checking it frequently.

Some distribute their goods freely, and they become wealthier. Others withhold unduly, and they are always in need. (Pro 11:24)

Areas to Examine:

- Do I find it hard to part with my money even when it comes to meet my most basic need or to pay my bills?
- Do I always have to be compelled to give?

- Do I get angry at my family members if they spend for their basic needs?
- Am I obsessed with checking my bank balance/ bank account?
- Do I waste money or spend unnecessarily?
- Do I misuse borrowed money?

Gift Culture

Exchange of gifts is widespread in developed countries where billions of dollars are spent every year during major holidays and festivals. Americans purchase nearly 600 million pounds of candy a year for Halloween. Close to 465 billion was spent during Christmas of 2017 in the US alone. Big money is spent each year on exchanging gifts. One should understand that the earth's resources are limited. Most developed countries are immersed deeply in a materialistic culture and lifestyle. Therefore, their love is also expressed in material terms. Gifts, according to many, is an expression of love. People have a wrong understanding of love. Although it is not a sin to give and receive gifts, one should see the larger picture behind this culture. Money, time, and natural resources are wasted, and at the same time, one-third of the world is living in poverty barely surviving.

Areas to Examine:

- Do I feel hurt when I do not get any gift?
- Do I feel obligated to give gifts during Christmas and other occasions?
- Do I see giving and receiving of gifts as an expression of love?
- Do I measure the love of a person by the gift, he or she gives?
- Do I waste too much money on gifts and holiday shopping?

Flaunting One's Wealth

People have an unhealthy affiliation toward brand names. They take great pride in showing off or telling others the kind of cars they drive, the gadgets they own, or the accessories they wear. There is a "show off" mentality or culture. This leads to wasting money on newer material. Old is unfashionable for many, and they have this urge to keep buying the newest design of clothes, gadgets, accessories, vehicles, etc.

Stealing from Nature

Every now and then, we hear certain groups of people, namely the environmentalists stressing on the need to save the planet or conserve energy or protect our earthly home. They are right about their claims. We are consuming natural resources at an alarming rate. Nature is abundantly generous to us, but its resources are limited. Our consumption levels have gone so high; there may come a time when certain minerals may run out, medicine producing crops may be wiped out, cattle may become extinct, and so on. Some of our practices are indirectly and directly harmful to the nature around us. Food consumption is at an all-time high. A good Christian is mindful of these threats and should do his best to prevent the damage being done to our earthly home.

Wastage of Food

Every day, tons and tons of food are wasted all over the world, and at the same time, a segment of the population goes hungry. There is an imbalance of allocation or consumption of food. Every Christian must do his part in fixing this problem, beginning with buying and consuming only what is needed and sharing the excess with others. More on this topic will be discussed under the topic of gluttony.

When they were filled, he told his disciples, "Gather the fragments that are left over, so that nothing may be lost." (Jn 6:12)

Wastage of Fuel / Energy

The fuel and energy we use are not unlimited either. The essential fuel for our vehicles and cooking is getting depleted at a quick rate. Until an alternate solution is figured out, we have the responsibility to conserve and use them wisely.

Deforestation

It is a scientifically proven fact that we depend on plant life for our oxygen needs. Excess deforestation also destroys the animal habitat, which in turn will destroy the ecosystem. A good Christian is mindful of these issues and does his part to preserve the world for the coming generations.

Harmful Scientific Experiments

The Church is not against science or scientific breakthroughs and inventions as thought by many. In fact, the Christian world welcomes all such achievements if it makes life better. At the same time, the Church vehemently opposes all researches that can cause harm to the natural world or any life form.

The earth and all its fullness belong to the Lord: the whole world and all that dwells in it. For he has founded it upon the seas, and he has prepared it upon the rivers.
(Ps 24:1-2)

Misuse of Nuclear Energy

The world around us has vast untapped energy, and if used wisely, can make life better. The same energy, however, if used unwisely, can wipe out all human, animal, and plant life. The world has witnessed what nuclear and atomic energy can do if used for the wrong reasons. Scientists have the responsibility of contributing only to the good of this world.

Areas to Examine:

- Do I waste food?
- Do I waste electricity or other energy that I use?
- Have I supported any scientific research that could potentially harm life or the natural world around us?
- Am I prompt in recycling?

The Eighth Commandment

You shall not bear false witness against your neighbor

The second commandment deals with how one must address God, whereas the eighth commandment addresses how one must talk to one's neighbor or speak about one another. Our speech is an integral part of who we are. The heart of a person is revealed in his speech and the words we utter tell the condition of our heart.

How can you speak good things, when you are evil? For out of the abundance of the heart the mouth speaks. (Matt 12:34)

We have not attained perfection in us if we still make mistakes in our speech. One who can control his tongue is spiritually mature.

Anyone who makes no mistakes in speaking is perfect, able to keep the whole body in check with a bridle. (Jas 3:2)

Our tongue is a small member of our body, yet it causes significant damage or good depending on how we use it. It can land us into trouble or get us out of trouble. It can bless or curse. Like every other aspect of our being, our speech also needs purification and taming.

With it we bless the Lord and Father, and with it we curse those who are made in the likeness of God. From the same mouth come blessing and cursing. My brothers and sisters, this ought not to be so. (Jas 3:9-10)

Our speech can be a powerful weapon if we know how to use it. The tongue is like a spark that has the potential to set fire to the whole forest (Jas 3:5). Death and life are in the power of the tongue (Pro 18.21). Our words can either make us holy or unclean. We are to give an account of every word we speak.

It is not what goes into the mouth that defiles a person, but it is what comes out of the mouth that defiles. (Matt 15:11)

Additional Reading: Matt 12:37, Jas 1:26

Use of Speech

It is important that we use our speech for what it is intended for. We will begin this section by how one ought to use the gift of speech and move on to how one ought not to use this gift.

Holy and Godly Conversation

The Gospel of Luke gives us a story from the life of Jesus when he was only 12 years old. Jesus was in the temple, sitting among the teachers, listening to them, and asking them questions. People were amazed and astonished at his wisdom and knowledge of God. Jesus always spoke about the heavenly Father. He glorified the Father with his speech. How many people genuinely enjoy talking about God? We are living in times where any conversation or discussion about God is unwelcome in many public places like schools, government offices, courts, etc. People talk about anything and everything other than God, who created them. God has given the gift of speech so that we glorify him through our words.

Let your conversation be with intelligent people, and let all your discussion be about the law of the Most High. (Sir 9:15)

Bearing Witness to the Truth

Standing up to the truth is also a Christian call. Voicing out against injustice, discrimination, and falsehood is our responsibility. Pontius Pilate, who though had the power to release Jesus, did not bear witness to the truth. There are many saints in the Church, who bore witness to the truth and were persecuted, and a great many were martyred. St. Stephen, St. Peter, and St. Paul were all examples of how to be bold and witness to the truth at any cost.

As they left the council, they rejoiced that they were considered worthy to suffer dishonor for the sake of the name. And every day in the temple and at home, they did not cease to teach and proclaim Jesus as the Messiah. (Acts 5:41-42)

Words of Encouragement

Our words have the power to transform and change people. It is each one's responsibility to speak the right words, encourage one another, discipline if needed, lift the down-trodden, and guide people to the truth.

Let no evil talk come out of your mouths, but only what is useful for building up, as there is need, so that your words may give grace to those who hear. (Eph 4:29)

Let us consider how to provoke one another to love and good deeds, not neglecting to meet together, as is the habit of some, but encouraging one another (Heb 10:24-25)

Additional Reading: Num 32:7,9

Power of Blessings

Not only is God's word and his blessing powerful, but all his followers also have the power to bless. Few people realize that a Christian's blessing is very powerful and effective. Christians should use this gift as frequently as possible.

Misuse of Speech

As mentioned in the previous section, the words of a Christian are powerful. Therefore, the gift of speech must be used only to bless, encourage, witness, exhort, and correct others. Often, we misuse the God-given gift of speech, which brings great harm to the one listening and the one speaking. Few people know that God hears every word we utter, and he is grieved by the misuse of speech in his children.

Then those who revered the LORD spoke with one another. The LORD took note and listened, and a book of remembrance was written before him of those who revered the LORD and thought on his name. (Mal 3:16)

Bearing False Witness

In the Old Testament days, during the period of Exodus, when the Israelites were in the wilderness, Moses and the elders were assigned to judge or mediate the problems arising amongst the people. The law was so strict that even the smallest of mistakes were sometimes punishable by death. Some of these crimes required a witness to testify and the life and death of an individual at times depended on the testimonies of these witnesses. A false witness could sometimes end a person's life. A person called to testify had a great responsibility to witness to the truth. This practice is valid even today in a court of law or at the workplace. Even at homes, if one child does something wrong, a parent may call a second child to testify. A false witness perverts justice.

Do not be a witness against your neighbor without cause, and do not deceive with your lips. (Pro 24:28)

Jesus himself was a victim of false witnessing. Although they could find no fault with him, they continued to testify falsely to persecute him. It was false testimony and witnessing that led to his sentencing.

The chief priests and the whole council were looking for false testimony against Jesus so that they might put him to death, (Matt 26:59)

Areas to Examine:

- Have I ever testified falsely in a court?
- Did I ever produce a false witness in a court to win a case?
- Did I ever, as a child, testify falsely against my sibling?
- Did I ever falsely testify at work resulting in penalties, suspension, or termination to any of my co-workers, subordinates, or superiors?
- Did I ever blame someone else for an accident I caused?

Additional Reading: Pro 25:18, Pro 12:17, Pro 14:5, Exo 20:16

False Accusations

False accusations, like false witnessing, can begin right at home with little children. Children sometimes falsely accuse others of wrongdoing. It could be out of sibling rivalry or jealousy or fear. Couples blame each other because of doubt and lack of trust. We destroy a person when we falsely accuse them. It is a grave sin against love. Jesus was more than once, charged with breaking the Old Testament laws. He was also accused of joining with the devil and performing his signs and miracles with the help of evil powers.

When the Pharisees heard it, they said, "It is only by Beelzebul, the ruler of the demons, that this fellow casts out the demons." (Matt 12:24)

Blaming others for our sins and wrongdoings (pointing of fingers)

When God questioned Adam about his sin, he pointed fingers at Eve. When God asked Eve about her failure, she in turn, pointed fingers at the devil. None of them took responsibility of their wrongdoing, instead blamed it on whoever they could find to blame. Each time we sin or commit a mistake, all that God wants to see is acceptance of our failure and repentance. Honesty is a virtue pleasing in God's eyes.

Cease to point your finger and to speak what is not beneficial. (Is 58:9)

Areas to Examine:

- Have I falsely accused anyone and have not repented?
- Do I have the habit of accusing others of wrongdoing without verifying the facts?
- Have I falsely accused anyone because of hatred, envy, or jealousy?
- Did I ever falsely blame someone for a mistake or an accident I caused?

Additional Reading: Deut 19:18-19

Accusations

In the Gospel of John, chapter 8, a woman caught in the act of adultery is brought to Jesus. The law was noticeably clear about such a sin. The woman ought to have been stoned to death. The accusation was real, and every Jew was bound by the law to execute punishment for such a crime. Jesus, when faced with such a situation, chose mercy above judgment. He forgave her. Be merciful as your heavenly Father is merciful, is the words uttered by Jesus in Luke, chapter 6. Compassion is more powerful than accusation. Accusation destroys a person, whereas compassion heals and builds up an individual.

The word 'Satan' in Greek means accuser or adversary. He is known as the accuser of the brethren. Accusing is one of the primary natures of Satan. A person who has this habit of blaming others is cooperating with the plan of the devil. On the contrary, God is merciful, loving, and compassionate. He convicts us but never accuses us.

Ridiculing / Mocking / Teasing / Making Fun

It is not godly behavior to ridicule, tease, mock, or make fun of another individual. Every person is a child of God, and they bear the image and likeness of the Father on them. What we do to the least of the brothers and sisters of Jesus, we do it unto him (Matt 25:40). Jesus was, on more than one occasion, ridiculed, mocked, teased, and made fun. Jesus understands what it is to go through such humiliation.

Love does no wrong to a neighbor; therefore, love is the fulfilling of the law. (Rom 13:10)

Areas to Examine:

- Have I teased people based on their looks?

- Have I teased people for their race, community, nationality, color, etc.?
- Have I teased people for their weaknesses and failures?
- Have I bullied other kids when I was a kid?
- Do I have the habit of imitating, making fun of my superiors behind their backs?
- Have I teased people for their accent or how they speak?

We live in a time where people make fun of others, especially political figures and celebrities, by forwarding and sharing videos and images on social media. It is a sin under the eighth commandment.

Judging

Judging is a sin we commit the most. As a matter of fact, we judge people all the time. We make our judgment based on our limited observations. We judge and come up with opinions based on outward appearances, words, actions, works, etc. Our judgments are not accurate because we are unable to see the motive and intention of a person. God sees each human heart, and he does not judge anyone while they are alive. It is a sin against love and he who judges fails to love.

Do not judge, so that you may not be judged. For with the judgment you make you will be judged, and the measure you give will be the measure you get. (Matt 7:1-2)

Repeated judgmental thoughts toward a person is a sign of unforgiveness or block in the flow of love. We take the place of God when we judge others. God alone has the right to judge us, and he does so only after we die, but we judge people daily.

Do not speak evil against one another, brothers and sisters. Whoever speaks evil against another or judges another, speaks evil against the law and judges the law; but if you judge the law, you are not a doer of the law but a judge. There is one lawgiver and judge who is able to save and to destroy. So, who, then, are you to judge your neighbor? (Jas 4:11-12)

We judge people in areas where we are strong, and they are weak. Judging others is also a sign of hidden pride in us.

Areas to Examine:

- Do I get repeated judgmental thoughts about anybody?

- Do I judge my superiors at work?
- Have I judged any religious person?
- Do I judge people for their work or performance?
- Am I a judgmental person?

Additional Reading: Luk 6:37, Rom 2:1-3

Prejudice

Having an unfavorable preconceived opinion, idea, or feeling about a certain ethnic or religious group is prejudice. Jesus too was a victim of prejudice. The people had nothing good to say about where Jesus came from.

Can anything good come out of Nazareth? (Jn 1:46)

Is not this the carpenter, the son of Mary and brother of James and Joses and Judas and Simon, and are not his sisters here with us? And they took offense at him. (Mark 6:3)

We are all created by God in his image and likeness. We have one Father, and we are all his children. Our God is a God of all humanity and therefore wants us all to love one another just as he loves us and not to have any kind of prejudice toward anyone.

There is no longer Jew or Greek; there is no longer slave or free, there is no longer male and female; for all of you are one in Christ Jesus. (Gal 3:28)

For there is no distinction between Jew and Greek; the same Lord is Lord of all and is generous to all who call on him. For, "Everyone who calls on the name of the Lord shall be saved." (Rom 10:12-13)

Additional Reading: Rev 7:9

Slander

Slander is the uttering of a false statement which brings harm and damage to a person's reputation. Slander is malicious lying. The Pharisees and the religious people of Jesus' time gave a wrong report about him to the Roman officials. They committed the sin of slander. Slander and gossip are a result of judgmental thoughts.

Put away from you all bitterness and wrath and anger and wrangling and slander, together with all malice. (Eph 4:31)

Lying

Lying is defined as concealing the truth, covering up the truth or speaking contrary to the truth. A lie is not always said to harm others. Most lies are harmless to others and cause little to no damage externally. But, in the spiritual sense, a lie wounds our relationship with God. We lose the presence of the Holy Spirit each time we lie.

Lying lips are an abomination to the Lord, but those who act faithfully are his delight. (Pro 12:22)

Jesus called the devil a liar. The devil is a liar from the beginning and those who lie become one with him. Satan spoke his first lie to man when he tempted Eve with the words," "You will not die;" He has been lying ever since. Every temptation is backed by a lie from Satan.

When he lies, he speaks according to his own nature, for he is a liar and the father of lies. (Jn 8:44)

Given below are some reasons why people lie.

- To escape some penalty or punishment
- To receive a favor
- Fear
- To cover up a mistake
- To make someone (the hearer) happy
- People are good at it
- People are addicted to it

There are many variations to the sin of lying depending upon its purpose and motive. God does not lie, and he does not approve our lying no matter what the purpose is. A lie is a lie, and it is sinful. A liar cannot be a friend of the Holy Spirit, and each time we lie, we grieve the Holy Spirit and also commit a sin.

White Lie

A harmless lie told to avoid hurting someone's feelings or to cheer the mood or spirit of a person. It is still a lie and needs to be dealt with. Jesus is the way, the truth, and the life and we cannot follow our Lord carrying falsehood and lies with us. All lies, smallest to the greatest must be given up through repentance and confession.

So then, putting away falsehood, let all of us speak the truth to our neighbors, for we are members of one another. (Eph 4:25)

Additional Reading: Sir 20:26

Omission of Facts

The omission of facts or concealing the truth is also a lie. Truth should not be hidden, and to speak the truth requires courage. Fortitude or courage is a gift of the Holy Spirit mentioned in Isaiah Chapter 11.

Truthful lips endure forever, but a lying tongue lasts only a moment. (Pro 12:19)

Exaggerating /Concocting / Fabricating

Exaggeration and fabrication are also a kind of a lie because it deviates from the truth. Fabrication or concoction is the deliberate invention of a false story. Children invent many stories when they are asked by the teacher the reason for not completing their homework. Exaggeration is enhancing the truth with lies to make it dramatic and more convincing.

Do not lie to one another, seeing that you have stripped off the old self with its practices. (Col 3:9)

Chronic, Pathological, Impulsive, and Compulsive Lying

A person who frequently lies without any guilt or regret. Whatever the name used, some of us need deliverance in this area from the spirit of lying. We approach God with the usual method, that of repentance and confession. God, upon seeing our heart, will free us from this addiction.

A lie is an ugly blot on a person; it is continually on the lips of the ignorant. (Sir 20:24)

Additional Reading: Ps 120:2

Lying for Making Profits (Businessman / Traders)

The financial world is another area where lying is so frequent, acceptable, and goes unchecked. Businesspeople, corporations, salespeople, marketers have all (most) resorted to lying to sell their products or stay in business or become successful. A lie makes it faster to sell a product because people buy into these lies. Greed and love of money force one to steal from others through lying.

The getting of treasures by a lying tongue is a fleeting vapor and a snare of death. (Pro 21:6)

Areas to Examine:

- Do I remember any instance in my life where I lied and brought harm or disrepute to another person?
- Am I a habitual or chronic liar?
- Do I lie to my superiors/ teachers to cover up my mistakes?
- Do I keep secrets and lie to my spouse about it?
- Do I (teenage children) lie to my parents about my whereabouts?
- Do I lie in order not to hurt people's feelings?
- Do I (businesspeople) lie to my customers about the product I am selling?
- Do I lie about my age or my children's age to get some benefit?
- Do I lie when I must take a day off from work?

Gossip

Our judgmental thoughts become gossip if we do not bring it to God in repentance and confession. It becomes a greater evil because more people are affected by it and become victims. A gossip affects at least three people; The one who shares, the one who listens and the one is the subject of the scandal. We generally do not gossip about our children because we do not judge them, and we do not judge them because we love them deeply. Gossip is an evil that wounds relationships, distorts the truth, spreads lies, and exaggerates facts.

One day Padre Pio said to a penitent: "When you gossip about a person it means that you have removed the person from your heart. But be aware, when you remove a man from your heart, Jesus also goes away from your heart with that man."

Gossip does not always mean spreading lies or exaggerating facts. For example, if a person comes to me and shares his marital problems asking for my prayers and if I share it with fifty other people asking for their prayers, without his consent, it has violated this man's privacy.

A gossip goes about telling secrets, but one who is trustworthy in spirit keeps a confidence. (Pro 11:13)

Rumors

There is a difference between gossip and rumor. A gossip may contain facts and truth, which should not be revealed, but a rumor is something heard from another person which is shared without verifying the facts.

You shall not spread a false report. You shall not join hands with the wicked to act as a malicious witness. (Exo 23:1)

Rash Judgement

We humans do not have access to all the resources for us to judge justly. Our judgments are mostly wrong, hasty, and rash. Our own mental and emotional state influences our judging ability. We see other's sins, weaknesses, and failures as unforgivable and at the same time, want everybody around us to sympathize and put up with us. Jesus tells us to look at the log in our own eye before trying to remove the speck in our neighbor's eye.

Why do you see the speck in your neighbor's eye, but do not notice the log in your own eye? (Matt 7:3)

Calumny

It is the unfair or unjust damaging of the good name or reputation of another by attributing a crime or fault of which a person is not guilty.

Do not speak evil against one another, brothers and sisters. Whoever speaks evil against another or judges another, speaks evil against the law and judges the law. (Exo 23:1)

Detraction

Detraction is the revealing or disclosing the faults, weaknesses, and failures of a person to people who do not know it.

Secrets

Every one of us has secrets that we have not shared with others. There are secrets within a family. There are secrets within every organization, business, and institution. One is expected to honor these secrets when one becomes a part of an institution. There are times when people have shared their secrets to us, trusting in us. A secret should be honored if it does not break any law or causes harm to an individual. To reveal secrets is a sin and violates the trust that others may place upon us.

Argue your case with your neighbor directly, and do not disclose another's secret; (Pro 25:9)

Areas to Examine:

- Have I gossiped?
- Do I actively and engagingly listen to gossip?
- Have I revealed or disclosed the faults, weaknesses, or failures of another person?
- Do I reveal the faults/ sins of my spouse or family member to a priest in the confessional?
- Do I reveal the faults of my loved ones or others to a third person, such as a counselor or coworker?
- Have I engagingly listened to the faults of other people shared by someone?
- Do I share the faults of celebrities/politicians that I receive on social media?
- Have I shared secrets that I am not allowed to share?
- Did I break any non-disclosure agreement?

Flattery (Failure to Correct)

Flattery is giving insincere or excessive praise or compliments for the advantage, benefit, and interest of oneself. Some are addicted to it, and they have what is called a flattering tongue. Flattery is different from encouragement. We encourage others to build them up and to grow, but flattery has hidden ungodly motives behind it.

Jesus was at the receiving end of flattery more than once. In the gospel of Mark, the Pharisees came to Jesus and began to flatter him to trap him. As always, Jesus was able to outwit them with the wisdom of God.

Then they sent to him some Pharisees and some Herodians to trap him in what he said. And they came and told him, "Teacher, we know that you are sincere, and show deference to no one; for you do not regard people with partiality but teach the way of God in accordance with truth. Is it lawful to pay taxes to the emperor, or not? (Mrk 12:13-14)

They came with praise and compliments only to trap him regarding the issue of paying taxes. Although they said good comments about Jesus, their motives were sinful.

Areas to Examine:

- Do I have the habit of praising others with an ulterior motive?
- Do I flatter for a return favor?
- Do I exploit the weaknesses in people?
- Do I correct and discipline people who are under my authority?

Additional Reading: Sir 2:11

Lovers of Praise and Glory

Some of us love the compliments and praises of people. We seek the approval of people and make ourselves available for such praise and honor. A godly and humble person will detest and flee from all compliments and admiration because it gives room to pride and arrogance.

They loved human glory more than the glory that comes from God. (Jn 12:43)

Additional Reading: Jn 5:44

Careless Words

A wise and prudent person will measure his words before he speaks. A prudent person knows when to talk and when to remain silent. An imprudent person lacks these qualities. We utter many careless and unproductive words daily that do not bring any good to us or to the person who listens to us. The ability to speak is a gift, if used wisely, can be a powerful and useful weapon.

When words are many, transgression is not lacking, but the prudent are restrained in speech. (Pro 10:19)

Additional Reading: Matt 12:36-37

Condemnation

God seldom condemns but convicts us for our good. Condemnation brings guilt in us, whereas conviction is meant to correct us. Our words should not condemn anybody, remembering that all of us are sinners, and we make mistakes from time to time. Every sinner must be given a chance to repent. Jesus was compassionate to the woman caught in the act of adultery, whereas the people around her condemned her. We are quick to condemn others and expect people to be forgiving and merciful toward us.

Indeed, God did not send the Son into the world to condemn the world, but in order that the world might be saved through him. (Jn 3:17)

Pride in Speech

Although pride is hard to detect, it can be seen in one's way of talking and speech. Boasting, arrogance in speech, always talking about oneself, self-praise, and haughtiness in conversation are some signs of pride in speech.

Boasting

Boasting is defined as talking with excessive pride about one's own abilities, achievements, and possessions. The root of boasting is pride and arrogance. Pride manifests in our speech in multiple ways, and boasting is one of them. A person who boasts fails to see and understand God's hand in his life. The sooner we grasp the fact that our possessions, abilities, talents, and achievements come from God, the more humble we will become. Jesus never boasted but glorified God in all his works, and he is rightly called the humblest one.

Do not let the wise boast in their wisdom, do not let the mighty boast in their might, do not let the wealthy boast in their wealth (Jer 9:23)

Additional Reading: Jas 4:13-16

Negative Speech

The negativity of a person is often reflected in his speech. Our sorrow and sadness are usually reflected in our countenance and attitude. In the gospel of John, Jesus met a man who sat by the pool, sick for a long time. When he spoke to this man, Jesus knew that this man had given up on his healing. His speech was very negative. Some of us bring a curse upon ourselves by our speech. When we dwell in negativity, faith cannot fully operate in us.

Hastiness in Speech / Swift Tongue

Hastiness in speech is not a sin, but a flaw or imperfection in speech. It can lead to sin or put one in trouble. Hastiness is a form of imprudence. Lack of wisdom, imprudence, and immaturity will cause a person to falter in speech.

Do you see someone who is hasty in speech? There is more hope for a fool than for anyone like that. (Pro 29:20)

Additional Reading: Eccl 5:2

Self-Praise

We are so accustomed to praise that if we do not receive praise from others, we begin to praise ourselves. We talk highly about ourselves; therefore, sin and evil in us go undetected. The Pharisee in the Gospel of Luke went on and on talking good about himself. He was not justified in the eyes of God.

Let another praise you, and not your own mouth – a stranger, and not your own lips. (Pro 27:2)

Areas to Examine:

- Do I seek and look for praise and compliments for what I do?
- Do I make myself available for praise or Do I praise myself?
- Do I speak carelessly?
- Do I judge people for their sins/ failures/ weaknesses or actions?
- Do I boast?
- Do I speak negatively?
- Do I speak hastily without much thought?

Cursing (Wishing Harm)

Do curses come true? Can a person curse someone who is blessed by the Lord? This topic is beyond the scope of this book to discuss, but people do curse others in a state of anger, to wish them harm. There are people who would go to the extreme level of cursing others or casting a spell with the help of occult. Cursing is a means of retaliation to the injustice suffered. Cursing is a sin because God has given the gift of speech to bless and encourage others.

No one has ever been able to tame the tongue. It is evil and uncontrollable, full of deadly poison. We use it to give thanks to our Lord and Father and also to curse other people, who are created in the likeness of God. Words of thanksgiving and cursing pour out from the same mouth. (Jas 3:8-10, GNT)

Additional Reading: Rom 12:14, 2 Sam 16:8

Critical Speech

There is a criticism that is positive, which comes from love. There is also negative criticism which can wound a person. Correcting a person when he or she is going astray is each one's responsibility. There should be hope in our correction. Criticism, especially public rebuking, can do more harm than good.

A soft answer turns away wrath, but a harsh word stirs up anger. (Pro 15:1)

Additional Reading: Pro 12:18

Verbal Abuse / Verbal Attack / Verbal Assault

Verbal abuse (verbal attack or verbal assault) is when a person forcefully criticizes, insults, or denounces someone else. Characterized by underlying anger and hostility, it is a destructive form of communication intended to harm the self-concept of the other person and produce negative emotions. *(Wikipedia)*

Some use it to control or manipulate, while others have abusive behavior. Some others become verbally abusive when under stress or in a state of anger. Verbal abuse is a grave sin that can cause severe wounds in others, especially if they are children.

You must get rid of all such things – anger, wrath, malice, slander, and abusive language from your mouth. (Col 3:8)

Areas to Examine:

- Have I cursed or wished harm to anyone?
- Have I wished the death of anyone?
- Have I prayed for somebody's harm or destruction?
- Have I criticized anyone publicly?
- Did I verbally abuse anyone?

Additional Reading: Job 2:9, 2 Sam 16:13, 2 Tim 3:2, Sir 18:18, Sir 23:15

Idle Chatter / Idle Talk

People engage in idle talk to kill boredom. Idle talk does not necessarily mean gossip or talking about others. People talk about topics that interest them. Movies, books, sports, hobbies, food, politics, news, and current affairs are some central topics in which people engage in a conversation. Gaining worldly knowledge and sharing it with others is what most people are interested in. The question is, what have I truly gained by filling myself with the knowledge of this world. To remain silent is also a virtue.

Timothy, guard what has been entrusted to you. Avoid the profane chatter and contradictions of what is falsely called knowledge. (1 Tim 6:20)

Foolish Talk / Crude Jokes / Profane Chatter / Bad and Obscene Language / Dirty Talk

As per worldly standards, if the speaker and the listener agree to the use of bad language, it is generally seen as harmless. The whole world is careful not to let children speak or listen to anything profane or dirty, but adults have no such restriction. In the eyes of God, all profanity is sin irrespective of who commits it; either adults or children. Profane chatter leads to impiety, and it grieves the Holy Spirit who resides in us.

Avoid profane chatter, for it will lead people into more and more impiety. (2 Tim 2:16)

Areas to Examine:

- Do I use impure language while speaking?
- Do I overly engage in a foolish, idle, or unproductive talk?
- Did I engagingly listen to impure conversations?
- Do I watch or listen to shows that use bad, and profane language?

Additional Reading: Eph 5:4

The Ninth Commandment

You shall not covet your neighbor's wife.

Covet means to yearn to possess or desire. Just because we have not committed any sexual sins listed under the sixth commandment, does not mean that we are free from the sin of lust. Jesus, speaking about adultery, said that even if we have desired to commit adultery, we are guilty of breaking the law. Yearning, craving, or desiring is the same as committing the sin, as per the words of Jesus. Desire is conceived in the heart but enters through the senses, namely our eyes. He who can master or control his vision has crossed a major hurdle in the path of attaining holiness. The mind heavily relies on the data provided by the eyes. Healthy eyes lead to healthy thoughts and healthy desires.

Purity of Vision

Looking with Lust

Looking at someone with lust is given the same treatment as adultery in the Bible, making it a serious sin. Most people struggle in this area. People find it hard to control themselves when they are around a beautiful person of the opposite sex. The human eye is the most dangerous of all organs and the weakest. Most desires and sin enter us through our eyes.

But I say to you that everyone who looks at a woman with lust has already committed adultery with her in his heart. (Matt 5:28)

Jesus also said that the eye is the most important part of the human body, and the health of the eye (vision) decides the health of the whole person.

The lamp of your body is your eye. If your eye is healthy, your entire body will be filled with light. But if your eye has been corrupted, your entire body will be darkened. If then the light that is in you is darkness, how great will that darkness be! (Matt 6:22-23)

Additional Reading: Sir 41:21

Voyeurism

This is the practice or habit of deriving sexual pleasure from watching others when they are naked, dressing or undressing, or engaged in sexual activity. It is a kind of sexual fetish. It violates the privacy of the person being watched and at the same time, disrespectful and invasive. It also reduces other human beings to mere objects of gratification for oneself. It is unlawful and immoral. The sin of voyeurism in mentioned in the book of Daniel, where the two judges secretly watch Suzanna while she goes to take a bath in the pool (Dan 13).

Turn away your eyes from a shapely woman, and do not gaze at beauty belonging to another. (Sir 9:8)

Areas to Examine:

- Do I find it hard to control my eyes when I come across a beautiful person?
- Do I make a sincere effort to look away from a beautiful person?
- Do I look at people with lust?
- Do I secretly look at the private parts of the opposite sex?
- Do I look at people while they are displaying affection in public?
- Do I enjoy watching the beauty of any celebrity/ media person on television or the internet?

Additional Reading: Job 31:1, Ps 119:37, Luk 11:34

Purity of Heart

Mere actions cannot give the full picture, and actions can also be deceiving. God looks deep into our heart and sees our intention behind every action. One can act or pretend to be a holy person on the outside but be evil and wicked in the heart. Jesus, referring to the Pharisees, said that their actions contradicted their motives and intentions. Jesus used the word, "hypocrite" when referring to people who exhibited holiness merely on the outside. As we examine ourselves, we will see if any of these questions apply to us?

Areas to Examine:

- Do I look at people of the opposite sex with lust?
- Am I fixated on the body parts of people?
- Do I mingle with people of the opposite sex with a secret sexual motive?
- Have I secretly desired or yearned for another person's spouse?
- Have I sexually fantasized about a person other than my spouse?
- Do I admire any movie or sports personality merely for their physical features?
- Did I take pleasure in impure thoughts or desires?

Modesty

If there is a subject of sin, there is also an object of sin. Jesus cautioned and warned those who cause others to stumble, saying, "Woe to the one by whom the stumbling block comes!" Modesty is the behavior, manner, or appearance intended to avoid indecency or impropriety. Causing another to sin through words and actions is also sinful.

Areas to Examine:

- Have I seduced anyone using words or actions?
- Do I have the habit of wearing indecent and revealing clothes?
- Do I flirt with the opposite sex, thereby tempting them and causing them to fall into sin?

Moral Permissiveness

The world, in general, is becoming more and more liberal when it comes to sexual freedom. Many practices that were considered taboo some decades ago are finding acceptance and endorsement from the mainstream population and from the religious. The content shown on television, especially for kids, is getting filthier by the day. The language that they are exposed to is deteriorating speedily. There is parental control with parents having little or no control. Sex, violence, and foul language are finding its way into our homes through the media that we have willingly subscribed.

This behavior or trend is nothing but man trying to act as his own boss. Man is trying to define life and its meaning without fully understanding or answering the fundamental questions about life; where did I come from? Where am I headed? And what am I doing here? Without first defining the origin, end, and purpose of life, trying to define or modify other things will only lead to the downfall of humanity.

Concupiscence

Concupiscence is the strong desire in us, which may be of any kind. It generally refers to lustful desires. It is not a sin in itself, but it can influence us to make poor moral choices. It inclines man to commit sins.

Etymologically, "concupiscence" can refer to any intense form of human desire. Christian theology has given it a particular meaning: the movement of the sensitive appetite contrary to the operation of the human reason. (CCC 2515)

Flesh vs. Spirit

There is a constant battle within us between the flesh and the spirit. St. Paul gives a glimpse of this battle in the book of Romans, chapter 7, verses 14 to 26. This inner conflict is fueled by our habits, practices, lifestyle, priorities, etc. In short, what we feed will get stronger in us and subdue the other. If we feed to the flesh, the flesh will get stronger and choke the desires of the spirit. If we feed to the spirit, the spirit will have control over the flesh. The spirit desires for God and the flesh desires for the world. The choice is ours!

What the flesh desires is opposed to the Spirit, and what the Spirit desires is opposed to the flesh; for these are opposed to each other, to prevent you from doing what you want. (Gal 5:17)

Additional Reading: Gal 5:24, Rom 8:9, Rom 8:7

The Tenth Commandment

You shall not covet your neighbor's goods

Unhealthy Desires

There are good desires, and there are also bad desires in us. There are godly desires, and there are also evil and sinful desires in us. There are healthy desires, and there are also unhealthy desires in us. Desire is a strong urge or feeling of wanting or possessing something or wishing something to happen. Desire stems from love. Love gives birth to desire. When we love God deeply from the heart, we have a strong desire to pray and read the Bible. Many positive desires are built in us when we have true love in us. Unhealthy love will produce unhealthy desires in us. How do we overcome evil and sinful desires? The answer lies in finding our true love. Our effort must be channeled toward love for God and neighbor. In doing so, we will eventually get freedom from all unhealthy desires, and sin will cease to control us.

Those who belong to Christ Jesus have crucified the flesh with its passions and desires. (Gal 5:24)

Amassing Earthly Goods Without Limit

Life is eternal, but life in this world is not. Lazarus, who was raised from the dead by Jesus, died again. In our present state, we are mortal beings. When the time comes, we will have to leave everything behind, including our loved ones. A life of greed and lavishness is a life wasted. If we look around and see the birds and the animals, they do not have big mansions or palaces. They do not have life's worth of savings. They do not have expensive clothing or gadgets with them, yet there is full of peace in their eyes. When we look at our own humankind, many have money enough for three generations. Still, there is no joy or happiness. The reason is, we have failed to live life the way it is intended.

Harming a Neighbor for Material Goods

King David, gripped by an uncontrollable passion for Bathsheba, went to the extreme and killed Uriah (Bathsheba's husband). He destroyed a family because of his adulterous lust and subsequent evil. Many such events take place even during our times. Harming a neighbor to covet his goods is a result of extreme greed rising from an evil heart. When love for the world dominates our heart, the love of neighbor dies within us which results in many crimes against others

Passion for Riches

Acquiring the riches of this world has become the purpose and aim of life for most people. Wealth is the single driving force or motivator for many in this world. We are a workaholic generation. We see our value in how much we have earned and how much we possess. We do not realize that if today, our life is taken away from us, all our toil becomes meaningless.

Then I considered all that my hands had done and the toil I had spent in doing it, and again, all was vanity and a chasing after wind, and there was nothing to be gained under the sun. (Eccl 2:11)

True Treasure

Who does not want to stumble upon a treasure? The problem is; what kind of a treasure am I seeking? Am I looking for an earthly treasure which can be consumed by moth or rust? Am I looking for a treasure that is with me today and is gone tomorrow? Am I storing treasures that thieves can break in and steal? There is another kind of treasure that is lasting and true. Take the example of St. Paul. He authored more than 70% of the new testament. His writings are recited in churches and homes all over the world even today. He accumulated a treasure that cannot be eaten by moth or rust or can be stolen by thieves.

Store up for yourselves treasures in heaven, where neither moth nor rust consumes and where thieves do not break in and steal. (Matt 6:20)

Areas to Examine:

- What is the driving force behind all my actions?
- Is becoming rich, the sole purpose of my life?
- Have I hurt or harmed anybody because of my greed or covetousness?

Capital Sins

(Seven Deadly Sins / Cardinal Sins)

What Are Capital Sins?

Capital sins are also called deadly or cardinal sins. These are the chief sins that give birth to other sins. There are seven capital sins, namely; pride, greed, envy, wrath, lust, gluttony, and sloth. It is believed that these are the seven qualities of the devil.

Vices can be classified according to the virtues they oppose, or also be linked to the capital sins which Christian experience has distinguished, following St. John Cassian and St. Gregory the Great. They are called "capital" because they engender other sins, other vices. They are pride, avarice, envy, wrath, lust, gluttony, and sloth or acedia. (CCC 1866)

Understanding the characteristics of capital sin will help us see how they operate in us and affect our lives. Knowledge of these sins will help us discern and detect their presence. Given below are some qualities of capital sins.

Root Sins

A root is hidden, and the longer it has existed, the deeper it has grown into the ground. Similarly, root sins are invisible, and they control many of our habits, personalities, and attitudes. Most of the sins we commit find its roots in one or more of the capital sins. Certain character traits, flaws, and behavior patterns seen in a person are also a result of the presence of capital sins within.

They are Hidden

The fact that they are harder to detect by oneself gives it the name "hidden sins." No matter how hard we try, we will have some unconfessed sins within us. We need the Holy Spirit to show us our hidden sins. Some vices blend so well with our personality that it is hard to discern and see them by ourselves.

Clear me from hidden faults. (Psalm 19:12)

They Give Rise to Other Sins

Sin has different layers and hierarchy. Sin gives birth to other sins. There are vices that feed off or depend on another sin or habit. Certain outward traits are controlled by some deeper evil within us.

They Blend With our Personality

One reason why it is hard to detect capital sins is that it is so deep in us, and it has become a part of who we are. Some people are proud, and it is hard to see them without their sin. Some others are selfish, and they have always been this way. Capital sins take control of our personality and behavior.

Capital Sins are Detected by Their Manifestations

Capital sins are best discerned by their manifestations or actions. Pride, for example, can be seen in the way one speaks, thinks, reacts, or treats other people.

They are Stubborn

Yes, you heard it right. Capital sins are stubborn sins and require much grace from God to overcome. Its hidden nature and its length of stay in us make it difficult to fight and defeat it, but with God's assistance, can be conquered. No evil is powerful enough to stop God and his works. The blood of Jesus can cleanse us from all unrighteousness.

Let us look at each of these seven capital sins to prepare ourselves for a good confession.

Pride

The first capital sin that we will examine is pride. Pride is the root of all sin, and it is a sin God hates the most. God is humble, and he wants us also to be like him. Pride is the nature of the devil, and he lost his position in heaven because of this vice. His pride made him rebel against God. Pride can be defeated only by humility, and we must always look for ways to humble ourselves. It can influence all aspects of our personality; namely thoughts, speech, and action. At times we must listen to our thoughts and see what their source is. A person who thinks too highly of himself will not be able to discern his sins. Pride can blind a person and lead to other sins. A proud person stays in the dark because his pride does not permit him to get help. These are people who find it hard to accept mistakes, forgive others, and seek help. We will study some basic areas of pride and how it manifests in us.

Haughtiness

Haughtiness means to look down at others and to show an attitude of superiority and also to look at people with contempt. The Jews of Jesus' time considered themselves superior to the Samaritans and hence looked down on them and wanted to do nothing with them. Haughtiness stems from pride.

Pride goes before destruction and a haughty spirit before a fall. (Pro 16:18)

Additional Reading: Is 2:17

Arrogance

Arrogance is the acting or showing oneself as superior in an unpleasant way. Arrogance is a strong sign of hidden pride. An arrogant person thinks highly of himself and expresses his superiority in an overbearing manner. God detests arrogance.

Talk no more so very proudly, let not arrogance come from your mouth; (1 Sam 2:3)

Boasting

Boasting is defined as proud speech or claims about one's abilities, achievements, and possessions. According to the book of James (Jas 4:16), boasting is a result of arrogance.

The wise man should not boast in his wisdom, and the strong man should not boast in his strength, and the rich man should not boast in his riches. But he who boasts should boast in this: that they know and understand me well. (Jer 9:23-24)

Additional Reading: Ps 5:5, Ps 12:3, Ps 75:4

Pride of Possessions

Riches and possession can open doors to pride if one is not careful. If a person receives financial blessings too quickly, he will find it hard to stay humble. The heart gets puffed up. People always get carried away by sudden wealth. Most people think that money is the answer to all their problems and hence tirelessly run after it. But the truth is, money brings its challenges and heartaches. It changes people and their priorities. It gives a false sense of power and authority. Wealth and humility do not get along very well.

By your great wisdom in trade you have increased your wealth, and your heart has become proud in your wealth. (Eze 28:5)

Pride in Abilities

This is another type of pride people struggle with. Every child of God is gifted and talented. We have our weaknesses and strengths. There is bitter competition among people about who is superior, who is more talented and gifted and who can do better. Parents compete with other parents about who's child is smarter and intelligent. This spirit of competition is everywhere. We take immense pride in our activities and how we work. I remember, in the country where I was born, people who do not speak good English are looked down upon.

Pride in Looks

Our looks, our youthfulness, physique, and body features give room to pride in us. The day we die, and if left unattended, we will begin to rot and decay within twelve hours. Each Lenten season, we begin our Lenten journey with Ash Wednesday. We are reminded that our body is mere dust and to dust, we shall return. Our outer nature and looks are perishable. All the beauty products in the world cannot keep us young forever. All the medicines and healthcare cannot keep us alive forever. People spend so much money trying to enhance and add value to things that are not eternal and pay little to no time or attention feeding their soul, which is the real person. There are people who feed on the looks of other people. They want to be seen and noticed. They get offended if they are not complimented or ignored.

Pride in Race / Creed and Culture / Family Tradition / Community / Color

People take extraordinary pride in where they come from, where they live, their family ancestry, family name, race, color, country, clan, caste, community, religion, language, etc. God's word is clear that all of us came from the same ancestor, and science also validates this claim to an extent.

From one ancestor he made all nations to inhabit the whole earth, and he allotted the times of their existence and the boundaries of the places where they would live. (Acts 17:26)

The New Testament explicitly tells us not to cause division based on any of the things mentioned above. We are one body in Christ. The world has seen enough violence, strife, and discrimination. The massacre in Rwanda, the Holocaust in Europe, and the war in Vietnam are some examples of how extreme man can take his values and belief system.

I say to everyone among you not to think of yourself more highly than you ought to think, but to think with sober judgment, each according to the measure of faith that God has assigned. (Rom 12:3)

Spiritual Pride

Spiritual pride is a topic for those who are religious or claim to be spiritual. Spiritual people can also be subjected to pride. If you have reached this point in the book, you are a reasonably religious person having an interest in godly matters. Foremost, we must remember and acknowledge that it is God who gives us the power, desire, and ability to do spiritual exercises. To be able to pray is a gift. To be able to spend time in adoration for long hours is also a gift. To be able to read the Bible for 30 minutes every day is another gift. To be able to attend Mass is a gift too. Everything we do for God is a result of his power and the Holy Spirit abiding in us, Peter had a great love for Jesus, but there was some hidden pride within him. When Jesus openly told the apostles that one of them would deny him. Peter, out of his pride, said that he would stand with Jesus even if all others left him. Peter did not rely on God's strength to stand with Jesus. As a result of this pride, he fell (denied Jesus) thrice before the cock crowed, as Jesus had predicted.

These are some of the manifestations of spiritual pride

- Angry with people who are not interested in spiritual matters
- Feeling good about oneself after accomplishing the daily spiritual activities
- Constant judgmental thoughts toward the Church and the religious
- Judging and gossiping about priests/ religious who are not serious about their ministry or vocation
- Hatred/hostility toward people outside the Church or other religions
- Trying to please God with our spiritual activities

- Anger and disappointment with self over failure to accomplish spiritual goals.
- Joy when someone compliments about our dedication to God

Intellectual Pride

Intellectual pride is deeply connected to spiritual pride. It is a significant block to opening our lives to God. It is this kind of pride that prevents us from learning and seeing what God wants to teach us and show us. It is a hindrance to our spiritual growth. We are at times stubborn to a certain kind of teaching or belief and refuse to submit to the truth that God wants to reveal. We attach certain infallibility to our judgment, discernment, ideas, and inspirations. We trust our senses too much and are deceived most of the time. A Christian should empty himself and be open to God for his inspirations and truths.

False Humility

False humility is also pride. We get a sense of satisfaction by portraying our humility to others. We like to be called a humble person. We are always trying to condemn people for their pride. We are always focused on our weaknesses and failures, and we talk about them all the time. There is hidden pride behind all such behaviors.

Areas to Examine:

- Do I have the habit of justifying myself (Self- Justification)?
- Am I open to corrections and submit to the one who is correcting me for my good?
- Am I always finding fault with others?
- Am I slow to find my own faults?
- Am I always critical of other people?
- Do I have the habit of pretending before others, trying to portray what I am not?
- Do I find it hard to seek help when I need it?
- Am I defensive when people try to correct me?
- Do I get irritated when I am contradicted?
- Am I hungry for praise and attention?
- Do I have a high opinion about myself?

- Do I look down upon others (haughty eyes)?
- Do I easily get angry when I do not get my way (a sign of wounded pride)?
- Do I find it hard to work under any authority or take orders?
- Do I find it hard to forgive people (it requires humility to forgive)?
- Am I of the viewpoint that my race, country, caste, color, etc. is superior to others?
- Do I feel offended if I am not acknowledged or thanked?
- Do I get repeated judgmental thoughts resulting in gossip?
- Do I easily get hurt by words and insults of people?
- Do I find it hard to serve others?
- Do I find it hard to seek forgiveness from others?
- Do I have the mentality that I deserve everything I have and more?
- Do I act humble only to receive praise from others?
- Do I find It hard to be thankful to others for their help and support?
- Do I find it hard to work as a team?
- Do I find it hard to submit before God? (A humble person will have no difficulty kneeling, raising his hands, prostrating during prayer)
- Do I have a show-off attitude?
- Am I arrogant toward people under me?
- Do I have a self-centered, selfish attitude, always thinking and talking about myself?
- Do I yield to other people's ideas and plans?
- Do I listen to people, and am I an approachable person?
- Do I put myself first in everything I do?
- Do I reject authority at home, work, and Church?
- Am I frustrated about my weaknesses?
- Do I boast about myself?

Avarice or Greed

Greed, the next capital sin in our list, is the excessive, inordinate, wasteful, and unhealthy love and desire for wealth and material possessions. It is a sin of excess. Greed leads to covetousness against the neighbor. Those who love God cannot love money and vice versa. Greed is one of the major causes of poverty in this world. One who loves money will never have enough. Sadly, the world measures growth by how much wealth one has accumulated in one's lifetime.

Take care! Be on your guard against all kinds of greed; for one's life does not consist in the abundance of possessions. (Luk 12:15)

Many of us think of this life and this world as a permanent place. Little do we know that we can take nothing out of this world, and we are not here permanently either. We do not even know who is going to use or enjoy all the wealth we make. Yet, we exert ourselves so much powered by greed. Jesus tells us to store up treasures in heaven where it will be with us forever.

Do not store up for yourselves treasures on earth, where moth and rust consume and where thieves break in and steal; but store up for yourselves treasures in heaven, where neither moth nor rust consumes and where thieves do not break in and steal. (Matt 6:19-20)

Greed and love of money is a strong force operating in this world. Most people are slaves to this vice. It works and operates in us in many ways. Looking deeper into our lifestyle and priorities will help us detect its presence.

Areas to Examine:

- Is getting rich, the primary goal in my life?
- Do I have a history of not paying back my creditors?
- Am I overworking to earn more money?
- Does it hurt me when I must give money to others?
- Do I make an excuse not to tithe?
- Do I have an unhealthy attachment to material possessions?
- Am I always into watching money related television shows or reading money related magazines and books?

- Am I involved in, or operating more businesses than what I can handle?
- Is money the driving force behind all my decisions and activities?

If you are attached to the things of this earth, you should give alms enough to enable you to punish your avarice by depriving yourself of all that is not absolutely necessary for life. (St. John Vianney)

Moderation

If greed is the vice, then moderation is the virtue. All blessings, given to us by God, if used in moderation, will turn out be good for us. Moderation is a virtue that one must practice in everyday life. Eating, sleeping, earning money, exercise and workout, work habits, recreation, etc. if carried out in moderation will lead to a healthy and satisfying life. Excess of anything is harmful.

Listen to me, my child, and do not disregard me, and in the end you will appreciate my words. In everything you do be moderate, and no sickness will overtake you. (Sir 31:22)

A good Christian exercises balance and self-control in everything. He is not controlled and dominated by anything even if it is a harmless habit like drinking coffee or tea. We are created for freedom, and not as slaves to the goods of this world.

Envy

The next capital sin that will be our focus is envy. Envy is the grudging admiration or a resentful longing and desire for another person's talents, possessions, abilities, qualities, etc. Envy is the sadness that fills us when others are blessed and the joy when others suffer or become needy. In the book of Genesis, we read that Cain was envious of Abel's relationship with God. He ended up killing his brother. St. Gregory saw envy as the root of violence, strife, and hatred in this world.

From envy are born hatred, detraction, calumny, joy caused by the misfortune of a neighbor, and displeasure caused by his prosperity. (St. Gregory)[7]

There is an apt definition of envy given in the book of Job. Rejoicing at the ruin of our enemy is envy.

If I have rejoiced at the ruin of those who hated me, or exulted when evil overtook them (Job 31:29)

Have you ever wondered why the devil hates humanity so much? It is because we are the children of God. The devil cannot see us have what he had lost; therefore, he is envious of us.

Through the devil's envy death entered the world, and those who belong to his company experience it. (Wis 2:24)

The Catechism defines envy as a form of sadness which goes against charity and generosity. It is rooted in pride and therefore, can be defeated only by humility.

Envy represents a form of sadness and therefore refusal of charity; the baptized person should struggle against it by exercising good will. Envy often comes from pride; the baptized person should train himself to live in humility: (CCC 2540)

Let us examine some practical areas where envy hides or manifests in a subtle manner

A Hardworking Person

Hard work is good and rewarding. The problem lies in the motive. Why do I work so hard? Is it to support my family or to be able to afford what others have? We see our friends who live in big mansions and deep inside we too long to buy a big house. Out of envy, we exert ourselves to get rich. The book of Ecclesiastes warns us not to fall trap to envy.

Then I saw that all toil and all skill in work come from one person's envy of another. This also is vanity and a chasing after wind. (Eccl 4:4)

False Happiness

Do I have to force myself to rejoice when others are blessed? Do I find it hard to congratulate and celebrate another person's success? Do I put up a false smile and give fake compliments on people's achievements? These are signs of envy working in me.

Sadness in Poverty

People who are poor are sad that they are not able to afford what the rich people have. When a person is busy looking at what the other person has, he will not be able to see his own blessings and become gloomy and discontent with life.

Gossip and Slander

Gossip and slander have their roots in envy and lack of love. We speak negatively about a person because deep down, we are not happy with their success or achievement.

Ingratitude

Ingratitude and complaints are also rooted in envy to a certain degree. For example, if there is no air-conditioner in this world or nobody has ever seen one or used one, then there will be less or no complaints about heat and other issues related to it. The fact that we sometimes complain about having no air-conditioner at home is because someone else has it and we are unhappy about it.

Competitiveness

Parents who compare their children's performance with other children become victims of envy. We live in an extremely competitive world, and the pressure to excel is instilled in the child from a noticeably early age. Parents want their child to be the topper in class and find it hard to accept another child getting better grades than their child. They are internally saddened by it and as a result, put more pressure on their own children.

Let us not become conceited, competing against one another, envying one another.
(Gal 5:26)

Areas to Examine:

- Have I ever been saddened by the success and achievement of my spouse?
- Have I ever been saddened or felt angry over the achievements or successes of my peers?
- Have I ever been saddened by the news of my friends or family member who is having a child before me or is getting married before me?
- Have I been saddened by the financial growth of others (family and friends)?
- Do I overwork or stress myself to have or afford what others have?
- Am I genuinely happy over other's successes?
- Do I show compassion and console people when they experience a loss?

- Do I, because of my envy, put undue pressure on my children with regards to their education and performance?
- Am I unhappy about my poverty or my financial condition?

Wrath or Anger

Anger is the next sin on our list. Anger by itself is not wrong or sinful. God himself has expressed his anger so many times in the Bible, and Jesus was also visibly angry when he saw the money changers and their practices in the temple. Parents get mad at their children almost every day. It is also natural for spouses to get upset with each other for a valid reason. Anger without a valid cause or for the wrong reasons is sinful. Some basic types of wicked, sinful or unjust anger are listed in this section.

Do I Have the Right to be Angry?

God asked Jonah whether he had any right to get angry. Jonah had many complaints against God. He was not happy about his vocation and call, and he was not pleased with the fact that it was too hot (Jonah 4). We have all been there, and we have questioned many things, sometimes directly to God. We have expressed our anger over so many things and to countless people, all of whom we cannot control. God is asking us the same question today. Do you have any right to be angry? Most of our anger is unjust and unwarranted.

There is no sin or wrong that gives a man a foretaste of hell in this life as anger and impatience. (St. Catherine of Siena)

Meaningless Anger

There is a kind of anger known as meaningless anger. Let us imagine a person driving on the highway. There is a traffic jam and cars are piled up for at least a mile. Cars are not moving at all. This person sitting in the car is getting very restless. His restlessness turns into anger. The question is, is this kind of anger, good or bad? The answer is plain and simple. Not only is this anger bad, but also meaningless. This anger will just take a toll on the person's health. If this man were to travel on this highway every day and experience similar traffic daily, he would soon end up getting some stress-related sickness. Most of the anger we experience or express is meaningless and unproductive.

Hidden Anger or Suppressed Anger

Some people are exceptionally good at hiding their anger. The anger has not gone anywhere but, buried deep inside. Hidden anger is still anger. It will manifest in other ways most unexpectedly. Those who try to suppress their anger will someday find themselves exploding. Anger needs to be dealt with, through repentance and confession. Hiding and suppressing it is not the solution.

Anger That Affects Love

Anger is an emotion, if used rightly, can bring the best out of a person. If anger is used by a person who does not know how to handle it, he or she may end up wounding the other person and the relationship. A person should master the art of taming his emotions from an early age. A sign of maturity is visible in how one controls one's feelings, namely anger. Many people have wounded their relationships, especially marriage, because of the wrong use of their anger. Anger is a sin if it harms people instead of building them up.

Anger that Affects Communication

How many times we have seen extended family members not talk to each other for a long period. Some silly and trivial problem in the past has triggered a rift where people do not converse with each other. The anger still festers inside, which prevents them from making peace with the other. There are cases where spouses do not talk to each other, and they are at the end of the marriage line nearing separation. Anger mixed with pride makes life complicated. A humble man makes peace with everyone and remains in peaceful terms with all.

Prolonged Anger

This group of people does not know how to come out of their anger. They become victims of their own anger. This can happen within families, or in a community or between nations. I have personally seen people who have so much hatred and anger for their neighboring country or an occupying country. They even pass it on to their successive generations. Over time people forget why they got angry in the first place but still hold on to their anger, or the anger is holding on to them.

Be angry but do not sin; do not let the sun go down on your anger, and do not make room for the devil. (Eph 4:26-27)

Anger without Restraint (Uncontrolled Anger) / Aggression

This is the most dangerous kind of anger where a person loses all control over himself. He may either slam the door behind and storm out of the house, engage in physical violence harming his near and dear ones or get into destructive behavior, throwing and destroying things. Such a person can terrify the people who live with him. There are cases where the husband has kicked his wife out of the house or hurt the children physically or even broken the television.

A fool gives full vent to anger, but the wise quietly holds it back. (Pro 29:11)

Additional Reading: Pro 29:22

Revenge

Revenge is the act of hurting, harming, or injuring someone in some way for the hurt received from them. All forms of hate, vengeance, retribution, and retaliation are sinful and wrong. Vengeance should be left to God.

You have heard that it was said, 'An eye for an eye and a tooth for a tooth.' But I say to you, do not resist an evildoer. But if anyone strikes you on the right cheek, turn the other also. (Matt 5:38-39)

Evil should never be repaid with evil. Love is our identity, and love is our weapon. Love and prayer have the power to defeat any evil in this world. Jesus, by accepting the cross, showed us the way to defeat evil.

Beloved, never avenge yourselves, but leave room for the wrath of God; for it is written, "Vengeance is mine, I will repay, says the Lord." (Rom 12:19)

Additional Reading: 1 Thes 5:15, Lev 19:18

Short Tempered / Quick-Tempered

Some of us are quick to lose our temper or become angry. Trivial matters bother and irritate us. We have little patience in us, and often the anger has no good reason. One must check what kind of fruit this anger produces.

Do not be quick to anger, for anger lodges in the bosom of fools. (Eccl 7:9)

Additional Reading: Jas 1:19-20

An Angry Person

There are some who brand themselves as an angry person. To begin with, God did not make any angry persons or sad persons. All of us are made in the image of God, which is love and mercy. Anger is an emotion given to us to use when needed, and we should not be controlled by it. Using it according to God's purpose will always bring the best results.

Those who are hot-tempered stir up strife, but those who are slow to anger calm contention. (Pro 15:18)

Additional Reading: Eph 4:31-32

Anger from Wounded Pride

Pride can be an underlying reason for most anger. Each time our pride is wounded, it makes us angry. A proud person considers himself above everyone else and is usually not open to ideas, suggestions, and corrections, Therefore, he is more prone to getting hurt. The more we humble ourselves, the more we will be freed from the spirit of anger.

Passive Aggressive Anger

A passive aggressive person does not directly show his anger. He finds other ways to demonstrate it. Non-co-operation and noncompliance are some methods adopted by them. They do not usually admit their anger either. This is another way of expressing one's anger. A husband or wife when they are angry may not sometimes communicate it directly with words, but subtly show it by lack of communication (limited communication with a yes or no answer) or omitting to do things around the house that they are supposed to do.

Avoidance

Avoidance is another way people express their anger. People sometimes do not mingle with certain people because of some unresolved anger. Anger, hatred, bitterness, strife, and unforgiveness block God's blessings and will keep us in darkness.

Pursue peace with everyone. (Heb 12:14)

Additional Reading: Ps 34:14, Rom 12:18

Wrong Desires Lead to Anger

Wrong, sinful, and evil desires in us lead to anger and strife. We pick a fight with those who do not agree with us or let us have our way. It is a struggle that most parents face when they deal with children and teenagers. For example, the child wants to watch television, and the parent insists on him doing his schoolwork. The parent tries to take away the television remote, and he is faced with rebellion, anger, tantrums, etc. The child's unfulfilled sinful desires are causing him to become angry. Are we angry because we do not get to do what we want? Are we angry that our freedom and privileges are taken away from us? When we identify our carnal nature and sinful desires in us and repent for them, anger will vanish by itself.

Those conflicts and disputes among you, where do they come from? Do they not come from your cravings that are at war within you? (Jas 4:1)

Lust

The capital sin of lust is defined as a strong or an intense desire or want. Lust is the opposite of love, and it dominates when love is absent. Lust can also be called unhealthy love. Love should primarily flow from and to God and neighbor. If this love for God and neighbor is blocked, it turns and becomes lust and starts to flow in every direction such as money, physical body, material goods, etc. All lustful desires must be given up, by abiding in true love and walking in it. Lust is the opposite of love. Absence of love gives birth to various lustful passions.

Lust of the flesh is generally referred to when speaking about lust. All sexual sins are committed because of lust. There is also lust for power, lust for money, food, etc.

Do not follow the lust of your heart and your own eyes. (Num 15:39)

Sexual Lust (Lust of the Flesh)

All sexual sins fall under this category. At the same time, the flesh can lust after many other things. Because of our sexual nature, most people find it hard to conquer or master this area. People are not able to restrain it, and it runs wild and causes havoc. Most people are not aware of the way sexuality affects the whole being. For some, it is a taboo and some others it is a way of liberating oneself. Some are conservative in their approach, and some others vouch for sexual liberty. Some see it as pleasure and while others see it as a commodity. Some see it as a way of livelihood, while others do not even want to talk about it. Some play it safe and follow the rules while others like to venture into the forbidden. Sex and sexuality have existed since the time of our first parents. It is part of the creation package, and its purposes are manifold. It is given to us for pleasure, expression of love, and procreation within marriage. It is an undeniable fact that we are sexual beings. It is in our DNA. Then what makes it wrong or evil, and why is it listed as one of the seven cardinal sins?

The answer to this lies in the distinction between the act of sex and lust. Let us try to understand with an example. A small bullet, an inch long is a piece of metal which we can hold in our hand, and it is harmless. The same bullet, if it is loaded in a gun, becomes powerful and lethal. It can harm and kill people. Sexuality and lust work in a similar manner. Sexual instincts if they are tamed, is not harmful and can serve the purpose of God. Uncontrolled sexual appetite and wrongful sexual desires are what is harmful. The sixth commandment deals in detail about how our lust manifests itself in different ways.

Let us look at some misconceptions about our sexuality, which will help us to overcome the sin of lust.

It is Dirty

Sex and the things related to it are seen as dirty and filthy by many. Our whole approach toward our sexuality is flawed. Sexuality is much more than what meets the eye. In marriage, it is an exchange of love between spouses. It is a holy and life-giving act.

Sex is Bad

Not only does the world see it as dirty, but it also labels sex as bad and evil. I remember, when growing up, I was told that all the smokers, alcoholics, and drug addicts are bad and evil and not to associate with them. Later, when I got hooked on to these addictions, I labeled myself as a wicked and evil person. Much later in life, I understood that these are just addictions, and bad and evil are entirely different. People with some sexual habits are not bad people, nor are we to see sex as bad. Sex, as per God's plan, is a holy and pure act.

It Must be Hidden

Sex is also seen as something dark and something that needs to be hidden. Young people are of the impression that their sexual acts or habits need to be hidden from the elders, or else they will get into trouble. As a result, they hide it more, and the more it stays hidden, the more power it has over the person. All darkness must be exposed in the light. Frequent confession (bringing to the light) will bring freedom from sinful sexual habits.

Take no part in the unfruitful works of darkness, but instead expose them. (Eph 5:11)

We do Not Talk About it

Because sex is considered dirty, evil, and dark, people do not talk about it in Church anymore. There is little to no knowledge and awareness about it, and people are living their lives by their own rules. The truth about sex and sexuality is diluted. For some, everything is acceptable, and for some others, everything is forbidden. Parents do not talk about it with children, and when children have questions, they do not know whom to turn to. They keep it private and secret and fall into many traps.

I am a Sexual Being

I am a sexual being, and I have needs, is the standard by which some of us live. I am sexually hungry, and I satisfy these needs without harming anyone, is what some people claim. The Bible verse most suitable for people with this way of thinking comes from St. Paul's second letter to Timothy,

Shun youthful passions and pursue righteousness, faith, love, and peace. (2 Tim 2:22)

Additional Reading: 1 Pet 1:14, Eph 4:22

Holiness is the Absence of Sexuality

Some of us are of the impression that holiness is a call only for the priestly and religious who are single and celibate. This was a theory believed by so many. It was also believed that married people who are involved in sexual intimacy, could not become holy. This teaching was put to an end in the 2nd Vatican council.

The classes and duties of life are many, but holiness is one – that sanctity which is cultivated by all who are moved by the Spirit of God, and who obey the voice of the Father and worship God the Father in spirit and in truth. (Lumen Gentium Ch 5)

Sexuality can be Restrained not Removed

Some who are yearning for a higher spiritual life may have prayed," God, please take away my sexuality." A noble prayer indeed, but not the right prayer. It is like someone asking God to take away his eyes so that he does not watch porn again. What they need is grace in times of weakness. Although our sexuality is here to stay, we have power over it with the help of the Holy Spirit.

I pray that, according to the riches of his glory, he may grant that you may be strengthened in your inner being with power through his Spirit. (Eph 3:16)

We are powerless over sin on our own, but the power of the Holy Spirit gives us freedom and victory over our lustful nature.

Mere Pleasure

Sex is seen merely as pleasure by people. "It has what I need; therefore, I go for it" attitude is approached by many. Although the world calls it "physical intimacy," it goes much deeper than the physical level. It involves the mind, soul, will, emotions, etc. Pleasure is an incentive in sex, but not everything. St. Augustine speaking about lust and pleasure, says that lust, although begins as pleasure, will end up as a need.

Lust indulged became habit, and habit unresisted became necessity. (St. Augustine)

It is Good

Finally, if sex is good and created by God, why can't everyone enjoy it? Why are there restrictions to it? A very valid question. Those who believe in the sex for all theory should accept the fact that in the future, a ten-year-old child may insist on having sex. How do you stop that? Therefore, God has restricted sex solely for marriage partners. Just as marriage calls for a certain degree of maturity in its members, so does sex. All forms of sex outside of marriage is gravely sinful.

Lust of the World

Materialism is driven by lust that is taking the whole world by storm. The standard of living has been on a steady rise over the past couple of decades, which has resulted in people being able to afford more. The more we buy, the more our needs increase. We have become greedy for goods. World spending levels are on the rise. People are materially rich and spiritually poor, and sadly, they are yet to recognize their poverty. We have a deep love for the world and the things of this world. Satan controls the entire world, and whoever loves the world is under the power of Satan.

We know that we are God's children, and that the whole world lies under the power of the evil one. (1 John 5:19)

Christians cannot be connected to the world and God at the same time. We will love the one and hate the other. We are called to be connected with

God and communicate to the world about his love. We live in the world, use the things of the world according to need, but we do not fall in love with it.

Do you not know that friendship with the world is enmity with God? Therefore, whoever wishes to be a friend of the world becomes an enemy of God. (Jas 4:4)

Lust of the Eyes

The eye is our window to the world. It collects all or most of the information from the world and sends it to the brain for processing. There are many passages in the Bible that speak about the human eye. Jesus said that the eye is the most important part of the body. The health of the whole being (mind, body, and soul) depends on the eye.

The lamp of your body is your eye. If your eye is healthy, your entire body will be filled with light. But if your eye has been corrupted, your entire body will be darkened. If then the light that is in you is darkness, how great will that darkness be! (Matt 6:22-23)

There are three primary areas of weakness when it comes to seeing. All of us are victims of one or more of these areas. We are attracted to beauty in the form of people, things, and places. It is hard for us to control ourselves when our eye meets a beautiful person, a beautiful object, or a scenic location.

Beautiful People

We have our opinions when it comes to defining a beautiful person. But, all of us are attracted to some form of beauty in a person. Some are attracted to the shape of a person, while others are attracted to the sexual features. Some are attracted to the facial looks, and some others are drawn to their clothing style or color of the person. Some take a quick glance while others find it hard to resist looking when there is a beautiful person around. It feels like they have no control over their eyes. Men have their preferences, and women have their own.

Is it wrong to look? We will try to answer this. Desires are conceived in the heart but enter us via the senses mainly through the eyes. If a person has never seen a monkey, not even a picture of it nor heard the word, he cannot visualize a monkey in his mind, or will there be a need to imagine. All the thoughts and fantasies of our mind are directly connected to what we see or choose to look at with our eyes. Pay attention to all the thoughts you are regularly getting, especially the repeated overpowering thoughts. You will notice that they are related to something of this world. Once again, going back to the scripture in Matthew's Gospel, we have a need to check the health of our eyes constantly. The blood of Jesus is powerful, and we must apply it every day to our eyes by praying a simple prayer, "Jesus, wash my eyes in your precious blood and fill me with our Holy Spirit." At the same time, we must put an effort to refrain from looking at all unholy and worldly things.

I have made a covenant with my eyes; how then could I look upon a virgin? (Job 31:1)

Beautiful Things

Beauty, in all its forms, always catches our eyes. No wonder, all the commercials that cater to us focus so much on the eye appeal of a product. This is a weakness that we all have and find it hard to resist. We tend to go for things that are visually appealing. At times, we stretch ourselves to acquire these things even though we are not able to afford them. So much of care, attention, and detail is given to the things we are surrounded with, the clothes we wear, the cars we drive, etc. The entire world is caught up in the battle of making things beautiful and attractive. Take the landscaping industry; for example; the US spends over 40 billion dollars a year to maintain its lawns.

Turn my eyes from looking at vanities; give me life in your ways. (Ps 119:37)

Some of us have a strong preference for color. We like a particular color, and our choices are dependent on it. There are people, especially women, who are always on the lookout for new colors in clothing and buy them. We put so much value on how things should look. We are victims of the lust of the eye.

Beautiful Places

This is another weakness in people. Most people go on vacation from time to time. They like to look at new places and scenic locations. If you have planned one, please proceed with it. It is not sinful or evil, and do not feel guilty about it. I am merely trying to bring to light, the culture that is existing in our times, and the connection between our actions and lust. We take great pride in the neighborhood we live in. How many of us who are wealthy would buy a house in a poorer community and live there? If we look at the life of Jesus, though he was the richest of rich, he chose to be born in a manger amidst all the cattle.

The world and its desire are passing away, but those who do the will of God live forever. (1 John 2:17)

The Restlessness of the Human Eye

Eyes are restless, and it is always leading the person into sin and trouble. One who can control his eyes has already won the battle over lust. I know a person who sits in front of the blessed sacrament for hours merely gazing at the Eucharist (host). Very few people can do this. Our eyes, when Looking at the face of Jesus, will receive strength to escape the lust of the eyes.

Turn away your eyes from a shapely woman, and do not gaze at beauty belonging to another; many have been seduced by a woman's beauty, and by it, passion is kindled like a fire. (Sir 9:8)

Gluttony

Gluttony is another capital sin. Gluttony is derived from the Latin word gluttirei which means-to gulp down. Gluttony is excessive and unhealthy attachment toward food and drink. It goes against the spirit of moderation and self-control. We should eat to live and not live to eat and not let our belly to become our God. Overconsumption and indulgence in areas of food and drink lead to many problems both in the physical and spiritual level.

Physical Sickness

It is a well-known fact that too much of anything is harmful to us, which applies to food and drink as well. Many diseases are related to our eating habits. We hear about and know many who are affected by illnesses related to cholesterol and sugar. God, in his word, had spoken about these things long before man discovered it.

Healthy sleep depends on moderate eating; he rises early and feels fit. The distress of sleeplessness and of nausea and colic are with the glutton. (Sir 31:20)

It is almost certain that excess in eating is the cause of almost all the diseases of the body, but its effects on the soul are even more disastrous. (St. Alphonsus Liguori)

Additional Reading: Sir 37:29-31

Love of Food

Worries and anxieties about food, always thinking about the next meal, no willingness or desire to fast are signs that food has entered our heart and it has become an idol for us.

Do not worry about your life, what you will eat, or about your body, what you will wear. For life is more than food, and the body more than clothing. (Luk 12:22-23)

Food and Spiritual Life

There is a strong connection between our eating habits and spiritual growth. Jesus began his public ministry by first fasting and praying and showed us its need and importance. Fasting is a sign of self-denial, mortification, and humility. Just as Jesus underwent the first temptation in the area of food, we too will go through many temptations in this area. Discipline and self-control in our eating habits are vital to our spiritual growth.

Unless we first tame the enemy dwelling within us, namely our gluttonous appetite, we have not even stood up to engage in the spiritual combat. (St. Gregory)

Food and Worldly Desires

Unhealthy love toward food is a sign of worldly desires lurking within us, namely lust and greed. Lustful habits have their roots in gluttony. Fasting and abstinence help in mastering and chasing out many vices that are inhabiting us.

Areas to Examine:

- Is there an unhealthy craving for delicious food in me?
- Am I always seeking a variety of food items or dishes?
- Does my eating habit conflict with my spiritual life and work?
- Do I fast regularly (if I am healthy)?
- Do I easily get irritated if the food is not tasty or if I do not get food on time?
- Do I eat hastily?
- Am I always thinking about food?
- Am I always eating?
- Am I fussy about a certain kind of food?
- Am I meticulous about eating only a particular cuisine?

Sloth

Sloth is one of the seven capital sins and the last in our list. Spiritual sloth and laziness in fulfilling our responsibilities are two main kinds. Sloth is more than laziness of the body, although it is one of the ways it manifests. Sloth is an attitude toward God, neighbor, work, and responsibilities.

Spiritual Sloth (Acedia)

Spiritual sloth or acedia is defined as a condition where one does not want to work or exert oneself for spiritual goods. It is the laziness associated with living out our faith and practicing virtues.

Acedia or spiritual sloth goes so far as to refuse the joy that comes from God and to be repelled by divine goodness. (CCC 2094)

St. Thomas Aquinas used the term, "sluggishness of the mind" when referring to spiritual sloth. Given below are some of the ways spiritual sloth expresses itself in us.

Aversion to Spiritual Matters

A strong dislike and disinterest in doing spiritual things such as prayer and Scripture reading is a sign of spiritual sloth. Such people just do not want to pray or read the Word of God. They see spiritual exercises as dry and fruitless.

Sorrow About Spiritual Good

Finding religious practices cumbersome and not experiencing the joy of salvation is a clear sign of spiritual sloth in us.

Underuse of God's Gift

People who are blessed with some supernatural gift but do not use them are victims of spiritual sloth. Gifts and charisms are used to build the body of Christ. Unwillingness to exercise the gifts is also a sign of spiritual sloth. A person with the gift to pray should pray for those who do not pray. A person who is good in writing or composing songs should do so for the glory of God.

Unwillingness to Make Sacrifices

Spiritual life calls for sacrifice. God made the ultimate sacrifice of sending his son on the cross so that we can be saved and be with him in heaven. We ought to also make certain sacrifices to fulfill our relationship with God. Every sacrifice we make takes us to the next level of our spiritual life. Unwillingness to make sacrifices is an indication of spiritual sloth.

Areas to Examine:

- Do I find it hard to make sacrifices for the Lord?
- Am I happy with my spiritual growth, or is it stagnant?
- Do I sincerely and joyfully use the God-given gifts for the kingdom?
- Do I find spiritual activities boring and tiring?
- Do I always look at the clock when I pray?
- Do I love sleep and rest more than I love God?

Laziness in Fulfilling Our Responsibilities

Oversleeping

Sleep is a naturally occurring phenomenon and is necessary for optimal health and functioning of the body. The problem lies in oversleeping which hinders our day to day functioning. Oversleeping can also be a result of depression or other clinical factors. Lack of discipline is also a reason. Oversleeping is a problem if it hinders our work, responsibilities, and prayer time.

Do not love sleep, or else you will come to poverty; open your eyes, and you will have plenty of bread. (Pro 20:13)

Additional Reading: Pro 6:9, Pro 24:33

Avoidance of Work (indolence)

Work is essential for the whole world to function. It is important that we enjoy our work. All that we use and utilize is somebody's hard work and contribution, and we contribute by offering our work and services to the world. A lazy person will hate and avoid work.

Work is a good thing for man – a good thing for his humanity – because through work man not only transforms nature, adapting it to his own needs, but he also achieves fulfillment as a human being and indeed, in a sense, becomes 'more a human being (Pope John Paul II)[8]

Indifference and Hatred of Work

Every task must be received from God and done for the Lord. We have one master who is God Almighty. It is this attitude which will help us contribute our best and be successful in what we do. Our earthly masters and bosses are a mere representation of God. People often hate their work when they develop a hatred for their boss or superiors. Jesus did not get angry with the people who prevented him from doing God's work. He continued without grumbling and complaining and accepted the cross from the heavenly Father.

Whatever your task, put yourselves into it, as done for the Lord and not for your masters, since you know that from the Lord you will receive the inheritance as your reward; you serve the Lord Christ. (Col 3:23-24)

Additional Reading: Gen 2:15, Pro 12:11

Procrastination

Procrastination is the avoidance of task by delaying or postponing it. Some of us are quick to begin new projects and tasks, but never have enough drive and motivation to finish it. The sin of sloth or laziness works in many subtle and mysterious ways. Always feeling too tired is also a sign of sloth.

The way of the lazy is overgrown with thorns, but the path of the upright is a level highway. (Pro 15:19)

Additional Reading: Pro 10:4

Idleness

It is rightly said that an idle mind is the devil's workshop. He who is idle works for the devil. Idleness, unwillingness to work, feeling too tired to work, etc. originate from the sin of sloth. One of the qualities of God is that he is a worker. He worked for six days creating the universe, and he works day and night to save us. We who belong to God, cannot be idle doing anything. We honor God when we work. We are given work by God, who uses it to purify us.

While we were with you, we insisted on this to you: that if anyone was not willing to work, neither should he eat. For we have heard that there are some among you who live in idleness, not working at all, but eagerly meddling. Now we charge those who act in this way, and we beg them in the Lord Jesus Christ, that they work in silence and eat their own bread. (2 Thes 3:10-12)

Additional Reading: Pro 14:23, Pro 10:26

Losing Interest in Life (Dejection)

God treats everyone equally, but life does not. Everything we do should be backed by purpose and meaning. Answering God's call and living a life for Jesus gives meaning and purpose to life. Everything worldly and carnal we seek in this life will eventually leave us empty and broken. The soul cannot be filled or satisfied with the goods of this world. It was not designed for it. We fail to realize this and end up being dejected and cast down. St. Paul, who was formerly known as Saul, was running aimlessly in life, until that profound moment when he encountered Jesus. It changed his life completely. Suddenly, he could see his life from God's viewpoint. Pleasing God became his primary mission and motive in life. It was not about him anymore. Writing to the Galatians, he says,

When God, who had set me apart before I was born and called me through his grace, was pleased to reveal his Son to me, so that I might proclaim him among the Gentiles (Gal 1:15-16)

Attitude Toward Work

There is a desire to get rich, but at the same time, there is an unwillingness to work. There is love for money, and at the same time, there is hatred for work. Offers such as "least investment and maximum returns" always catch our attention. Hatred and resentment toward work and responsibility stem from the sin of sloth. A godly person receives everything from the hands of God, including the sufferings and hardships in this life. Jesus did not blame Judas, or the Jews, or Pontius Pilate for his cross. He accepted it willfully from the Father (Jn 10:17).

The lazy do not roast their game, but the diligent obtain precious wealth. (Pro 12:27)

Areas to Examine:

- Am I always looking for quick ways to make money without any desire to work?
- Am I losing interest or meaning to life?
- Do I see work as a burden?
- Do I make false excuses to avoid work?
- Do I see work solely to earn money?
- Do I procrastinate?
- Am I thankful to God for work?
- Does my sleep habits hinder my work, responsibilities, and prayer time?
- Is money the only driving force for all the work I do?
- Do I do all my work to the best of my ability?

The Precepts of the Church

Whoever listens to you listens to me, and whoever rejects you rejects me, and whoever rejects me rejects the one who sent me. (Luk 10:16)

The precepts are general rules of the Catholic Church meant to guarantee the basic or necessary minimum one must fulfill in spiritual matters. In addition to the Ten Commandments, it is a good practice to regularly examine our conscience based on the precepts of the church to see if we are following the fundamental laws. The precepts were covered in detail within the commandments in this book; therefore, no further explanation is given here.

A word of caution to the reader; if we base our life on the bare minimum, little of what is left will be taken away from us. We should strive to excel and reach perfection in our faith life. Our love for God is not genuine if we try to fulfill only the minimum requirements of the church.

Therefore, just as you have received the Lord Jesus Christ, live your lives in him. Be rooted and continually built up in Christ. And be confirmed in the faith, just as you have also learned it, increasing in him with acts of thanksgiving. (Col 2:6-7)

Additional Reading: CCC 2042-2043

The First Precept

You shall attend Mass on Sundays and holy days of obligation and rest from work.

The Second Precept

You shall confess your sins at least once a year.

The Third Precept

You shall receive Jesus in the Eucharist at least during the Easter season.

The Fourth Precept

You shall observe the Church's prescribed days of fasting and abstinence.

The Fifth Precept

"You shall assist to provide for the material needs of the Church.

Conclusion

A Catholic is foremost expected to be faithful and committed to his parish. People come together to form a parish. Without the people of God there will be no parish. Praying with the parish and for the parish is the duty of every parishioner. A parish needs intercession and prayer support to operate. It is important that we understand and play our role in our parish and the mother Church. The next chapter looks at another important teaching which summarizes all that we learnt so far.

The Great Commandment

Just as I have loved you, you also should love one another. (Jn 13:34)

Commandment of Love

All the old testament commandments can be summarized to two commandments in the new testament; love for God and love for neighbor. The two commandments can be combined into one, which is the only commandment to obey and follow. Love is the only commandment and the greatest. He who loves has fulfilled the law. Sin is the absence of love, and to love is what we owe to our God and neighbor.

Owe no one anything, except to love one another; for the one who loves another has fulfilled the law. (Rom 13:8)

Love for God

God is love, and he created everything in love, for love, and to love. He created us in love and filled us with his love. Original sin wounded our capacity and ability to love. Our love is wounded because of our iniquities. It is not steadfast, abundant, and free-flowing. It is selfish and centered toward self. As a result, it takes an effort to love. We are fully capable of loving, and it is not impossible for us. Jesus modeled love for us. Therefore, meditating on the gospels and the life of Jesus will teach us to love like him. All things must be done with love, including our spiritual activities. To love God with all our heart, mind, body, soul, and spirit is the first commandment.

To love him with all the heart, and with all the understanding, and with all the strength,' and 'to love one's neighbor as oneself,' – this is much more important than all whole burnt offerings and sacrifices." (Mrk 12:33)

Jesus combined the love for God and love for our neighbor as one commandment making it inseparable. Therefore, our love for God is demonstrated in our ability to love our neighbor, and the love of neighbor can be fulfilled only if we deeply love God.

Those who say, "I love God," and hate their brothers or sisters, are liars; for those who do not love a brother or sister whom they have seen, cannot love God whom they have not seen. (1 Jn 4:20)

True love casts out all sin and evil. We cannot do evil to somebody we truly love. Love by itself has the power to destroy all evil. God is love, and those who abide in love abide in God, and God abides in them. Jesus, through his unconditional love for the father and all mankind, won victory over evil and death.

Love for Neighbor

Do I love my neighbor the way I want to be loved by others? By far, this is the easiest commandment to explain, but the hardest to follow. Jesus used the words, "love your neighbor as yourself" leaving us a lot to work on. How do I want to be loved? I don't want to be hurt by anybody. Therefore I have no right to hurt anybody either. If I want others to be compassionate and forgiving toward me, I should also be returning that treatment to others. What we look for in people, they look in us for those qualities. We should be willing to do to others as we would want them to do for us.

The commandments, "You shall not commit adultery; You shall not murder; You shall not steal; You shall not covet"; and any other commandment, are summed up in this word, "Love your neighbor as yourself. (Rom 13:9)

Additional Reading: 1 Jn 4:7, 1 Jn 4:11-12, Luk 6:31

Conclusion

This concludes our study on the examination of conscience. We used four main tools to examine ourselves, namely; The Ten Commandments, the capital sins, the precepts of the Church, and the great commandment. In addition to this, one must also read Scriptures daily and frequently. God's Holy Word opens our heart and mind and reveals our inner darkness.

Repentance

I have come to call not the righteous but sinners to repentance. (Luk 5:32)

Acknowledge Your Sins

Once we have examined our conscience, it is time to write down our sins. A good practice is to write our sins each day and take it with us to confession. It is important that no one sees it. God is merciful, but your spouse may not be. The next step is acknowledging these sins. To acknowledge means to admit or to accept and take full ownership and responsibility of our sins. The prayer during the Mass for the forgiveness of venial sin goes like this," I *have sinned through my own fault, in my thoughts, and in my words, in what I have done, and in what I have failed to do"*

In the above prayer, we acknowledge sin as our own fault without any justification. This is the first step of confession. Confession begins with admission and acceptance of our sins and weaknesses. In the book of Jeremiah, God asks the people to acknowledge and admit their wrongdoing,

Only acknowledge your guilt, that you have rebelled against the Lord your God (Jer 3:13)

A person, who defends, justifies, and conceals his sins, makes an insincere confession whereas a person who acknowledges his fault will receive pardon and grace from God.

You say, "I am innocent; surely his anger has turned from me." Now I am bringing you to judgment for saying, "I have not sinned." (Jer 2:35)

Years ago, I had met with an accident. I had hit a car from behind, and it was entirely my fault. The next day my insurance agency called me, and one of the first things they told me was to deny that it was my fault. They did not want me to acknowledge my mistake. Similarly, each time we fall, Satan tells us to deny our wrongdoing and sin. We yield to his voice, and we either justify or minimize the seriousness of it or blame it on somebody else. The prodigal son, when he came to the father, made an honest confession. He took full responsibility for his wrongdoing and did not make any excuses for his behavior. Pride often prevents us from admitting our faults, and we make a half-hearted confession.

Basics of Repentance

Most Catholics are familiar with the words, confession, reconciliation, and penance, but very few are aware of the importance of repentance, let alone know its meaning. Repentance or to repent means to be genuinely sorry for one's sins. It also means a change of heart or to turn back from one's sinful ways. The Greek word for repentance is "Metanoia," which is translated as a transformation of heart or spiritual conversion. Repentance is a crucial aspect of salvation. We are all headed in the wrong direction and to get back in the right direction; we must make a sharp U-turn. In the spiritual sense, a total conversion must take place.

Repentance and faith are the two pillars of our religion. Jesus began his public ministry by proclaiming repentance from sins and faith in God (Jesus).

The time is fulfilled, and the kingdom of God has come near; repent, and believe in the good news. (Mrk 1:15)

John the Baptist and the Apostle Peter, too, began their sermon with a cry to repent and to turn back to God.

In those days John the Baptist appeared in the wilderness of Judea, proclaiming, "Repent, for the kingdom of heaven has come near." (Matt 3:1-2)

Peter said to them, "Repent, and be baptized every one of you in the name of Jesus Christ so that your sins may be forgiven; and you will receive the gift of the Holy Spirit. (Acts 2:38)

Repentance is a theme or topic covered throughout the Bible. From the early pages to the book of revelation, God is calling his people to return to him. Repentance is the opposite of sin. Sin and repentance are the choices we make, which lead us either to life or death. Let us look at some biblical language to get an in-depth meaning and definition of repentance and what God wants from us.

Coming to our Senses

The phrase, "coming to our senses" is mentioned three times in the Bible (1 Kgs 8:47, 2 Chron 6:37, 2 Mac 9:11) and each time it refers to a sinner who returns to God. To repent means to come to our senses. Formerly we acted foolishly in ignorance. A person who heads on the path of destruction is either foolish or ignorant. The Bible describing the prodigal son's condition uses the words, "he came to himself."

Rend your Hearts

God, through the prophet Joel, tells the people to repent from the heart and not just perform an external ritual. God wants us to have a deep inner experience of remorse for the sins we have committed. Mere words and confession cannot change a person. It is confession rooted in repentance that is powerful and effective.

Yet even now, says the Lord, return to me with all your heart, with fasting, with weeping, and with mourning; rend your hearts and not your clothing. (Joel 2:12-13)

Humble Yourselves

Repentance is an act of humility. The root of every sin is pride and to forsake our evil deeds and to return to God is a sign of humility in us.

If my people who are called by my name humble themselves, pray, seek my face, and turn from their wicked ways, then I will hear from heaven, and will forgive their sin and heal their land. (2 Chron 7:14)

Turn Back

If I am walking in a direction and I want to head in the opposite direction, I must first turn back and then start walking again. We must face our backs to sin and evil, and our eyes toward Jesus.

Turn back to the Lord and forsake your sins; pray in his presence and lessen your offense. Return to the Most High and turn away from iniquity, and hate intensely what he abhors. (Sir 17:25-26)

Return to God

Sin, by definition, is an act of walking away from God's love, whereas repentance is a journey back to God. The prodigal son in Luke, chapter 15, took the money that belonged to him and traveled to a distant country. The more a person sins and the longer he stays in that state, the more he goes away from God. Once the prodigal son comes back to his senses, he starts the process of repentance. He journeys toward his father. Repentance with confession is a journey toward our loving Father.

Repentance is Conversion

A person who has repented for his sins is no longer attracted to it. Change of heart leads to a change of mind, behavior, and attitude. People who do not repent or go through a conversion experience keep falling back into the same sin again and again. One may wonder; is God not powerful to free a man from his addictions? The answer is that the person is still attached to his sin deep within. No inner conversion has taken place.

Amend Your Ways

Our ways will change only when our heart changes. Sin is conceived deep in the heart. The human heart is the birthplace of sin. For our thoughts, words, and actions to improve, we must go through a change of our heart.

For it is from within, from the human heart, that evil intentions come: fornication, theft, murder. (Mrk 7:21)

God be Merciful to Me a Sinner

The sign of a repentant heart is the longing for God's mercy and forgiveness. We develop a deep thirst for his mercy and kindness. It is demonstrated in our ability to weep and pray. We begin to experience what is called "tears of repentance." The tax collector, mentioned in Luke, chapter 18, is an example of a man cut to the heart, longing, and pleading for God's mercy. This is true repentance.

The tax collector, standing far off, would not even look up to heaven, but was beating his breast and saying, 'God, be merciful to me, a sinner!' (Luk 18:13)

Hatred for Sin

We must develop a strong dislike and loathing for all things sinful. God hates sin, and he who abides in God must have the heart and mind of God and flee from sin. One who hates sin will flee from sin and avoid all sinful situations.

Flee from sin as from a snake; for if you approach sin, it will bite you. Its teeth are lion's teeth and can destroy human lives. (Sir 21:2)

Remove All Sinful Objects

This is another important step in repentance. It is a practical step of removing or getting rid of all those substances, objects, friendships, and lifestyle that cause us to fall into sin. Examples are; pornographic material, adult videos, bad company, tobacco products, alcohol, drugs, occult literature, occult objects, etc. Our repentance is ineffective if we still hold onto the object of sin, and we are more likely to fall into the same sin again.

You need always to exercise very great care and to avoid all occasions of sin and any kind of company which will not help you to get nearer to God. (St. Teresa of Ávila)

Practical Steps of Repentance

- Find a quiet place within your home. A spot where you usually pray
- Recall all the sins that the Holy Spirit showed you while you were examining your conscience
- If you have a piece of paper where all the sins are written down, read them in your mind
- Ask God sorry for all the sins you have committed
- Ask God sorry for walking away from his love
- Meditate on how much you hurt God with your sins, by looking at a crucifix in front of you
- Feel free to shed tears
- Resolve never to sin again
- Nurture a deep hatred for sin
- Resolve to put away all sinful objects and never associate with anything that leads to sin
- Resolve to avoid all people who tempt you to sin
- Accept all your weaknesses and surrender them to God
- Resolve never to leave God's presence and strive to live in his love every day by doing things pleasing to God
- Thank God for his love and mercy

- Read Psalm 51

Conclusion

God is pleased when we repent. In the gospel of Luke, Jesus says that the whole heaven rejoices when we repent. Understanding God and his love will help us go through a profound conversion experience, which will be covered in the next section.

God and Sinner

In this section, we will see the whole picture from God's perspective. It is God who created us and blessed us with everything, including our free will. Man uses his free will and chooses sin over God. God is hurt but sees man as helpless, therefore comes to his aid by sending his son. This is how the story opens in Genesis. It is essential for us to understand the person and personality of God. The story of the prodigal son is an excellent example of how all of us behave. We want to take what belongs to us and travel far away from God. Only when this man lost everything in life, did he repent for his sin. He began to understand the love of the Father. Without knowing the love and mercy of God, our repentance is incomplete. When we journey back to God, we strive to have a deeper understanding of God's love. God is not a police officer or a strict lawgiver. He is merciful, full of love, forgiving, and compassionate. Let us look at some of the traits of God as we prepare for our confession.

God Calls Every Sinner to Repent

Jesus shares three parables in the gospel of Luke, chapter 15, to make us understand how God reaches out to a sinner who is lost and helpless. In the first parable, the shepherd leaves the ninety-nine sheep and goes after the one sheep that is lost. This shows that every sinner is valuable in the eyes of the Father. The second parable is about a lost coin. Some of us are like the coin which cannot find its way back to the owner unless the owner searches for it. In the third parable, we see the father waiting expectantly for the son, showing us that our heavenly Father will also never forget about us and will wait eagerly for our return.

While he was still far off, his father saw him and was filled with compassion; he ran and put his arms around him and kissed him. (luk 15:20)

It is useful and vital to know that each time we go to confession, Jesus is already waiting there for us. Conversion of heart is the highest spiritual experience, and the whole heaven rejoices when a sinner returns to God.

God Hates Sin

God accepts the sinner, but not his sin. His outlook on sin has not changed since the beginning of creation. God hates sin, and he cannot and does not sin. He has not committed a single sin in all eternity. Sin is the nature of Satan, and those who cooperate with him yield to sin.

Do not say, "It was the Lord's doing that I fell away"; for he does not do what he hates. Do not say, "It was he who led me astray"; for he has no need of the sinful. The Lord hates all abominations; such things are not loved by those who fear him. (Sir 15:11-13)

God Does not Tempt

God does not tempt anyone, nor has he given anyone permission to sin. God is never the source of our sin. One may ask, why did not God stop me from sinning, or why does God allow sin and evil in this world. The answer to this question can be found in the Bible. Sin and death entered through the devil's envy. God, who created our free will, does not curb it or restrict it. He inspires us to be holy but never forces it on us.

He has not commanded anyone to be wicked, and he has not given anyone permission to sin. (Sir 15:20)

Additional Reading: Jas 1:13

God Does not Hate a Sinner

Jesus gave Judas the same treatment and importance that he gave to the other apostles. Jesus washed the feet of Judas and shared the Eucharistic meal with him. God does not hate us just because we have sinned. His love for us is unconditional. We are the apple of his eye, and every sinner is valuable to God. A sinner is so precious that God gave his only son to save him. Jesus did not die for the holy and righteous who needed no salvation, but for all sinners.

God proves his love for us in that while we still were sinners Christ died for us. (Rom 5:8)

God Convicts a Sinner and Does Not Condemn

God condemns our sinful deeds but never condemns us. He convicts us to forsake our sinfulness and return to him. God knows that we are weak and unable to overcome sin on our own. Therefore, he is very patient with every sinner by giving them many chances and opportunities to return to him. He draws every sinner to repentance, and he is never tired of reaching out to us.

Jesus said, "Neither do I condemn you. Go your way, and from now on do not sin again." (Jn 8:11)

Additional Reading: Ps 34:22, John 3:17

God is Merciful to the Sinner

If there is any weakness in God, that is his mercy. He is very merciful to every sinner. The sacrament of Reconciliation is a sign of God's abundant mercy, and he is compassionate to all those who cry to him. God understands human weaknesses, and he is able to sympathize with us.

For we do not have a high priest who is unable to sympathize with our weaknesses, but we have one who in every respect has been tested as we are, yet without sin. (Heb 4:15)

God Wants to Forgive Us

Our God is waiting to forgive us each time we plead for his mercy. He never withholds mercy and forgiveness to the sinner who approaches him. The prophet Isaiah writes that no matter how grave our sin is, God has the heart and power to forgive us. He values our fellowship. Therefore, it is essential that we are not shy or afraid to go to him for mercy and forgiveness.

Let us therefore approach the throne of grace with boldness, so that we may receive mercy and find grace to help in time of need. (Heb 4:16)

God Does Not Remember Our Past Sins

Man finds it hard to forget the sins committed by others, whereas God does not remember our sins once confessed. God deletes it from his memory forever and does not keep count of our confessed sins. God does not treat us based on our past actions or failures. The prophet Isaiah writes about this quality of God,

I, I am He who blots out your transgressions for my own sake, and I will not remember your sins. (Is 43:25)

St. Paul is saying the same words in his letter to the Hebrews,

I will be merciful toward their iniquities, and I will remember their sins no more. (Heb 8:12)

God Loves Us

This is the foremost quality of God that one must understand to grasp other truths about God and our Christian faith. If we cannot understand his love, it will be hard for us to understand all other revealed truths about God. God is love, and he cannot stop loving us. Love is his nature, hobby, occupation, passion, and everything. He loves us with all his heart. Every other trait and quality of God must be understood in the light of his love.

For the mountains may depart and the hills be removed, but my steadfast love shall not depart from you. (Is 54:10)

God Rejoices When We Repent

God grieves over a hardhearted person and the increasing sin and evil in this world. It breaks God's heart to see his children walking away from him and closer to their death. The wages of sin is death, and he who clings to sin clings to death. Jesus describing the atmosphere in heaven says that all the angels and the host of heavenly beings rejoice when a sinner repents.

There will be more joy in heaven over one sinner who repents than over ninety-nine righteous persons who need no repentance. (Luk 15:7)

Conclusion

Every sinner is valuable and important to God, which is what he demonstrated on the cross. Once we understand God's love and God's perspective, we have one more important area to focus before we can head to the confessional.

Forgiveness

Why should I forgive the person who hurt me, and how is it connected with my confession? Well, it has got everything to do with it. If we look closely at the Lord's prayer, what do we say about forgiveness? The words go like this, "forgive us our trespasses as we forgive those who trespass against us." Each time we do not forgive others and go and confess our sins, we tell God not to forgive us. At every Mass and at the confessional, Jesus offers forgiveness to all humanity. Jesus, on the cross, forgave all those who crucified him. He interceded for them and also asked God to forgive them. This is what God wants from us as well.

Then Jesus said, "Father, forgive them; for they do not know what they are doing." (Luk 23:34)

Unforgiveness is a major obstacle to our spiritual growth because it blocks the flow of love in us. Without love, we cannot attain holiness and sainthood. Below are some reasons why it is important to forgive others unconditionally.

Forgiveness and Prayer

Our prayers remain unanswered because of our unwillingness to forgive. Communion with God and neighbor go hand in hand. We cannot have one without the other. Forgiveness is not a sign of weakness, but it demonstrates our courage and humility. Jesus on the cross maintains a healthy relationship with his Father and at the same time, forgives all his enemies. Unforgiveness obstructs our faith. We read in the book of Sirach that when we overlook the wrong that others have done to us, our prayers will be heard, and our sins will be forgiven too.

Forgive your neighbor the wrong he has done, and then your sins will be pardoned when you pray. (Sir 28:2)

Forgiveness and God's Mercy

Each time we pray the Lord's Prayer, we use the words, "Forgive us our trespasses as we forgive those who trespass against us." In the true sense, we are telling God not to forgive our sins if we are not willing to forgive others. This is like cursing ourselves. Each time we go to confession and without releasing forgiveness to others, we waste our time because God has not forgiven us. God's love is unconditional; his forgiveness is not. Therefore, it is essential that we release forgiveness and God's love to all those who have hurt us.

For if you forgive others their trespasses, your heavenly Father will also forgive you; but if you do not forgive others, neither will your Father forgive your trespasses. (Matt 6:14)

Additional Reading: Sir 28:4

Forgiveness is Not an Option

Forgiveness is not an option in the kingdom of God. People who are unwilling to forgive cannot experience the love of God, although God loves and cares for them. They will cut themselves off from God by their refusal to forgive. Many of our sicknesses and problems in life are related to unforgiveness.

Be on your guard! If another disciple sins, you must rebuke the offender, and if there is repentance, you must forgive. (Luk 17:3)

A child of God cannot afford to live in hatred and bitterness. Every broken relationship is a sign of darkness and absence of love. Satan tries to take control of such people and expands his kingdom through them.

Anyone whom you have forgiven of anything, I also forgive. And then, too, anyone I have forgiven, if I have forgiven anything, it was done in the person of Christ for your sakes, so that we would not be circumvented by Satan. For we are not ignorant of his intentions. (2 Cor 2:10-11)

To Forgive is Important Than all the Spiritual Activities

All our devotions and sacrifices we make for the Lord will amount to nothing if there is unforgiveness in us. A Christian call cannot be answered without love. Jesus always invited people to come to him, but there is one place in the Bible where he tells us to make peace with our neighbor and then make the offering.

When you are offering your gift at the altar, if you remember that your brother or sister has something against you, leave your gift there before the altar and go; first be reconciled to your brother or sister, and then come and offer your gift. (Matt 5:23-24)

Always Forgive

Most of us confess the same sins repeatedly. We have our weaknesses and keep falling into the same sin again and again. Each time we confess, God forgives and accepts us with open arms. God is never tired of seeing us in the confessional. We find it hard to cope with people who repeatedly hurt us. At one point, we lose our ability to forgive them, but Jesus tells us to forgive as many times as it requires. God is willing to help us in this area if we are determined to forgive. The more we forgive, the more we become like Jesus.

Then Peter came and said to him, "Lord, if another member of the church sins against me, how often should I forgive? As many as seven times?" Jesus said to him, "Not seven times, but I tell you, seventy-seven times." (Matt 18:21-22)

The Sacrifice of Jesus Cannot Save Us

If we are stubborn and unwilling to forgive, even the sacrifice of Jesus cannot save us. There is a parable in the Gospel of Matthew called "The Parable of the Unforgiving Servant" where a man refuses to forgive his neighbor despite himself being excused by the king. This king, upon hearing this, revokes his forgiveness and sentences him to prison. Jesus concludes by saying that the kingdom of God works similarly.

If a mere mortal harbors wrath, who will make an atoning sacrifice for his sins? (Sir 28:5)

Additional Reading: Matt 18:35

Things to Avoid

Sin affects a man at various levels and those who fall victim to it also experience its after-effects, which manifests in one or more ways. How many of us can say that we are at total peace after having had an argument with our spouse or after having committed a mortal sin? We soon realize that our peace is taken away, and we are troubled and disturbed. In this section, we will deal with some of the consequences of sin and why one should not fall prey to it.

Guilt

Guilt is an emotional experience one goes through because of committing a sin or action or inaction. Guilt is different from repentance. Guilt is a feeling of hopelessness, whereas repentance is full of hope. Repentance frees us from sin and leads us to God, whereas guilt traps us and condemns us. A sinner should always look to Jesus for hope. The blood of Jesus is more powerful than all our sins. There is no sin that God cannot forgive. Satan tries to trap us in his chains of guilt, shame, and condemnation. He will not succeed if we keep our focus on Jesus.

For godly grief produces a repentance that leads to salvation and brings no regret, but worldly grief produces death. (2 Cor 7:10)

An excellent example in the Bible is the case of Peter and Judas. Peter denied Jesus and Judas betrayed Jesus. Both sins are forgivable by God, and in fact, Jesus did forgive Judas even before he died. We read that Peter was saved and went on with his mission, but Judas took his own life. Why was one saved and the other not? The answer lies in what kind of grief they expressed. Peter expressed godly sorrow and repentance that led to his salvation, whereas Judas was trapped in guilt. Guilt leads to hatred of self. We condemn ourselves and feel unworthy and unloved.

Self-hatred

Self-hatred is another trap laid for sinners, and those who are not secure in God's love fall prey to it. We should hate the sin we commit but never once hate ourselves. God hates the sin but loves the sinner. This should be our attitude as well. Self-hatred can take us deeper into a life of sin and evil. There may be habits and addictions in us that is controlling or enslaving us for an awfully long time. We may even be loathing ourselves for lack of strength. We may be in a state where we love God very much, but some hidden sin is always pulling us away from God. In addition to frequent confession, we must also learn to accept our weaknesses and surrender them to God to find freedom. God's grace is enough for us, and his power is made perfect in our weaknesses.

There is an excellent example in the Bible on this topic. Joseph, in the Old Testament, was sold by his brothers into slavery. They even tried to kill him. Joseph ended up in Egypt, and after years of suffering and trials, became the second most powerful person there. His brothers, on the other hand, having lost everything in a bitter famine, came knocking at Joseph's door. At first, they did not recognize him. Later, Joseph revealed himself to them. They were filled with guilt and self-hatred. It is then that Joseph consoled and encouraged them with these words,

Do not be distressed, or angry with yourselves, because you sold me here; for God sent me before you to preserve life. (Gen 45:5)

Joseph saw divine purpose behind all his sufferings and the harm done to him, whereas his brothers were stuck in guilt and self-hatred.

Self-Condemnation

Every sinner has a future with God. It is important that we learn to leave behind the things of the past and move forward in love. Moving forward means to move closer to God. Sin tends to hold us back and keep us away from God's presence. We blame ourselves in despair without looking at Jesus and his sacrifice for us. This is self-condemnation. Jesus forgave the woman caught in the act of adultery and told her that he did not condemn her, and St. Paul is repeating these words in the book of Romans.

There is therefore now no condemnation for those who are in Christ Jesus. For the law of the Spirit of life in Christ Jesus has set you free from the law of sin and of death. (Rom 8:1-2)

Unworthiness

We try to find our worth and value in the amount of money we have, our good looks, the educational qualifications we have earned, the size of our house, our achievements, accomplishments, and so on. No wonder, we are holding onto these things and derive our joy and peace from it. We do good things, and we feel happy about ourselves. When we sin, we feel unworthy and valueless. This is not how God looks at us. We are valuable to the Father just as we are. God loves us very much, and we are of so much value to him that he sent his only son to save us. We should boast of the cross and tell the world how each one of us is valuable to the Father. Sin does not diminish our self-worth for we are the apple of his eye.

For even if we sin, we are yours, knowing your power;
but we will not sin, because we know that you acknowledge us as yours. (Wis 15:2)

Additional Reading: Matt 6:26, Is 43:4, Luk 12:6-7

Feeling Unloved

Our definition of love comes primarily from our parents and family. No matter how loving they were, we were trained and raised in human love. Human love is conditional and has its limitations. Our mood, selfishness, self-centeredness, and many other factors influence our ability to love, and it is far from perfect. With this weak understanding of love, we enter a relationship with God. We treat God like a human being. It is very natural that If I do something terrible to you, you may not talk to me or take my calls or respond to my emails. We are used to this treatment, and we are prepared to face it. Coming back to our relationship with God; we feel that every time we sin, God is unhappy and will not love and accept us. As a result, we feel unloved. This is a wrong approach toward God. He is not human, and he does not behave like us. His love for us never diminishes. It is unconditional, everlasting, and steadfast. He loves us with all his heart.

The steadfast love of the Lord never ceases, his mercies never come to an end; they are new every morning; great is your faithfulness. (Lam 3:22-23)

Shame

One of the consequences of sin is that it brings a sense of shame upon the person. When Adam and Eve were created, they were naked, and their nakedness did not bother them. They were not ashamed to come before each other and God in a state of nudity. Sin changed everything. They became self-conscious. Sin turned man from a God-conscious person to a self-conscious person. Adam and Eve hid from God. People living a life of sin are away from God and the Church. They have stopped praying, going for Mass and confession. In short, man continuous to hide from God.

Spiritual Dryness

Spiritual dryness or spiritual drought is the absence of emotions during prayer. For example, if we meet a person we like or love, there is a sudden increase in feelings. We feel thrilled or jubilant. There are also people that may cause us to feel sad or angry. Our emotions are triggered, and it is a good sign. Spiritual dryness is a state where we are emotionally absent when we engage in religious matters. A state where prayer does not excite or thrill us. One of the reasons for lack of consolation in prayer is sin. It is a reality for not just those who sin, but also for the saintly and holy people. Many of the saints have gone through this experience. In this section, we will focus only on the dryness because of sin.

Then they will cry to the Lord, but he will not answer them; he will hide his face from them at that time, because they have acted wickedly. (Mic 3:5)

Your sins have hidden his face from you so that he does not hear. (Is 59:2)

We should never give in to dryness but persist and persevere in prayer even if we have fallen out of grace. A sinner should not lose heart. God came to save sinners like you and me. Therefore we should not get deterred by anything that tries to separate us from God.

Additional Reading: Is 59:2

Conclusion

Repentance is the key to a good confession and freedom from sin. Now that we have covered all the major areas, we are ready to make the trip to the Church and confess our sins. The next chapter focuses on the Sacrament of Reconciliation. It will help us rediscover the validity and the power of the sacrament.

Sacrament of Reconciliation (Confession)

Confession is an act of honesty and courage – an act of entrusting ourselves, beyond sin, to the mercy of a loving and forgiving God. (Pope John Paul II)[10]

What Is the Sacrament of Reconciliation?

- The sacrament of reconciliation is also known as confession or penance service
- It is one of the seven sacraments of the Catholic Church
- At confession, we receive pardon and forgiveness from God for the sins committed and are reconciled with God and his Church
- Confession, though an external act reflects the interior conversion of a sinner
- Confession is to be made use by Catholics as often as possible.
- Confession is done in person to a priest and not over phone or email
- Confession brings remission of the eternal punishment incurred by mortal sins
- The Sacrament of Reconciliation consists of three steps; Repentance, disclosure of sins to the priest, and reparation
- All mortal sins must be confessed to a priest in order to be forgiven. Confession of venial sins is also recommended

Why Should I Confess My Sins to A Priest?

We confess our sins to a priest, first and foremost, because Jesus said so. The tradition of confessing one's sins to a priest comes from two scriptures in the Gospels where Jesus gives this authority to the apostles and their successors.

And I say to you, that you are Peter, and upon this rock I will build my Church, and the gates of Hell shall not prevail against it. And I will give you the keys of the kingdom of heaven. And whatever you shall bind on earth shall be bound even in heaven. And whatever you shall release on earth shall be released, even in heaven." (Matt 16:18-19)

He said to them again: "Peace to you. As the Father has sent me, so I send you." When he had said this, he breathed on them. And he said to them: "Receive the Holy Spirit. Those whose sins you shall forgive, they are forgiven them, and those whose sins you shall not forgive them, they are not forgiven." (Jn 20:21-23)

If we look closely at the above verse in the Gospel of John, chapter 20, Jesus says, "as the Father has sent me (to forgive sins), so I send you (to forgive sins)." It is an extension of Jesus's ministry, and Christ himself gives a priest this power. Therefore, this practice is biblical and also commissioned by God. The Catechism goes on to say that it is God, in the person of the priest, who forgives our sins.

Only God forgives sins. Since he is the Son of God, Jesus says of himself, "The Son of man has authority on earth to forgive sins" and exercises this divine power: "Your sins are forgiven. "Further, by virtue of his divine authority he gives this power to men to exercise in his name." (CCC 1441)

Jesus has also made appearances to saints in which he stresses the importance of confession. Through a vision to St. Faustina, he communicates the validity of the Sacrament of Confession.

My daughter, just as you prepare in My presence, so also you make your confession before Me. The person of the priest is, for Me, only a screen. Never analyze what sort of a priest it is that I am making use of; open your soul in confession as you would to Me, and I will fill it with My light. (St. Faustina, Diary, 1725)

Scripture is again confirming this in St. Paul's letter to the Corinthians.

So if anyone is in Christ, there is a new creation: everything old has passed away; see, everything has become new! All this is from God, who reconciled us to himself through Christ, and has given us the ministry of reconciliation; that is, in Christ God was reconciling the world to himself, not counting their trespasses against them, and entrusting the message of reconciliation to us. So, we are ambassadors for Christ, since God is making his appeal through us; we entreat you on behalf of Christ, be reconciled to God. (2 Cor 5:17-20, NRSVCE)

Is Confession Biblical?

Confession, like every other Church doctrine and sacrament, is biblical and can be traced back to the old testament times. Jesus, himself instituted this sacrament. There is evidence from both the Old and New Testament about the practice and authenticity of the sacrament of confession. Confession has always existed in some form or other because without it, repentance is not complete.

David Confesses to Nathan

The incident where King David confesses to Nathan is a classic example of a person confessing to a man of God or prophet. Nathan was sent by God to counsel David after the latter had committed adultery and murder. David, upon coming to his senses, confesses the sin to Nathan.

David said to Nathan, "I have sinned against the Lord." And Nathan said to David: "The Lord has also taken away your sin. You shall not die. (2 Sam 12:13)

People Confessed in the Presence of John the Baptist

People came to John the Baptist, who was the forerunner of Christ, to be baptized by him. They also confessed their sins. He prepared them to receive Jesus. Similarly, we too receive Jesus in the Eucharist by baptism and confession.

People went out to him from all the region of Judea and all those of Jerusalem, and they were baptized by him in the river Jordan, confessing their sins. (Mrk 1:5)

People Confessed Their Occult Practices Publicly

The early Christians, who converted from other faiths and communities, openly confessed their sins by disclosing their shady practices.

Many who became believers confessed and disclosed their practices. Then many of those who had practiced magic brought together their books, and they burned them in the sight of all. (Acts 19:18-19)

Zacchaeus Makes his Confession to Jesus

Zacchaeus was a tax collector and a greedy man. He unfairly collected taxes from the public. In Luke, chapter 19, we read that Zacchaeus, upon knowing that Jesus was passing by, was curious to see him. Jesus surprises him by asking if he could stay at his house. Zacchaeus is touched by the words of Jesus and repents of all his sins. He makes his confession to Jesus and also makes restitution for the damage he had caused to others.

Zacchaeus stood there and said to the Lord, "Look, half of my possessions, Lord, I will give to the poor; and if I have defrauded anyone of anything, I will pay back four times as much." (Luk 19:8)

Confession of Sins in the Temple During Baruch's Time

It was a frequent practice during the Old Testament days to have public repentance services on special occasions. Kings and prophets, when they needed a special favor or divine intervention, would call the whole land to fast and pray as a sign of repentance. The temple used to be the meeting place of the Jews, and people would openly weep, wail, and repent for their sins. The below verse taken from the book of Baruch, speaks about repentance and confession and its origin from the old testament days.

Pray also for us to the Lord our God, for we have sinned against the Lord our God, and to this day the anger of the Lord and his wrath have not turned away from us. And you shall read aloud this scroll that we are sending you, to make your confession in the house of the Lord on the days of the festivals and at appointed seasons. (Bar 1:13)

Blessings and Graces in Confession

Confession and Holiness

Confession is a sacrament, or an outward sign instituted by Jesus to pour his graces upon us. Confession, like every other sacrament, puts us on the path of holiness. Every sacrament is an encounter with Jesus. We meet Jesus in the confessional, who sanctifies us and makes us holy.

"Do you want to become saints? Here is the secret: confession is the lock; confidence in your confessor is the key. This is how you open heaven's gates." (St. John Bosco)

Confession is an Act of Conversion

The prodigal son decided to get up and go to his father and confess his sins. This act is necessary for conversion. Conversion, although an inner experience, is supported by a physical sign. Confessing our sins with our mouth is an act of letting go of our sins and not holding on to them.

I will get up and go to my father, and I will say to him, "Father, I have sinned against heaven and before you; I am no longer worthy to be called your son; treat me like one of your hired hands." (Luk 15:18-19)

Confession Frees Us

Confession frees us from the fangs or chains of sin. Sin enslaves us into bondage while, repentance and confession open us to freedom. A person who frequently falls into the same sin should keep confessing until that sin is defeated and kicked out of his life.

Our Lord himself I saw in this venerable sacrament. ... I felt as if my chains fell, as those of St. Peter at the touch of the Divine messenger. My God, what new scenes for my soul! (St. Elizabeth Ann Seton)

Confession Strengthens Us

We sin because we are weak. Confession strengthens our conscience and helps fight evil and sinful tendencies. Frequent confession is a sign of humility and dependence on God in times of weaknesses.

Indeed, the regular confession of our venial sins helps us form our conscience, fight against evil tendencies, let ourselves be healed by Christ and progress in the life of the Spirit. (CCC 1458)

It Restores Peace in Us

Sin gives Satan access to our life and our blessings. It gives him permission to steal, kill, plunder, and destroy us. A sinner can never be at peace. Peace is one of the first fruits we lose to sin. In the book of Genesis, there is a story about two brothers, Cain and Abel. At some point, Cain became jealous of Abel and murdered him. Cain, after killing Abel, was very disturbed and troubled. We get back in confession what we lose to sin; namely joy, happiness, and peace. The psalmist also confirms this.

While I kept silence, my body wasted away through my groaning all day long. (Ps 32:3)

Confession Heals Us

If sin brought sickness into this world, Jesus, through his sacraments, brought healing to this world. The wages of sin are sickness and death, whereas Jesus came to save us from death and eternal damnation. In the gospel of Mark, Jesus heals a person with paralysis by forgiving his sins. In other words, when Jesus speaks the words of absolution, the person with paralysis receives instant healing.

Confess your sins to one another, and pray for one another, so that you may be healed. (Jas 5:16)

The Lord Jesus Christ, physician of our souls and bodies, who forgave the sins of the paralytic and restored him to bodily health, has willed that his Church continue, in the power of the Holy Spirit, his work of healing and salvation, even among her own members. This is the purpose of the two sacraments of healing: the sacrament of Penance and the sacrament of Anointing of the Sick. (CCC 1421)

Confession Gives us an Encounter with Jesus

Jesus is accessible to every sinner, and he is aptly called the friend of sinners. Jesus eagerly waits for us at the confessional, and he reconciles us with the Father and gives us a new life by paying the price himself. Every confession is an opportunity for us to meet Jesus and commune with him.

When you approach the confessional, know this, that I Myself am waiting there for you. I am only hidden by the priest but I Myself act in your soul. (St. Faustina, Diary, 1602)

Confession and Forgiveness of Sins

Confession gives the assurance of God's forgiveness. If we pay attention to the Gospels, Jesus spoke the words of forgiveness to the sinners who came to him for healing and mercy. It makes a substantial difference when the words of forgiveness are spoken to us. In the confessional, the priest acting in the person of Jesus speaks the words of absolution. This prayer is a guarantee and assurance of God's forgiveness. We come out forgiven, restored, healed, and united with God.

If we confess our sins, he who is faithful and just will forgive us our sins and cleanse us from all unrighteousness. (1 Jn 1:9)

Confession Brings the Mercy of God Upon Us

Every sin demands the judgment of God, yet God is merciful to the sinner and willing to reconcile with him. If a man is willing to amend his ways, he will see and experience the mercy of God in his life. God is in the business of saving man from his wickedness, and he uses confession to accomplish this.

No one who conceals transgressions will prosper, but one who confesses and forsakes them will obtain mercy. (Pro 28:13)

Confession Restores our Fellowship with God and Man

The story of the prodigal son shows us the heart of the Father and his forgiving and generous love. Upon seeing his son, the father wastes no time and restores his sonship and inheritance. This is precisely what happens at each confession. We get back all that sin stole from us.

The father said to his slaves, 'Quickly, bring out a robe – the best one – and put it on him; put a ring on his finger and sandals on his feet. (Luk 15:22)

Confession Helps us to Fight Sin

Confession is an act of humility, and those who humble themselves receive grace from God to overcome sin and evil. Confession is a weapon for us to fight Satan and his tactics. Each time we confess our sins, Satan is defeated, and his power over us diminishes.

Confession Frees us From Guilt

Sin brings guilt with it. Guilt is a powerful weapon used by Satan to keep us in chains. Many people are trapped in guilt because of some grave sin they committed in the past. Thanks to God for the sacrament of confession, which not only brings pardon and forgiveness but takes away the guilt associated with it. He who confesses his sin receives freedom also from the guilt associated with it.

Then I acknowledged my sin to you, and I did not hide my iniquity; I said, "I will confess my transgressions to the Lord," and you forgave the guilt of my sin. (Ps 32:5)

How to Confess Our Sins

You may kneel and not reveal yourself to the priest or sit face-to-face with the priest. The Church does not permit remote confession either over the phone or through the media.

- Begin your confession with the sign of the cross (In the name of the Father, and the Son, and the Holy Spirit, Amen)
- Bless me, Father, for I have sinned. My last confession was______ (days/weeks/months/years) ago.
- List out your sins. You may use the paper where you have written down all the sins. Confess all the sins and how many times you committed them.
- Conclude by saying, "I am sorry for these sins and the sins I fail to remember."
- Wait for the priest's advice. Listen carefully to what the priest has to say. Most priests encourage the sinner by drawing them out of guilt and taking them to the love and mercy of God. They may also suggest or give some practical advice to overcome certain sins.

Act of Contrition

At this time, the priest will ask the penitent to recite the act of contrition. Some priests may ask the repentant to say this prayer along with the penance, outside the confessional. This prayer is essential and must be recited at some point, either in the confessional or when saying the penance, because it opens our heart to God. It is our way of telling God that we have hurt and wounded him and would like to return to him. There is more than one form of this prayer. One may choose whichever kind one is comfortable praying. The prayer goes like this,

O my God, I am heartily sorry for having offended Thee, and I detest all my sins because of Thy just punishments, but most of all because they offend Thee, my God, who art all-good and deserving of all my love. I firmly resolve, with the help of Thy grace, to sin no more and to avoid the near occasions of sin.

or

My God, I am sorry for my sins with all my heart. In choosing to do wrong and failing to do good, I have sinned against you whom I should love above all things. I firmly intend, with your help, to do penance, to sin no more, and to avoid whatever leads me to sin. Our Savior Jesus Christ suffered and died for us. In his name, my God, have mercy.

or

O my God, I am heartily sorry for having offended you, and I detest all my sins because I dread the loss of heaven and the pains of hell. But most of all because I have offended you, my God, who are all good and deserving of all my love. I firmly resolve with the help of your grace, to confess my sins, to do penance and to amend my life. Amen.

The above prayer is simple, but a complete prayer of repentance. We will break it down for better understanding.

- The prayer is addressed to God
- We are sorry for our sins
- We imply that this prayer is coming from the heart
- We agree that we have hurt God with our actions (sins)
- We hate sin just as God does
- God is just in his punishment
- We have rejected his love by falling into sin
- We resolve not to sin again
- We ask for his grace to live a life without sin
- We will avoid the near occasion of sin
- We will love God above all things
- We will do penance for the sins we have committed
- We are pleading for God's mercy

Penance

Followed by the act of contrition, the priest will give a penance to the penitent. It is an exercise for the spiritual good of the repentant. Penance can be in the form of a prayer, namely; the Our Father, the Hail Mary or any prayer that the priest may recommend offering it for the victim of sin if there is any. Some priests recommend reading a chapter of the Psalms or other books in the Bible. Others may instruct the penitent to spend some quiet time in front of the Blessed Sacrament. It is up to the priest at the confessional.

Go to your confessor; open your heart to him; display to him all the recesses of your soul; take the advice that he will give you with the utmost humility and simplicity. For God, who has an infinite love for obedience, frequently renders profitable the counsels we take from others, but especially from those who are the guides of our souls. (St. Francis de Sales)

Absolution and Final Blessing

Finally, the priest will recite the prayer of absolution. To absolve is to free someone from guilt or blame or sin. At this time, the penitent listens carefully to the words of the priest. The formula is universal and goes like this.

God, the Father of mercies, through the death and the resurrection of his Son has reconciled the world to himself and sent the Holy Spirit among us for the forgiveness of sins; through the ministry of the Church may God give you pardon and peace, and I absolve you from your sins in the name of the Father, and of the Son and of the Holy Spirit.

The above prayer can be broken down for better understanding

- God, the Father of mercies, is the source of all forgiveness
- God makes this forgiveness possible by the death and resurrection of Jesus
- God brings sinners back by the working of the Holy Spirit
- God uses the prayer and the ministry of the Church to reconcile sinners back to him

Thank the priest and leave the confessional. Find a quiet corner in the church. If the Blessed Sacrament is exposed, you may sit before the Lord or sit where the tabernacle is located. Do the penance with all sincerity. Thanking the Lord for his mercy and forgiveness is an excellent way to conclude. A sample prayer is included below.

Prayer of Thanksgiving

O Almighty and merciful God, whose mercy is boundless, and the riches of whose goodness are infinite, I give Thee thanks with all my mind and heart for the amazing and exceeding goodness which Thou hast now shown me in so graciously pardoning all my sins and restoring me to Thy grace and favor. Blessed be Thy Divine compassion, O my God, and blessed be the incomprehensible love of Thy beloved Son, which constrained Him to institute so gentle and so mighty a remedy for our sins. Wherefore, in union with all the thanksgivings which have ever ascended to Thee from truly penitent hearts, I sing aloud Thy glad praises on behalf of all in Heaven, on earth, and in Purgatory, forever and ever. Amen. (St. Gertrude the Great)

Do's and Don'ts of Confession

Do Not Justify Your Sins

We tend to justify our actions, and this is one of the main reasons why we do not get total freedom from sin. We either minimize the seriousness of our sins or find something or somebody to put the blame. We are not willing to take full responsibility for our thoughts, words, and actions, and as a result, our confession is insincere and ineffective. Adam, when he was questioned, blamed it on God and Eve. Eve on her part blamed it on the devil. We continue to blame others and God for our sins. The truth is, we are weak and do not call on God in times of temptations. Hence, we sin. Below are some of the excuses that people give.

- I did not know it was a sin
- Everybody in the world is doing it
- The Christian laws are too old and not applicable to our times
- The other person tempted me
- It is legal
- It does not harm anyone
- It relaxes me and gives me peace
- This is how I am
- The other person or the situation provoked me
- Life is meant to be enjoyed
- Where does it say that it is a sin?
- I lost control

The problem of justifying and blaming others started with our very first parents. The Book of Genesis has a detailed narrative of the fall of Adam and Eve and the consequence of their sin. Let us look at the verse where Adam makes a false confession.

The man said, "The woman whom you gave to be with me, she gave me fruit from the tree, and I ate." Then the Lord God said to the woman, "What is this that you have done?" The woman said, "The serpent tricked me, and I ate." (Gen 3:12-13)

Do Not Confess Without Repentance and Preparation

Confession, like other spiritual activities, can at times become mechanical. We are very quick to confess our sins without proper repentance and examination of conscience. Most of the time, we are not sure of what to admit. We make a quick list on the way to the confessional. As a result, we repeat the same sins and confess repeatedly without any remorse. We profess and confess our faith with our lips, but our hearts are far from God.

Repentance should be part of our daily prayer activity. Each day, if we examine ourselves and see where we have fallen and feel sorry for those areas, we will go closer to the Lord. Repentance is a quality most pleasing to the Lord, as mentioned in the Bible many times.

A sin that is not quickly blotted out by repentance is both a sin and a cause of sin. (Pope St. Gregory the Great)

Do Not be Too Detailed About Sin

This is another mistake people make in the confessional. We are not in the confessional to tell our stories to the priest. The more we speak, the more we tend to justify and deviate from the truth. The advice is, keep the confession short and spend more time in repentance. Sadly, we do the very opposite. Our confessions are long with little or no remorse outside of it.

Do Not Leave Out Any Sin

Sin is like cancer. Just as cancer can grow back if not entirely removed, sin and sinful tendencies can also return if not thoroughly dealt with. The book of Sirach compares sin with a deadly and poisonous snake. Just as we would not rest until we kill the snake that has entered our house, so should we deal with sin. We forget some of the major sins we have committed and remember the smallest sins or injustice perpetrated against us. A good practice is to keep a journal and write down the sins committed daily.

In failing to confess, Lord, I would only hide You from myself, not myself from You. (St. Augustine)

Do Not be Afraid to Go to a Familiar Priest

We are people who care about our reputation and value in front of others. Some of us find it hard to confess to a familiar priest, namely one's own parish priest. A priest is a servant of God and fully understands the weak and sinful nature of man. A priest is one among us and one like us with weaknesses and frailties. There is no judgment in the confessional, only love and mercy. Hiding sins from a known priest can also be a sign of pride in us.

A confessor is there to help us grow closer to God. Another problem with sin is, it is most powerful when it is hidden. Sin brought to light loses its power. Opening our heart to a priest we know will bring our sin to view and give us strength and power over it.

For once you were darkness, but now in the Lord you are light. Live as children of light. (Eph 5:8)

Do Not Postpone Your Confession

We put off our confession for some silly and trivial reasons. Some of us do not know what to confess, and most of us have not experienced the power of this sacrament. Busy schedule, laziness, lack of faith, lack of knowledge, and other reasons add to why we are not regular. An age-old way of knowing something or understanding it lies in spending time with it. The same applies to confession. The problem lies not solely with us, but our parents are also partly responsible for our actions. This habit or tradition of going to regular confession was not nurtured in us by our parents. Our parents knew well about the importance of brushing the teeth every morning. Therefore, they trained us very well to brush our teeth every day. They prepared us very well in areas where they were enlightened. Sadly, their knowledge of the sacrament of confession was feeble, and therefore, it was not enforced in our lives. I have said this not to blame it on our parents, but to throw some light into our spiritual condition. It is never too late to develop a new habit. I started going for regular weekly confessions only after I turned 30. It has been that way ever since. Every visit to the confessional is a life-changing event for me. The writer of the book of Sirach is urging us not to delay or postpone our confession.

Do not delay to turn back to the Lord, and do not postpone it from day to day. (Sir 5:7)

Additional Reading: Jer 6:26

Do Not Receive Communion in a State of Mortal Sin

The Eucharist is our food, our strength, and above all, our God. Jesus deserves a holy place. We, the tabernacle, cannot be defiled under any circumstance. Jesus knowing our fallen nature has given us a way to cleanse ourselves so that we can have full communion with him in the Eucharist. We wound Jesus every time we receive him in an unworthy manner. Jesus is unable to unleash his full power in us because a part of us is still in sin. There are faithful Catholics who will never receive communion on Sundays without first confessing their sins. I remember a rule that was followed at my home when I was a child. Every evening, after we returned home after playtime, my grandmother would refuse to serve us dinner without first taking a shower. We were never allowed even to touch anything at home before a nice shower. Confession is our spiritual shower, and Eucharist is our food. So, no food without a proper shower.

Additional Reading: CCC 1385

Confess Only Your Sins, Not Problems

Some of us confuse confession with counseling. The confessional is not a place to open our problems and sufferings to the priest. The purpose of this sacrament is to receive pardon and peace for a sinner who has broken communion with God. Sin and only sin should be disclosed and discussed in a confessional.

Do not Confess the Sins of Others

Some of us have the habit of making a group confession. We are particularly good at confessing the sins of people who have hurt us or who are being mean to us. We are more focused on what evil the other person has done to us. If you ever sit for a counseling session for couples, you will notice that the husband lists out all the sins and wrongdoings of the wife and the wife does the same about the husband. In the confessional, it is vital that we take full responsibility for our sins and stick to our sins alone.

Be Mindful of the Priest's Time and Others in Line

There are over 1.2 billion Catholics today. Leaving out the population who are below the age of receiving the sacrament, it still leaves us with close to a billion Catholics worldwide. The number of priests currently serving is close to half a million (500,000). A sizable number of them may not be working in dioceses or parishes. Let us do the math. If every Catholic were to go for weekly confession, a priest must listen to over 2000 confessions every week. Why am I giving these figures? Merely to put forward the fact that a priest's time is valuable. We should in no way waste a priest's time and also be mindful of the people who are in line waiting to confess their sins. By discussing matters other than sin, we are guilty of stealing the priest's and people's time.

Be Considerate with Your Priest

There are times when we are desperate to go for confession only to find that there is no priest available or the priest turns down our request owing to prior commitments. We may even feel angry toward the priest and the Church. One must understand that hearing confession is not the only job of the priest. Every parish has a window for the parishioners to make their confessions, and they should make use of this opportunity unless it is a matter of life and death to confess their sins before this allotted time.

If in Doubt, Confess

Not all sins can be marked as either mortal or venial. The situation and other factors decide the gravity of sin. For example, murder and killing in a battle are not the same though both involve killing another human being. The best way to deal with it is by asking the priest in the confessional.

Do Not be Ashamed to Confess

Remember that a priest's life involves hearing the sins of other people. Our sins are in no way going to surprise or shock the priest. We should not be ashamed to confess our sins. Holiness and freedom from sin are more important than reputation. We should be ashamed of sinning, not confessing them. No sin is more powerful than the blood of Jesus.

Do not be ashamed to confess your sins. (Sir 4:26)

Do Not Hide Your Sins

Let us imagine we are standing in line for confession, and when it is our turn, we come in face to face with a familiar priest. What is our attitude? Do we go on with our confession that we had prepared or quickly hide some sins that we do not want to confess? Some of us may be familiar with what I am talking about. A church is not a human institution, and the sacrament of confession is not a human-made tradition. Every hidden or concealed sin comes back to overpower and master us. It is to Jesus we confess, and it is Jesus who forgives our sins at the confessional.

Have you sinned, my child? Do so no more, but ask forgiveness for your past sins. (Sir 21:1)

False and insincere confession

Exaggeration of sins, diminishing the gravity of our sins, lying in the confessional, failure to do penance, and lack of repentance is what is called an insincere confession. Lying in the confessional is the same as lying to God.

Make an Effort to Come Out of Sin

All our spiritual activities, including confession, will be fruitless without repentance and contrition of heart. Every confession should be seen as the last and the only opportunity to return to God. Confession is not a license to sin.

Do not say, "I sinned, yet what has happened to me?" for the Lord is slow to anger. Do not be so confident of forgiveness that you add sin to sin. (Sir 5:4-5)

Additional Reading: Sir 34:31

Humility in Confession

Every sin is a result of pride. Pride is the root of all sin. Repentance, which is the opposite of sin is a way of expressing our humility. In the Gospel of Luke, we read about two people who come to the temple to pray. The Pharisee was boasting about his spiritual life, whereas the tax collector would not even look up to heaven but was beating his chest and asking for God's mercy. A sinner needs God's mercy. God hears the prayer of the humble and resists the proud.

Do not Confess the Same Sins Repeatedly

Some of us have the habit of confessing the same sin repeatedly, although we do not commit that sin anymore. We are ridden by guilt and find it hard to come out of the memories associated with past sins. We are not fully assured of God's mercy and forgiveness. There is a beautiful promise given in the book of Isaiah, which tells us that God's mercy is more powerful than all our sins.

Come now, let us argue it out, says the Lord: though your sins are like scarlet, they shall be like snow; though they are red like crimson, they shall become like wool. (Is 1:18)

Do I Willingly go for Confession?

God wants us to have a deep love for him in and through the sacraments. We as Catholics are called to develop a deep and personal relationship with Jesus in the sacraments, namely, the sacraments of Eucharist and Reconciliation. Without love for the sacraments, it is difficult to grow in it.

When is There a Need for Confession?

All Catholics who have received the sacrament of penance should go for confession whenever they have committed a mortal sin. Confession of venial sins is also strongly recommended by the Church.

All mortal sins of which penitents after a diligent self-examination are conscious must be recounted by them in confession, even if they are most secret and have been committed against the last two precepts of the Decalogue; for these sins sometimes wound the soul more grievously and are more dangerous than those which are committed openly. (CCC 1456)

How Frequently Must I go for Confession?

Regular weekly confession is recommended to maintain a healthy spiritual life. There are practices and advice we can follow from saints' and popes' lives. For example, Pope John Paul II confessed his sins almost every week. All the saints we know of had a deep love for this sacrament and made use of this sacrament often.

It would be illusory to desire to reach holiness – according to the vocation that each one has received from God – without partaking frequently of this sacrament of conversion and sanctification. (Pope St. John Paul II)[9]

I did not Commit any Sin to Confess

If you have not committed any sin since your last confession, please email us your information. The entire world needs to know who you are, and you deserve to be honored along with Jesus and Mary. All of us have sinned and fallen short of the glory of God. If we claim that we have no sin in us, it makes us a liar, and God is not abiding in us.

If we say that we have no sin, we deceive ourselves, and the truth is not in us. (1 Jn 1:8)

Additional Reading: Rom 3:23, Rom 3:10

That brings us to the question, why we are not able to see our sins. In the next section, we will look at some reasons why.

Knowledge of Sin

Be in the world and not of the world and be filled with divine wisdom and not just the knowledge that comes from this world. God created the world and the things around us, and he has given us specific guidelines about the use and care of everything in this life. For example, we sometimes see that a product comes with a warranty, and if the product is handled in a way other than recommended by the company, the warrant becomes invalid. Similarly, life and the laws of this life are given to us by God. We are unable to see sin in us because we are busy looking at the world around us and trying to adapt and imitate its ways. Our moral standards are dictated by the secular and liberal environment around us.

When I was a child, my mother used to force me to go for confession every week. Sometimes I used to argue that I had not committed any sin since my previous confession. It was later in life that I understood why I could not come up with any sin to confess. As a young man, I started to question the purpose and meaning of life. It was in Jesus that I found the answer to all my questions. We came from God, and we are going back to God. We are here in this life to fulfill his will and to be obedient to him. His laws are for our good.

Self-Justification

We go to great lengths to justify our actions and behavior, although we are wrong most of the time. Our practice is sometimes contrary to our beliefs. We rationalize our mistakes, and at some point, we fail to differentiate between right and wrong. Every passing generation is moving farther and farther away from God, and our moral and ethical standards are deteriorating drastically. Each one has become his own God. For example, the institution of marriage has been in existence long before any of the present forms of government or kingdoms emerged. Therefore, no one has the right to alter it or tweak it according to their needs. Sadly, people today are trying to define what marriage is. People want to live together without any commitment. Marriage is no longer just the union of a man and a woman. Younger people are no longer attracted to marriage and are postponing it well into their thirties and forties. Cohabitation, free union, trial marriage, and live-in relationships have become the norm of our times. If the law of the land allows it, I have the right to do it, is the attitude of many.

Self-Righteousness

To be self-righteous is having a feeling that we are entirely correct or morally superior. We rate people based on the sins that they have committed and have placed ourselves in the highest position of that chart. According to us, rapists, terrorists, murderers, and child abusers are at the lowest level. We are also glad that we are not like them. People we do not like are also placed at a level below us. We are pleased with our lifestyle and the way we treat others. We are content with what we do with our time and money. We are proud of the way we attend to our family needs. It is this approach to our life that also prevents us from seeing our sinfulness. Jesus, in the Gospel of Luke, speaks about a Pharisee who comes to pray. He was busy bragging to God about all the good works he was doing and at the same time comparing himself with the tax collector who was praying next to him. He considered himself superior to the tax collector. His self-righteous attitude prevented him from seeing his sinfulness.

The Pharisee, standing by himself, was praying thus, 'God, I thank you that I am not like other people: thieves, rogues, adulterers, or even like this tax collector. I fast twice a week; I give a tenth of all my income.' (Luk 18:11)

The Bible sees human righteousness as equivalent to filthy rags. God's standard of righteousness is what we must strive to achieve. Our righteousness can make us "good people." But merely being good cannot take us to heaven. Heaven is for holy people who rise to God's standard of righteousness.

We have all become like one who is unclean, and all our righteous deeds are like a filthy cloth. We all fade like a leaf, and our iniquities, like the wind, take us away. (Is 64:6)

Weak Conscience

Conscience is a God-given natural ability to discern good and bad. All of us, irrespective of faith and creed are given this gift. It is the immune system of the mind. It works most of the time in most people. Conscience does help in preventing major sins happening in this world. There are some who do not have a conscience or act like one when they kill other people in the name of religion. A vast majority of us do not fall into this category. However, repeated sinful behavior can cause the slow death of the inner conscience. For example, the first time you lied, it hurt you for some time and you may have regretted it. If you continue to lie, you will slowly lose that inner voice that warns you.

To the pure all things are pure, but to the corrupt and unbelieving nothing is pure. Their very minds and consciences are corrupted. (Tit 1:15)

We have killed our conscience or weakened it in so many areas, and we are no longer able to hear the inner voice warning us or prompting us to repent. More and more sins have become acceptable to us. We move from one sin to the next, one deadlier than the earlier. Frequent confession heals and strengthens our conscience, which is wounded.

Lack of Discipline

Sin and evil have a lot to do with discipline or the lack of it. Discipline builds one's character. To the one who is not disciplined, everything is acceptable. We were not restrained in many areas, the result of which is our sinful lifestyle. Our parents were exceptionally good at giving us the importance of academics to earn a living. Although we may be financially and economically successful, our knowledge of sin and evil is weak. We are cautious to avoid the major sins like murder, rape, terrorism, etc., but the small vices or the little foxes still control us. Selfishness, self-centeredness, and other hidden sins were never dealt with. We are unable to see them and repent.

Whoever heeds instruction is on the path to life, but one who rejects a rebuke goes astray. (Pro 10:17)

The Holy Spirit

By the kind of life we lead, it is evident that we are blinded by the sin and evil of this world. Once we understand why we are unable to see the sin in us, we can now focus on some positive steps that need to be taken to see the sin in us and repent for it. One of the reasons the Holy Spirit is given to us is to provide us with the knowledge of good and evil. The Holy Spirit brings us to the understanding of sin and righteousness and convicts us of wrongdoing.

When he comes, he will prove the world wrong about sin and righteousness and judgment. (Jn 16:8)

The Holy Spirit will teach us about everything, including sin. We do not have a good understanding of sin because we have a broken relationship with the Holy Spirit. Communion with the Holy Spirit is essential if one were to grow in the ladder of holiness. We cannot attain holiness without the Holy Spirit.

Building a healthy relationship with God's spirit is essential to growing spiritually. This is done by praying every day to the Holy Spirit, asking his help, listening to him, and doing his will.

Additional Reading: Jn 16:13

Word of God

The Word of God is the sword of the Spirit. The Spirit works in us through the Word of God. Without God's Word, our Christian life will be shallow and weak. The Word of God was written for our edification and correction and to help us discern what is right and wrong. St. Paul, in his letter to Timothy, gives us the purpose of God's Word.

All scripture is inspired by God and is useful for teaching, for reproof, for correction, and for training in righteousness (2 Tim 3:16)

Regular Bible reading and meditating on God's word is key to knowing sin and truth.

Daily Eucharist

The Eucharist is Jesus, and those who honor Jesus in the host will have a deeper relationship with our Lord. The Eucharist has the power to open our eyes and show what is right and wrong.

Conclusion

Each time we confess our sins, we are washed, sanctified, and justified in Jesus' name. We become a new creation. We have given up the old life with its desires and passions. We are ready to live for Jesus and his kingdom. In the next chapter, we will meditate on what this new life in Christ means.

Post Confession

A New Life in Christ

Confession offers hope to every sinner. It signifies, leaving our former ways behind and adopting a new life; a new life in Christ. St. Paul exhorts us in the book of Ephesians to put away our old sinful life. Sin took us nowhere but, robbed and ruined us. Confession, on the other hand, gives us a second chance. We are washed, sanctified, and robed in righteousness; the righteousness that comes from God.

Set aside your former way of life, the former man, who was corrupted and deluded by its lusts, and so be renewed in the spirit of your mind, and so put on the new self, who, in accord with God, is created in true righteousness and holiness. (Eph 4:22-24)

A godly life, though it may sound tedious or strenuous in the beginning, is enriching and more rewarding as one grows spiritually stronger. Though there will be temptations and trials all along the way, God's presence will hover over us and protect us from the evil one. In this chapter, we will discuss what one must do to grow in the Lord and not fall back to sin and evil.

Live for Jesus

All sin has to do with selfishness and self-centeredness. A spiritual death of self must take place, and Jesus must become alive in us. In other words, we must surrender our lives to Jesus completely. We must make ourselves available for Jesus and his kingdom. Coming out of oneself and living for Jesus is the way out of sin. St. Paul, talking about his life, tells us about his spiritual death and conversion in the book of Galatians.

I live; yet now, it is not I, but truly Christ, who lives in me. And though I live now in the flesh, I live in the faith of the Son of God, who loved me and who gave himself for me. (Gal 2:20)

St. Paul formerly was a persecutor of Christians. He had a divine encounter with Jesus, and that changed his life radically. Upon meeting Jesus, he dedicated himself to the kingdom of God, and it is evident in all his letters. A life lived for Jesus is a meaningful and fruitful life. There is no hope and life outside of Jesus. So, what is "living for Jesus" and how does one walk with God? These are some of the questions answered in the coming section.

Daily Eucharist

The Eucharist is the source and summit of our Christian life. We draw our strength and energy from the heavenly food called Jesus. Jesus strengthens and nourishes us with his body and blood in the Holy Eucharist. According to the Catechism, the Eucharist has the power to keep us free from sin and preserve us from mortal sin.

Daily conversion and penance find their source and nourishment in the Eucharist, for in it is made present the sacrifice of Christ which has reconciled us with God. Through the Eucharist, those who live from the life of Christ are fed and strengthened. "It is a remedy to free us from our daily faults and to preserve us from mortal sins." (CCC 1436)

Many of us may not be able to attend the Holy Mass daily because of work and family commitments. Foremost, if we desire from the heart, God will make way for us to participate in daily Mass. God fulfills the desire of those who delight in him. Secondly, we should participate whenever it is possible.

Daily Word

Daily Scripture reading is necessary to grow spiritually. Most people neglect Bible reading, and they are not able to see the full power of the Word of God. God's Word is living and active, and it gives us the strength to stay away from sin and sinful tendencies. There are many Bible verses that speak about the connection between the Word of God and holiness. Meditating on them will help us understand why it is important to take God's word seriously.

How can young people keep their way pure? By keeping to your words. (Ps 119:9)

The verse quoted above shows us the direct link between the Word of God and sin. Daily Bible reading has the power to draw us out of sin and evil. The Word of God must be read meditatively. God speaks to us through his word. Those who have experienced the power of his Word are spiritually mature Christians who hold fast to his Word and ponder upon it, day and night.

Additional Reading: Jn 8:31, Ps 37:31, Ps 119:165, Ps 119:11, Ps 1, Josh 1:8, Ps 119:148

Personal Prayer

The identity and mark of a Christian is his prayer life. A good Christian gives foremost priority to his time with God. Our daily activities, when it revolves around our prayer life, will bring joy and satisfaction in us. Jesus tells us to be in a state of prayer always. We cannot afford to enter a state of spiritual slumber but be ever alert and vigilant in prayer. Sin is all around us, and to escape its chains, we must be continuously connected with God in prayer.

Stay awake and pray, so that you may not enter into temptation. Indeed, the spirit is willing, but the flesh is weak. (Matt 26:41)

Jesus never compromised on prayer. However busy he was, he always dedicated time for his Father. Prayer is a sign of humility and dependence on God, telling him that we are nothing without him. Prayer keeps us enveloped in God's love and presence. Those who take refuge in his presence will receive protection from sin and evil.

Additional Reading: Luk 18:1, 1 Thes 5:17

Pray the Rosary

The benefits and blessings of the Rosary are many. The rosary prayer invokes the presence of the Blessed Mother, who also has power over the evil one. Jesus gave Mary to us as a mother, protector, and intercessor. Satan, the propagator of sin and evil, will flee from us when we prayerfully invoke the intercession and presence of the blessed mother through the Rosary. We meditate on the life of Jesus when we pray the Rosary. The prayers of the Rosary are extracted from the Bible, which makes it even more powerful and effective. The Rosary can be prayed individually or as a community.

The Rosary is a powerful weapon to put the demons to flight and to keep oneself from sin...If you desire peace in your hearts, in your homes, and in your country, assemble each evening to recite the Rosary. Let not even one day pass without saying it, no matter how burdened you may be with many cares and labors. (Pope Pius XI)

Additional Reading: CCC 2675

Family Prayer

The family is the nucleus of the Church; therefore, it is essential that every Christian family dedicate some time for common prayer each day. It symbolizes oneness and harmony within the family. A family that prays together is spiritually healthy, and its members are protected from the attacks of the evil one. It acts as a wall against the wiles of the devil.

When the parents had gone out and shut the door of the room, Tobias got out of bed and said to Sarah, "Sister, get up, and let us pray and implore our Lord that he grant us mercy and safety." So she got up, and they began to pray and implore that they might be kept safe. (Tob 8:4-5)

Praise and Worship

Praise is a weapon that is rarely used by Christians these days. Our praise and worship are limited to what we sing in church during Mass. We leave the responsibility of praising God to the choir and the music minister. The reason is that we have not understood its real purpose and have not tapped into its hidden powers. King David, in the old testament, is known for his praises to God. Many of his psalms are sung in churches even today. He recognized the power of praise. Praise frees us from all sinful and evil inclinations. It keeps us in the comfort and protection of God's presence. Praise is an attitude of the heart. When I praise, I exercise faith in God.

The worship of the one God sets man free from turning in on himself, from the slavery of sin and the idolatry of the world. (CCC 2097)

Thanksgiving

Thanksgiving goes with praise. A thankful person can freely praise and worship God from the heart. Being grateful for the smallest blessing and the crosses in life is a sign of faith and trust in God. Praise, along with thanksgiving, takes away all the negativity and fills a person with joy and peace.

Weekly Fast

Fasting has many benefits, and a healthy Christian should fast regularly, at least once a week. Fasting expresses our self-denial to God. It helps in overcoming many stubborn sinful inclinations in us. Are you struggling with some addictions? Fast and pray. It is a way of mortification. Jesus fasted regularly and commanded us to do the same, and it is good for our physical body and spiritual growth. Jesus, before beginning his public ministry fasted and prayed for forty days, and he was able to resist the temptations of the devil successfully. Fasting gives us power over the devil and his attacks.

Fasting is an expression of humility and repentance. In the Old Testament, an act of contrition always went with fasting and weeping. Fasting expresses our love for God more than our passion for food. Fasting also strengthens the soul, which is at constant war with the flesh.

On that day they fasted, and in that place they said, "We have sinned against the Lord." (1 Sam 7:6)

Additional Reading: Matt 6:16-18, Is 58:3-7

Daily Repentance

When I was a child, we had two cats at our house. I noticed that cats were very particular about cleanliness. They always licked their paws and tried to keep themselves clean. This is what is expected of us as well with regards to the examination of our conscience and repentance. Daily and regular analysis of our thoughts, words, and actions will bring to light all hidden sins in us. God is always pleased with acts of repentance. God's mercy for us is abundant, but it cannot be ours if we do not claim it. Praying the Chaplet of the Divine Mercy daily is an excellent way to plead for God's mercy.

If repentance is neglected for an instant, one can lose the power of the Resurrection as he lives with the weakness of tepidity and the potential of his fall. (St. John Chrysostom)

Weekly Confession

A person can remain clean and smell good only if he showers every day. Similarly, a person can maintain his holiness only by making use of the sacrament of confession regularly. We are continually sinning in our thoughts, if not in actions. Even Pope John Paul II needed to go for confession every week. Confession is our spiritual shower. Just as a person can never say that he or she will not need a shower anymore, we can never say that we will not require another confession. There will be a need to confess our sins until the last day of our life. We should make a set time and day for confession every week and stick to it.

By receiving more frequently through this sacrament the gift of the Father's mercy, we are spurred to be merciful as he is merciful. (CCC 1458)

Community Worship

Community worship is powerful, and Jesus has promised that if we gather in his name, he would be there amongst us. Jesus prayed to the Father for our unity knowing that we are stronger against the evil one when we are together. A Christian should never be alone. Satan is a loner, and those who belong to his company behave likewise. It is important that we be in a community and grow as a community. Judas, in the Bible, was a loner. Many times, he would distance himself from the other apostles. He became an easy victim of Satan who tricked him into deceiving Jesus.

And so, I beg you, brothers and sisters, by the name of our Lord Jesus Christ, that every one of you be in agreement, and that there be no divisions among you. So may you become perfect, with the same mind and with the same purpose. (1 Cor 1:10)

Additional Reading: Rom 12:5, Jn 17:22-23, Acts 2:42, Ps 95:6-7, Acts 2:46

Love Unconditionally

Love covers a multitude of sins, and he who loves has fulfilled the law. Sin is nothing but love flowing in the wrong direction. If the love in us is not flowing toward God or our neighbor, it will flow toward the world. To successfully come out of sin, one must love God and neighbor unconditionally. Forgive everyone, bear with one another, encourage one another, be patient, be gentle and kind to all. We will, and we can never sin against the person we love, be it God or neighbor.

Those who fear the Lord will not be unbelieving toward his Word. And those who love him will keep to his way. Those who fear the Lord will seek the things that are well-pleasing to him. And those who love him will be filled with his law. (Sir 2:15-16)

Additional Reading: Rom 13:8, Rom 13:10

Serve God

A Christian has a much bigger call than getting a job, making money, getting married, and having children, although all these are also important. A Christian is a property of Christ. A Christian is here in the world to do the will of God and the work of God. God has sent us with a specific purpose, and all of us have a ministry in the kingdom of God, beginning with praying for the conversion of souls. Praying for others, a.k.a. intercession can be done right at home. One of the ways to escape a life of sin is by stepping out of oneself and ministering to God in the way he wants us to. Either being part of the parish or some prayer community or helping in the evangelizing efforts are some ways we can give a hand and contribute. We can also pray and seek for a specific ministry. A life lived serving God and others is a complete and satisfying life. As St. Paul says in the book of Acts,

I dread none of these things. Neither do I consider my life to be more precious because it is my own, provided that in some way I may complete my own course and that of the ministry of the Word, which I received from the Lord Jesus, to testify to the Gospel of the grace of God. (Acts 20:24)

A sinner is selfish. We misuse our God-given freedom to indulge in sinful activities and thereby lose our freedom. Every sinner is a slave to the sin he commits. Instead, the Bible tells us to use our freedom to love and to serve one another.

For you, brothers, and sisters, have been called to freedom. Only you must not make freedom into an occasion for the flesh, but instead, serve one another through love. (Gal 5:13)

St. Paul, in his letter to the Romans, again tells us what the kind of life one ought to be living.

None of us lives for himself, and none of us dies for himself. For if we live, we live for the Lord, and if we die, we die for the Lord. Therefore, whether we live or die, we belong to the Lord. (Rom 14:7-8)

Life in The Spirit

All the spiritual exercises mentioned above, to be achieved day after day and week after week is a daunting task if we are to do it by ourselves. Thanks to God, we are not alone, and we have a helper; the Holy Spirit who can achieve all this in us. We must seek the help of the Holy Spirit in our walk with God. He is waiting to unleash his power upon his children. We need strength to live our Christian life. Jesus, speaking about the Holy Spirit, says that when he comes, we will receive power to become his witnesses.

You shall receive power when the Holy Spirit has come over you. (Acts 1:8)

Jesus lived a spirit-filled life and did not yield or submit to sin. We are also called to live a life in the Spirit. What do we mean by living in the Spirit, and how does one build a relationship with the Holy Spirit? Let us look at some simple ways.

Seek / Long / Thirst for the Holy Spirit

Christians who thirst for money, power, and fame cannot have a thirst for the Holy Spirit and therefore cannot be filled. There must be a deep thirst for God and holiness in us to be filled with the Holy Spirit. Jesus commanded his disciples to wait and pray for the Spirit. Waiting is a sign of deep desire and love. We, too, when we wait and pray, we will be filled with the Holy Spirit.

I will pour out waters upon the thirsty ground, and rivers upon the dry land. (Is 44:3)

Ask and Invite the Holy Spirit

"Jesus, fill me with your Holy Spirit," is a simple prayer that can be prayed multiple times, repeatedly, showing God, how much we long and thirst for the Spirit. Jesus promises that whoever asks will receive. God is pleased to pour his Spirit upon his children.

Therefore, if you, being evil, know how to give good gifts to your children, how much more will your Father give, from heaven, the Holy Spirit to those who ask him? (Luk 11:13)

Additional Reading: Luk 11:9

Be Filled with the Spirit

The inheritance of every believer of Christ is the Holy Spirit. God wants his children to have the greatest gift that is out there, which is the Holy Spirit. Jesus was full of the Spirit. No part of him was in sin or in the flesh. He gave himself completely to the Holy Spirit, who was able to do mighty things through him. When we allow the Holy Spirit to take control of us, we too can live a life like Jesus- a life without sin. Filled with the Spirit, the apostles could do great deeds for the lord.

When they had prayed, the place in which they were gathered was moved. And they were all filled with the Holy Spirit. And they were speaking the Word of God with boldness. (Acts 4:31)

Be Led by the Spirit

Once we are full of the Spirit, He will take total control over us. He will influence the way we speak, the way we think, and the way we act. In short, we will become like Jesus. Jesus was led by the Holy Spirit in all that he did. He never did anything out of his flesh. The Spirit was fully operational in him. Jesus promises us that we too can experience this power if we wait, pray, and seek for the Spirit of God.

For all who are led by the Spirit of God are children of God. (Rom 8:14)

Restitution and Reparation

The sin of Adam and Eve is not an isolated incident that happened thousands of years ago. We are all paying the price of this sin by inheriting a sin nature and sinful inclinations in us. Similarly, our sins wound our relationship with God and neighbor. The relationship with God is restored through repentance and confession, whereas the relationship with our neighbor is restored through reparation in addition to confession. We are not the only victims of our sinful actions. In a spiritual sense, all humankind is connected in Christ and become victims and sufferers of sin committed by all.

We, being many, are one body in Christ, and individually we are members one of another. (Rom 12:5)

Every sin that a husband commits also affects the wife. Marriage unites the man and woman in an inseparable bond where although they are physically two people, spiritually they are one. All sexual acts the husband commits outside of marriage also affect the wife. So, what is the remedy to this problem and how to fix the wound caused by sin? The answer lies in reparation and restitution. The making of amends for a wrong one has done is reparation. Restitution is the restoration or compensation of something lost or stolen to its proper owner.

The sacrament of Penance is a whole consisting in three actions of the penitent and the priest's absolution. The penitent's acts are repentance, confession or disclosure of sins to the priest, and the intention to make reparation and do works of reparation. (CCC1491)

Spiritual Reparation

It becomes the duty and obligation of every sinner to pray for all those affected by the sin. Praying the Rosary and Divine Mercy Chaplet, Offering Holy Mass, and fasting are some ways a person can offer reparation for the damage caused.

Some common areas where spiritual reparation should be offered is given below.

- Pray for all those I abused sexually (if any)

- If I caused another person to commit adultery, pray for their marriage and family
- Pray for all those who incurred financial or other losses because of my words or actions
- Pray for my parents whom I may have wounded while living with them?
- Pray for all those who were introduced to sin by me
- Pray for all those who were affected by my sinfulness
- Pray for our family members who live and bear with us despite our sinfulness and weaknesses
- Pray for all those who are struggling with addictions because of me

Material Restitution

Most of the sins we commit directly affect another person. Gossip, judging, slander, stealing, etc., cause damage or disrepute to people. Each person, within his or her strength, should restore what the other person has lost. Zacchaeus, when he met Jesus, was cut to the heart and repented for his sins. In addition to that, he pledged to restore to all those whom he had defrauded. Sin damages relationships; be it man with God or man with man. Through confession and restitution, we reverse the effects of sin on mankind.

A man or a woman, when they have done anything out of all the sins that often befall men, or if, by negligence, they have transgressed the commandment of the Lord, and so have committed an offense, they shall confess their sin. The person shall make full restitution for the wrong. (Num 5:6-7)

Abbreviations Used

CCC-Catechism of the Catholic Church
GNT-Good News Translation (Bible)
Gen-Genesis
Exo-Exodus
Lev-Leviticus
Num-Numbers
Deut-Deuteronomy
Josh-Joshua
Judg-Judges
Ruth-Ruth
Sam-Samuel
Kgs-Kings
Chr-Chronicles
Neh-Nehemiah
Job-Job
Ps-Psalms
Pro-Proverbs
Eccl-Ecclesiastes
Sir-Sirach
Is- Isaiah
Jer-Jeremiah
Lam-Lamentations
Eze-Ezekiel
Dan-Daniel
Hos-Hosea
Joel-Joel
Amos-Amos
Obad-Obadiah
Jon-Jonah
Mic-Micah
Nah-Nahum
Hab-Habakkuk
Zeph-Zephaniah
Hag-Haggai
Zech-Zechariah
Mal-Malachi
Matt-Matthew
Mrk-Mark
Luk-Luke
Jn-John
Acts-Acts
Rom-Romans
Cor-Corinthians
Gal-Galatians
Eph-Ephesians
Phil-Philippians
Col-Colossians
Tit-Titus
Phlm-Philemon
Thes-Thessalonians
Tim- Timothy
Heb-Hebrew
Jas-James
Pet-Peter
1 Jn- 1 John
Jude-Jude
Rev-Revelation

Bibliography

1. St Augustine; Sermon on the Mount; Homilies on the Gospels
2. Pope John Paul II's talk to a group of Charismatics in January of 1980.
3. *Guidelines for evaluating Reiki as an alternative therapy; Committee on Doctrine United States Conference of Catholic Bishops, 25 March 2009.*
4. Letter to the Bishops of the Catholic Church on some aspects of Christian meditation/ Pope Benedict XVI/ www.vatican.va / October 15, 1989
5. Jesus Christ the bearer of the water of life, A Christian reflection on the "New Age"- Pontifical Council for Culture & Pontifical Council for Interreligious Dialogue
6. A Catholic Response to the NEW AGE Phenomenon", The Irish Theological Commission 1994
7. St. Gregory; The Great Moralia in Job
8. Pope John Paul II's Encyclical; Laborem Exercens, 14 September 1981
9. Pope John Paul II Addressing the participants of a course on the "internal forum" organized by the Tribunal of the Apostolic Penitentiary, May 29, 2004.

Made in the USA
Middletown, DE
23 December 2021